Community Action and Climate Change

T0330885

The failure of recent international negotiations to progress global action on climate change has shifted attention to the emergence of grassroots sustainability initiatives. These civil society networks display the potential to implement social innovation and change processes from the 'bottom up'. Recent scholarship has sought to theorize grassroots community-based low carbon practices in terms of their sustainability transition potential. However, there are few empirical examples that demonstrate the factors for success of community-based social innovations in achieving more widespread adoption outside of their local, sustainability 'niche'.

The book seeks to address two significant gaps related to grassroots climate action: first the continuing dominance of the *individualization of responsibility* for climate change action, which presupposes that individuals hold both the ability and desire to shift their behaviours and lifestyle choices to align with a low carbon future. Second, the potential for community-based collectives to influence mainstream climate change governance, an area significantly under researched. Drawing on empirical research into Australian Climate Action Groups (CAGs) and related international research, the book argues that grassroots community-based collective action on climate change holds the key to broader social change.

This book will be of great interest to students and scholars of climate change, citizen participation, environmental sociology and sustainable development.

Jennifer Kent is an Honorary Associate at the Institute for Sustainable Futures at the University of Technology Sydney and Senior Environmental Officer at the Green Living Centre, a community sustainability resource centre in Sydney, Australia.

Routledge Advances in Climate Change Research

Community Action and Climate Change

Jennifer Kent

LONDON AND NEW YORK

from Routledge

First published 2016
by Routledge

2 Park Square, Milton Park, Abingdon, Oxfordshire OX14 4RN
711 Third Avenue, New York, NY 10017

Routledge is an imprint of the Taylor & Francis Group, an informa business

First issued in paperback 2017

British Library Cataloguing-in-Publication Data
A catalogue record for this book is available from the British Library

Library of Congress Cataloging-in-Publication Data
A catalog record for this book has been requested

ISBN: 978-1-138-92040-8 (hbk)
ISBN: 978-0-8153-5785-8 (pbk)

Typeset in Sabon
by Florence Production Ltd, Stoodleigh, Devon, UK

To my Mum, MCs and
all the people and communities working
against climate change everywhere

Contents

Figures

Acknowledgements

I decided to embark on my most recent academic journey (the result of which lies in this book) at mid-life as a time to reflect, restock and embrace change. The wisdom of this decision may become more apparent down the track as, to say the least, the journey has been a challenge to my intellect, my stamina and my passion. I am indebted to the many people who have assisted and supported me along this path and were required to deal with my moods, abstraction and complaints.

I sincerely appreciate the opportunity that Routledge UK has provided in publishing this book and the editorial assistance of Annabelle Harris and Helen Bell.

I acknowledge the support I received to complete my PhD from which this book is drawn. For the financial support provided by the Australian Government through an Australian Postgraduate Award and the University of Technology Sydney for a Thesis Completion Equity Grant and travelling scholarships. I am highly grateful to have had two wonderful PhD supervisors in Dr Chris Riedy and Dr Simon Fane. Both stuck with me through the whole journey and provided invaluable intellectual, emotional and practical support. I have appreciated their attention to detail and critique, boundless enthusiasm for my research, feedback and good humour.

I would like to further offer my appreciation to all the students and staff involved in the postgraduate programme at ISF and a special thanks to my fellow students, colleagues and friends Viv Benton, Dr Dena Fam, Tania Leimbach, Dr Jane Palmer and Dr Tanzi Smith for being wonderfully supportive and caring through the difficult times. I don't know what I would have done without your hugs Viv!

To Dr Johannes Behrisch I give my heartfelt thanks for realizing my diagrams from my poorly drawn efforts.

I thank my family and in particular my sister Jan and my mother for having to put up with my distractions throughout work on this book. To JP, Jaz, Zac and Bella – as always thanks for having me as part of your family and to Jack, a special thanks for your enduring friendship, support and advice. To my friends and fellow yogis I owe thanks for dealing with my emotional, physical and mental absences.

Finally, I wish to thank all those climate change activists who took part in my research and especially the members of the eight Climate Action Groups who gave their time and expressed beautifully their passion, commitment and drive to create political and social change. Your words, feelings and actions continue to inspire me. I dedicate this book to community activists everywhere striving to create a cleaner planet, a more just society and a better future.

Abbreviations

CAG	Climate Action Group
CANA	Climate Action Network Australia
CAN-I	Climate Action Network International
CBDR	Common but Differentiated Responsibility
CO_2	carbon dioxide
CO_2eq	carbon dioxide equivalents
COP	Conference of the Parties
CPRS	Carbon Pollution Reduction Scheme
CRAG	Carbon Rationing Action Group
CSG	coal seam gas
ENGO	environmental non-government organizations
GHG	greenhouse gas
GI	grassroots innovation
IPCC	Intergovernmental Panel on Climate Change
MLP	multi-level perspective
NGO	non-governmental organisation
NSM	New Social Movement
PCA	Personal Carbon Allowance
RCT	rational choice theory
STT	sustainability transition theory
UNFCCC	United Nations Framework Convention on Climate Change

Abbreviations

1   Introduction

Future weather will not be like past weather; future climates will not be like past climates.

(Hulme 2010, p. 1)

Contemporary societies are faced with many challenges to a sustainable future: broad-scale environmental degradation, economic crises, poverty and climate change. Human activity now breaches the Earth's ecological limits across many areas vital to continued human existence. While top-down policy, science and engineering responses continue to dominate, there are questions whether such approaches can meet the scale and pace of trans-formative change required. Increasingly there are calls for forms of radical innovation that can shift global social-ecological systems away from crisis. Such innovations should not be limited to science and technology but social institutions and practices should play a fundamental role.

Climate change represents just one global crisis in a series of accelerating and interlocking 'bads' threatening the ability of the Earth's systems to sustain human life (Leach *et al.* 2012). The anthropogenic impact on the Earth's atmosphere, which has been accelerating since industrialization began, is disrupting global climate systems (IPCC 2014a). This is creating complex and uncertain impacts, defining climate change as a 'wicked probl-em' (Rittel & Webber 1973), that is, one which defies simple solutions and cannot simply be addressed by the same type of thinking that created it.

The 'super wickedness' (Levin *et al.* 2012) of climate change is defined by the following four features: 'time is running out; those who cause the problem also seek to provide the solution; the central authority needed to address it is weak or non-existent; and, partly as a result, policy responses discount the future irrationally' (Levin *et al.* 2012, p. 124).

The complexity of climate change is evident as increasing levels of green-house gas (GHG) emissions released into the atmosphere cause differential impacts to the Earth's climatic systems. The uncertain and long-term extent of climate change that impacts both spatially and temporally creates impacts that are distant from its causes. The inequitable nature of climate change can be seen in how it is effecting often the poorest and most disadvantaged who have contributed least to the problem. Each of these defining characteristics represents an area where existing moral prescriptions are inadequate, contributing to what Gardiner (2006; 2011) describes as a 'perfect moral storm'. Who should bear the responsibility for the costs and burdens of responding to climate change is unclear as there is no single causal agent that can be identified as responsible for the problem. This positions climate change 'as the moral challenge of our generation' (Ki-moon 2009) as it throws up ethical contestations not only between nations but also between each government and its citizens; and between present and future generations.

Addressing the 'super-wicked' problem of climate change therefore demands an unprecedented level of global cooperation.[1] However, despite more than 20 years of concerted international effort to lessen the probability of catastrophic warming, no effective global treaty has been reached that would deliver a safe temperature target[2] (Climate Analytics Ecofys and PIK 2013). In order to resolve the 'super-wicked' problem of climate change we need to accomplish the following: first, we need to rapidly shift away from our currently unsustainable trajectory, which is based on a politico-economic system that embeds continued high use of fossil fuels; second, such a transition won't be achieved through the same way of thinking that got us to this point – we need new ways of thinking and doing to achieve such a transformation; finally, we need to move beyond relying purely on scientific and technological innovation to include social innovations as central to our future aims for long-term sustainability and a liveable planet. Traditionally, economic and technological innovation driven from the top down has been favoured by governments and policy makers. However, as complex global crises such as climate change require us 'to modify, or even transform existing ways of life' (Giddens 2009) social innovations are becoming of even keener interest than economic factors or technical innovations (Howaldt *et al.* 2010, p. 22). As the focus of governments and policymakers shifts towards involving and empowering citizens within local communities to resolve social challenges, governments are eager to foster social innovations from the 'bottom up'.

Climate change

The hottest year since records began in 1880 was 2014.[3] The latest report from the Intergovernmental Panel on Climate Change (IPCC) declares that the 'warming of the climate system is unequivocal' (IPCC 2014a, p. 1). It is human influence, through anthropogenic emissions of GHG, that is the driving force behind this climate heating. Despite the growing number of climate change mitigation policies and reduced carbon intensity of energy supply, total global GHG emissions continue to rise, now exceeding 400 ppm CO_2eq – the highest level since human existence began (Robinson *et al.* 2011).

This post-industrial climate forcing[4] (Butler 2010; Lacis 2010) is largely the result of a build-up of GHG, mainly carbon dioxide (CO_2) created from the burning of fossil fuels. These gases act on the Earth's climate system, producing complex and uncertain impacts. These impacts spread spatially, so that the source of greenhouse gases can be distant from their greatest impact, and temporally, so that greenhouse gases can take up to 100 years or more to break down (IPCC 2007). Their effect is not only cumulative but also delayed. While global warming is 'unequivocal', the actual impacts remain unclear. For example, the IPCC reports refer to modelling that shows a range of potential temperature rise by the year 2100 based on different action scenarios. The two degree 'cap' to prevent dangerous levels of climatic disruption equates to approximately 450 ppm CO_2eq in the atmosphere and the IPCC scenarios model predictions between 430 and 720 ppm CO_2eq. This puts us in a temperature range of between 1.5 and 5.8 degrees before the end of the century depending on what technological, economic and behavioural changes are enacted (IPCC 2014b, p. 13). The uncertainty of impacts is further complicated by the complexity of the Earth's climate systems along with the potential for reaching 'tipping points' (Hansen 2008; Robinson *et al*. 2011) that would lead to more sudden and catastrophic disruption.

According to the IPCC's latest report (2014b), the Earth's vast oceans are the primary sink for this amplified warming, causing: increased acidity; the loss of ice sheets, glaciers and snow cover; and rising sea levels. The impacts of climate change range widely across natural systems effecting migration patterns, geographic ranges of species and shifting crop growing seasons. Most notable is the rise in extreme weather events such as droughts, heat waves, floods and wildfires. As temperatures continue to rise these are predicted to worsen, risking 'severe, pervasive and irreversible' impacts on both people and ecosystems (IPCC 2007, p. 8). People from less developed countries, the poor and disadvantaged, are likely to bear the brunt of these impacts. Climate change creates unequal impacts, falling most heavily on the poorest and future generations that are least responsible for creating the problem (World Bank 2014).

Limiting global temperature rise below two degrees by 2100 is the widely accepted climate change mitigation policy target. It remains the benchmark for GHG emissions reduction despite the continuing dislocation between ambition and reality (UNEP 2014). Meeting the target has a particular significance for the current global energy system. Setting a defined limit on GHG emissions or a 'carbon budget' means decarbonization of energy supply must proceed rapidly and requires known fossil fuel reserves to remain in the ground (McGlade & Ekins 2015). Yet the increasing use of coal to fuel the world's energy requirements has overtaken mitigation efforts (IPCC 2014a, p. 4). There is, in fact, a perverse race to explore for and exploit the Earth's remaining fossil fuel reserves despite the clear knowledge that such actions will hurtle global temperature rise above the supposed safe level of two degrees (McGlade & Ekins 2015, p. 187).

The governance of climate change

The complex and uncertain scientific evidence that underpins climate knowledge has co-emerged with the global governance of climate change. Global governance systems are characterized by their increasingly complex, networked, multi-scale arrangements in response to the 'widening and deepening' (Newell 2008, p. 511) range of concerned actors. The current climate governance regime represents one such system bound by the UNFCCC and the Kyoto Protocol, informed by scientific discourse through the IPCC, and enacted, principally, through nation states.[5] Beyond these sites of international cooperation there has emerged a complex array of climate governance arrangements, consisting of non-state actors that operate to influence the existing regime, fill gaps where the regime has failed and 'open political spaces' (Biermann *et al.* 2009; Bulkeley 2005).

The Copenhagen climate change talks held in 2009 intended to secure a binding agreement to slow and ultimately reverse the trend of growing GHG emissions with the ultimate aim of preventing a global temperature rise of two degrees before the end of this century. However, despite 20 years of international negotiations under the UNFCCC, Copenhagen failed to achieve an effective policy response to secure this aim (Parks & Roberts 2010). Recent international negotiations have reinforced the necessity for a new global agreement to halt the Earth's temperature rise to below dangerous levels (for example, Cancun 2010, Durban 2011, Doha 2012, Warsaw 2013, Lima 2014, Rio+20 2012).[6] Consecutive annual UNFCCC Conference of the Parties (COPs) have made small advances, especially in relation to financing the least developed countries for climate change adaptation; however, national pledges to reduce GHG emissions sit well below what is needed (IPCC 2014b, p. 4). The complexity and scientific uncertainty that underpins climate change tends to favour governments delaying action (Meadowcroft 2009) and this is evident as nations are failing to meet their stated commitments for GHG emission reductions (Climate Analytics Ecofys and PIK 2013). The current climate governance regime has thus far proven incapable of addressing what is becoming a deepening, more urgent and 'diabolical' (Garnaut 2008) global dilemma.

Role of the state and civil society in climate change governance

While effective means of governing climate change at the international scale have thus far proven elusive, the emergence of multiple actors operating transnationally – public and private, state and non-state, across varying scales from the local to the international level – has drawn attention to the respective roles of the state and civil society in the climate change regime.

States play a central role in the spatial hierarchy of climate change governance. States act as a party to international negotiations, formalize agreements, and on the domestic front set national policy on climate change, as well as engage citizens in their climate change mitigation and adaptation efforts (Meadowcroft 2009). However, states can only indirectly influence or control the multiple, decentralized and independent decisions made by the public and corporations that generate greenhouse gas emissions (Bulkeley & Newell 2010). In response, there is growing interest in the actions made by local institutions, communities and individuals to reduce their carbon emissions (Agyeman *et al.* 1998; Meadowcroft 2009).

The status of civil society, in terms of its relationship with climate change governance, remains less clear. Civil society engages in the formal governance processes at the international scale. The United Nations formally recognizes civil society representatives as valuable actors in environmental decision-making. Principle 10 of the Rio Declaration states that 'environmental issues are best handled with the participation of all concerned citizens'.[7] However, while civil society participation may be encouraged in theory, in reality there are practical and structural limitations that prevent 'all concerned citizens' from engaging discursively with the formal United Nations negotiations on climate change, or even from attempting to ensure that their individual or national interests are represented (Saward 2008).

Civil society also participates in more informal ways through the public sphere where opinion formation and protest plays a role in countering entrenched political ideologies and business-as-usual pathways. Following Copenhagen, the World People's Conference on Climate Change and the Rights of Mother Earth was held in Cochabamba, Bolivia with the aim of challenging the dominant ecological modernization discourse (Hajer 1995) under the UNFCCC and to propose an alternative, grassroots and indigenous-focused 'green radicalism' (Stevenson & Dryzek 2012). More recently at COP19 in Warsaw, 800 civil society representatives walked out in protest at the lack of ambition of states as well as the deliberate blocking of advances towards a global agreement and the overt influence of the fossil fuel industry (Stevenson & Dryzek 2014). These examples demonstrate the fractious nature of civil society's relationship with the formal processes of the climate regime.

Civil society interventions that can shape and transform institutional structures (Gupta *et al.* 2008) face the inherent inertia of climate governance institutions, such as the UNFCCC processes described above. These institutions tend to be reactive and conservative, locked in to varying temporal scales and rates of change, such as: political and electoral (democratic) cycles; established patterns of production and consumption; and cultural and social norms. Yet, unanticipated events may provide 'powerful external shocks' (Meadowcroft 2009, p. 11) that can shift institutional inertia and open up opportunities for change.[8] However, in discussions on climate change governance, rarely does the grassroots warrant attention as a site of potential power, democracy or innovation. The focus remains largely on international developments under the UNFCCC and the central role of the state (Archibugi & Held 2011; Meadowcroft 2009). While there have been efforts to translate the views of citizens (as representatives of their states) directly into the wider formal debate, these have been largely unsuccessful in terms of shifting the political agenda (Riedy & Herriman 2011). The inherent difficulties of ensuring civil society participation in global talks, harnessing representative citizen views across the globe and bringing diverse peoples together in fruitful deliberation (Lidskog & Elander 2010) expose the need for broader civil society participation in climate change governance. However, it is difficult to see any progress in this regard. In the absence of a mobilizing social movement around climate change (North 2011; Rootes *et al.* 2012), citizen engagement in the global governance of climate change needs to overcome the significant privileging of participation by well-resourced states and other powerful stakeholders with the most to lose through ambitious climate action, such as the fossil fuel industry.

Individualization of responsibility for climate change action

National governments often emphasize responsibility for climate change action at the individual and household level, that is, from the 'bottom up'. They assume that the summation of local actions is (or can be) linked to national efforts and that this will lead to global-scale change (Crompton 2008). Current prescriptions for action on climate change rely at the global scale on internationally agreed GHG emission reduction targets and at the local scale on individuals instigating changes within their homes and lifestyles. Neither of these approaches has thus far achieved the dramatic shifts required in order to maintain the Earth's climate within safe limits. Nor do they address the continuation of the traditional economic growth model which is at odds with transforming from a fossil fuel based economy to a zero carbon one (Marsden *et al.* 2014).

Recent policy trends towards smaller government and bigger community responsibility for matters traditionally under state control (such as health, social services and the environment) has also called the attention of governments to the role of communities in climate change mitigation. Western governments operating within the neoliberalist tradition are increasingly transferring government services towards the private and community sectors. The UK government's 'Big Society' policy agenda serves as one example. Big Society aims to: 'help people to come together to improve their own lives. It's about putting more power in people's hands – a massive transfer of power from Whitehall to local communities' (UK Cabinet Office n.d.). Increasing citizen engagement at the local and community scale is a key component of democratic reform, assists in building social capital and ultimately transforms the relationship between governments and civil society around important social issues (Parkinson & Mansbridge 2012). However

Big Society's ideologically driven localism can be seen as a further attempt to drive increasing privatization of the public sector at the expense of an already stretched third sector (Civil Exchange 2012; Whelan & Stone 2012). Localism entrains the idea that individuals possess sufficient power and agency and are better placed to accept responsibility for systemic social issues. The individualization of responsibility thereby promotes private-sphere action in the form of voluntary changes in individuals' behaviour and lifestyles (based around notions of individual choice) without regard for the existing institutional arrangements that serve to embed unsustainability (Shove 2010).

A grassroots governance of climate change?

The absence of concerted state action highlighted above has generated calls for new approaches to the governing of climate change (Biermann *et al.* 2009; Held *et al.* 2011; Meadowcroft 2009). Centralized international climate change governance is being usurped by a more pluralistic and polycentric conception (Hoffmann 2011). Rather than states, cities are taking the lead as locales of experimentation in climate change mitigation and adaptation (Bulkeley *et al.* 2015) and local communities are being looked to as fundamental sources for climate change response. The IPCC's latest report (2014b) states it this way:

> Vulnerability to climate change, GHG emissions, and the capacity for adaptation and mitigation are strongly influenced by livelihoods, lifestyles, behaviour and culture. Also, the social acceptability and/or effectiveness of climate policies are influenced by the extent to which they incentivize or depend on regionally appropriate changes in lifestyles or behaviours.
>
> (p. 29)

Leach *et al.* (2012) argue that a dichotomy exists on the global governance of sustainable development. On the one hand, international treaties and conventions have developed in response to the complex, global and inter-twined issues of sustainability; on the other, grassroots and community-level responses have been increasingly encouraged. They call for increased efforts to link up the global scale with the local, mirroring the persistent tension between the global and the local that continues to play out in relation to the governance of climate change.

A bellwether year for grassroots mobilization – 2006

The year 2006 was a bellwether year for public and political attention to climate change globally (McGaurr & Lester 2009). It coincided with the aftermath of Hurricane Katrina and the release of the Stern Review on the

Economics of Climate Change. In the same year, former US Vice President Al Gore's film, *An Inconvenient Truth* was released internationally. The film attracted a very wide audience and it was during this coalescence of globally significant events that many grassroots organizations concerned with climate change arose within their local communities.

The lead-up to the United Nations Climate Change Conference held in Copenhagen in December 2009 represented an apex in citizen concern regarding climate change. Heightened media attention preceding Copenhagen matched with a series of natural weather-related disasters focused worldwide attention. Unprecedented numbers of civil society representatives attended the Conference (Fisher 2010) with 100,000 people marching the streets of Copenhagen as thousands took to the streets in cities and towns all over the world to encourage political leaders to take strong action on climate change.

By all accounts Copenhagen should have heralded not only a globally agreed pathway to prevent dangerous climate change but also the coming of age of a transnational social movement coalescing around the world's greatest challenge. However, successive climate talks have failed to secure ambitious action and citizens' interest waned following the disappointing Copenhagen outcome. The promise of a global environmental justice movement around climate change has so far failed to eventualize, as has the citizen momentum required to shift political agendas and force governments to respond with the urgency and scale that climate change demands (North 2011).

Instead there has been a dramatic rise in grassroots initiatives, which demonstrate the potential of civil society networks to implement social innovation and change processes within their local communities. Transition Towns, CRAGs, community renewables schemes and CAGs, to name just a few, are examples of this emergent phenomenon where bottom-up, community-based collectives engage in both the practice and politics of lowering carbon emissions. Increasingly, debates over climate change response are recognizing the political potential of these local, community-based and private-sphere forms of action (Paterson & Stripple 2010; Seyfang & Haxeltine 2012).

Sustainability transitions

An emergent theme in the climate governance literature is the potential for a more local, grassroots and devolved governance model (Meadowcroft 2011). Recent scholarship has sought to theorize bottom-up community-based low carbon practices in terms of their sustainability transition potential (Grin *et al.* 2010; Seyfang & Haxeltine 2012). Sustainability transition theory (STT) offers one prospect for normative understanding of the participation of grassroots community-based collectives in a decentralized climate change governance system (Meadowcroft 2009, 2011; North 2011). The sustainability transition model simplifies the complexity of considering transition interactions that cross scales and involve multiple and varied actors (Haxeltine *et al.* 2008), which is particularly pertinent to considerations of climate change governance where an increasing number and diversity of actors interact across multiple scales (Abbott 2011; Bulkeley & Newell 2010; Bulkeley *et al.* 2012).

STT is being increasingly applied to research into grassroots level climate change responses. STT provides an avenue for conceptualizing and exploring the complex spatial architecture of the social responses to climate change. Research on non-state niche actors (such as community-based Climate Action Groups) can also contribute to a better understanding of the role of grassroots actors in climate change governance. Yet few scholars have explored this potential. One of the aims of this book is to contribute to understanding how a local scale, community-driven governance of climate change might be realized.

Grassroots social innovations

Social innovation, according to Howaldt *et al.* (2010), 'does not occur in the medium of technical artefact but at the level of social practice' (p. 21). Social innovations involve collective action to develop 'new social relationships and structures', are triggered by some event or impetus and result in 'acts of change' (Neumier 2012, p. 51 cited in Kirwan *et al.* 2013). Social innovations involve 'new forms of civic involvement, participation and democratization ... contributing to the empowerment of disadvantaged groups and leading to better citizen involvement' (op cit., p. 53). Social innovations, thereby, build the capacity of local communities to bring about changes in social processes, institutions and behaviours rather than material products. However, rather than being mere conduits for top-down policy response, community collectives are more likely to form in response to institutional failure (Mulgan *et al.* 2007, p. 9). It is likely that they will spontaneously develop rather than be steered from above.

These types of social innovations that arise from the grassroots of civil society and are engaged in bottom-up transformations towards sustainability have been conceptualized as 'grassroots innovations' (GIs) (Seyfang & Smith 2007). Seyfang and Smith (2007, p. 585) define GIs as:

> Networks of activists and organisations generating novel bottom-up solutions for sustainable development, solutions that respond to the local situation and the interests and values of the communities involved. In contrast to mainstream business greening, grassroots initiatives operate in civil society arenas and involve committed activists experimenting with social innovations as well as using greener technologies.

Seyfang & Smith (2007) identify two main benefits of GIs. First are the 'intrinsic benefits' that individuals and the community derive from their actions in developing skills, enterprises and employment. Second are the 'diffusion benefits', which may lead to broader scale social, economic, cultural and political transformations. Though much empirical research has focused in recent years on the nature of these grassroots organizations, questions remain about their ability to contribute to broader scale societal change. For example, whether such groups can mobilize beyond their particular local community to grow and spread their influence more broadly and provide alternate paths for sustainability (Smith & Seyfang 2013). As such groups remain largely powerless and invisible to policy makers, generating calls for a 'need for better understanding of "the internal dynamics and external factors that limit and enable success", (Mulugetta *et al.* 2010, p. 7544) and the "preconditions, contexts and dynamics" of grassroots innovations' (Feola & Nunes 2014, p. 234).

Clearly individuals face significant challenges to creating the scale of change necessary to combat dangerous climate change and climate change requires actors across all scales to contribute to the solution (Rootes *et al.* 2012). Moreover prioritizing individuals as the focus of climate change mitigation, rather than collectives, tends to depoliticize civil society responses. While there are signs of a growing global climate movement within civil society, mass mobilization and large scale shifts in political responses and public opinion have not been realized (Rootes *et al.* 2012). Yet the increasing numbers of community-scale collectives engaged in a range of climate change mitigation and sustainable development practices perhaps signals a social movement derived from the grassroots. This suggests that theories of change need to consider what motivates individuals to join grassroots collectives in order to take action and the potential for these grassroots collectives to seed broader scale social change.

Climate action groups – a case study

To illustrate this point I provide a case study of grassroots climate action. Climate Action Groups (CAGs), consisting of highly motivated and publicly engaged citizens who devote their volunteer efforts to working collectively on climate change, have emerged in recent years in Australia. CAGs are a distinct kind of group within the broader movement for community-based climate change action. They are usually small groups strongly associated with place that rely on the commitment of a cohort of volunteers drawn from their local area. CAGs are diverse. They vary in size from a few members to larger groups (which can have several thousand members), all drawn from their local communities. They are involved in different forms and scales of action: from radical direct action and civil disobedience centred on sites of fossil fuel production or pollution, to bulk-buying schemes of solar goods, and advocacy and awareness-raising, such as creating human beach signs. They are largely non-partisan groups that may not subscribe to a particular political ideology yet share commonality in that they have come to see climate change as the most important target of their voluntary time, energy and resources.

I argue that CAGs are a type of organization that is distinct from the more established environmental non-governmental organizations (ENGOs) actively participating in climate change policy and advocacy work within Australia. CAGs have emerged from their local communities to take voluntary grassroots action on climate change. They engage their individual members in collective action and so express a collective agency. The CAG case study provides insight into the characteristics and motivations of individuals concerned about climate change, who choose to come together in local community-based groups in order to attain agency collectively. As a type of grassroots social innovation, CAGs, I will argue, hold the potential to stimulate broader social change on climate change.

Approach and book outline

In this book I adopt a transdisciplinary approach which incorporates knowledge from diverse sources to examine the complex problem context and breadth of stakeholder engagement in climate change action and governance (Carew & Wickson 2010). Scholars interested in global environmental change are now commonly calling for transdisciplinary approaches (Biermann 2007; Brown *et al.* 2010, p. 4) define transdisciplinarity as:

> the collective understanding of an issue; it is created by including the personal, the local and the strategic as well as specialized contributions to knowledge. This use needs to be distinguished from a multi-disciplinary inquiry, which is taken to be a combination of specializations for a particular purpose, such as a public health initiative, and from interdisciplinary, the common ground between two specializations that may develop into a discipline of its own, as it has in biochemistry. . . . 'Open' transdisciplinarity includes the disciplines, but goes further than multi-disciplinarity to include all validated constructions of knowledge and their worldviews and methods of inquiry.

Thus transdisciplinary work: tackles complexity and challenges knowledge fragmentation; deals with problems from heterogeneous planes such as climate change; encompasses the hybrid, non-linear and reflexive, thereby transcending individual discipline boundaries; and accepts local contexts and uncertainty (Lawrence 2010, pp. 17–8). Transdisciplinarity in accepting multiple knowledge constructions calls for a social constructivist approach.

Pettenger (2007b) describes social constructivism as consisting of three key aspects, which lie 'nested within the broad theme of power and knowledge'. These are: ideational and material factors; agent and structure duality; and process and change (Pettenger 2007a, p. 6). The objective of utilizing a social constructivist approach to climate change lies in its ability to reveal why and how actors take responsibility for climate change, how responsibility (in all its meanings) is formulated in climate change policy development, and the interplay of responsibility, power and knowledge in the responses to and development of climate change discourses.

Social constructivism has been increasingly adopted by scholars to investigate climate change from a different viewpoint – one which allows a broader framing of climate change and acknowledges the variety of actors, social structures and system processes that underpin its breadth and complexity. For this reason, climate change research is tending to breach the bounds of disciplinary scholarship, extending its reach widely so as to reveal the complexity of climate change as both a problem and a field of study and its central import in the concerns and imagination of the public mind (Hulme 2009; Weber 2010). I apply a social constructivist lens throughout but in particular focus on how climate change knowledge is constructed in Chapter 1.

In Chapter 2 I discuss the contemporary framing of climate change knowledge within its social and cultural contexts and examine some of the discourses that influence our understanding of and action around climate change. In particular, I argue here that how we *know* climate change patterns and potentially limits society's response. I put forward three main propositions in relation to the social construction of climate change. First, I discuss the limited role that the social sciences have traditionally played in relation to both our understanding of and reaction to climate change and argue for a balancing of the hegemonic techno-scientific and economic bias with a social perspective. Second, I position climate change in relation to the discourses that commonly contribute to the different social and political views and responses. Lastly, I select a social theory that adopts risk and uncertainty as the central characteristics of a post-industrial world (Beck's risk theory) to illustrate how climate change occupies its contemporary position in our individual and collective psyches and for illuminating potential pathways for social change.

The second core component of the theoretical framing of the book, discussed in Chapter 3, is individualization (Beck & Beck-Gernsheim 2002) and, in particular, how an individualization of responsibility for climate change, arising from the global conditions of risk and synony-mous with 'second modernity' (Beck 1992), is manifest. Beck and Beck-Gernsheim's scholarship prompts the question here: *can the individualization of responsibility create the conditions for social action on climate change?* I explore this question initially through three areas of literature that are concerned with the role of individual agency in climate change action. These are: individual responsibility as a product of neoliberalism; Beck and Beck-Gernsheim's (2002) individualization thesis; and psychological theories of behaviour change which privilege the individual. Each of these bodies of literature raises questions about the social, political and cultural contexts through which societal change is mediated. Governments and global institutions state that any successful climate change mitigation strategy will require significant changes in lifestyles and behaviours (Garnaut 2008; IPCC 2007; Stern & Stern 2007); and '"lifestyle" connotes *individual* responses to/responsibility for social and environmental change' (Evans & Abrahamse 2009, p. 501). This highlights an important role for individual action in meeting climate change imperatives. The nature of these voluntary acts, how they are enacted and the relationship between the actions of institutions (whether global, national or local) and individuals becomes critical. I conclude this section by bringing together theoretical perspectives on the individualization of responsibility for climate change drawn from the social, political, psychological, cultural and philosophical literatures to argue that the individualization of responsibility prioritizes *individual agency* over *structural responsibility* (Middlemiss 2010) and that the theories associated with these perspectives fail to inform us how the *constraints* to individual agency around climate change can be overcome. I proceed to identify three *constraints* to individual agency: lack of personal empowerment; lack of reflexivity; and lack of political trust. This leads me to argue that individual agents, in coming together in small groups (such as CAGs, the focus of my empirical study), express forms of collective agency which may overcome these constraints.

Chapter 4 provides a historic and international overview of the rise of grassroots collectives engaged in voluntary climate action. The chapter commences by describing the rise of grassroots social innovations as a distinct response to the high levels of community concern on climate change following significant global weather and cultural events around 2006. The chapter then turns to consider particular examples of grassroots collectives internationally in relation to their specific social, political and cultural contexts: CAGs within Australia; Transition Towns and Carbon Rationing Action Groups in the UK; and CAGS in the USA. I consider why research into CAGs can enhance understanding of both individual and collective motivations and behaviours targeted towards climate change mitigation. I draw on socio-technical (Sustainability) Transitions Theory (STT). STT seeks to understand broad scale change that emerges from the 'bottom up'. For example, Smith and Seyfang (2007) conceive that civil society collectives operating within their local communities act as 'grassroots innovations'. 'Grassroots innovations' possess the potential to influence or otherwise destabilize the incumbent regime in order to bring about change. This theoretical perspective contributed significantly to establishing CAGs as the focus of my empirical investigation.

In Chapter 5, the role of agency in climate action is discussed, bringing together theoretical understandings of individual and collective agency on climate change together with my case study results. I draw on my findings to argue that CAG members can be distinguished from others within their communities based on a process of engagement with climate change as an issue. Vitally, CAGs provide insight into how agency can be activated within the broader community. I detail my observation on participant and group characteristics to support my contention that CAGs represent distinct grassroots groups consisting of a particular 'elite' that formed under conditions of 'moral shock' (Pearse *et al.* 2010). Participants demonstrate both their individual and collective agency through their voluntary actions to address climate change and have overcome the constraints of lack of empowerment, lack of trust and lack of reflexivity.

The question of CAGs as agents of change is examined further in Chapter 6 where I utilize the sustainability transitions literature. CAGs are conceptualized as GI with the potential to translate community-focused climate action into more mainstream settings. I establish here a pathway for understanding broader social change processes that emanate from community-based collectives and transform themselves into wider social movements. This pathway incorporates the two complementary theoretical frames of the green public sphere and polycentrism. Both emphasize that social change occurs as a messy and disordered process and argue for the critical involvement of collectives in climate change action arising from the grassroots of civil society.

Having opened up a space for discussion on community-based social change on climate change in Chapter 7 I conclude by presenting a series of questions and ideas for further research. In particular I present some ideas that further conceptualize understanding of the role of CAGs in social change processes. I am attracted here to the metaphors of rhizome and arborescence (following Delueze) to describe dual pathways of social change – one horizontal and the other vertical – that complement STT, and suggest that the social change potential of grassroots niches can be conceived as a 'complex contagion' (Centola & Macy 2007).

Notes

1   The IPCC (2014b, p. 17) states: 'Climate change has the characteristics of a collective action problem at the global scale, because most greenhouse gases accumulate over time and mix globally and emissions by an agent (e.g. individual, community, company, country) affect other agents'.
2   The United Nations Framework Convention on Climate Change (UNFCCC) sets a goal of keeping global temperature 'at a level that would prevent dangerous anthropogenic (human induced) interference with the climate system' (Article 2 of the Convention). In 2010 governments agreed to keep global temperature rise below two degrees centigrade (http://unfccc.int/essential_background/items/6031.php, accessed 8 June 2015). Analysis by Climate Action Tracker indicates that current global agreements are on track to deliver a temperature rise in the order of 3 degrees, http://climateactiontracker.org/news/222/Emissions-Gap-How-close-are-INDCs-to-2-and-1.5-pathways.html, accessed 20 September 2015.

3   NOAA National Climatic Data Center, State of the Climate: Global Analysis for December 2014, published online January 2015, www.ncdc.noaa.gov/sotc/global/2014/12, accessed 26 January 2015.
4   Climate forcing is a 'change' in the status quo of the 'radiative energy budget' (IPCC 2007) within the Earth's atmosphere. The long-lived greenhouse gases (carbon dioxide, methane, nitrous oxide and halogenated compounds) are contributing both the greatest and most uncertain impacts on the Earth's climate (Butler 2010).
5   Of nation states (plus the European Union) 195 are signatories to the UN Framework Convention on Climate Change and 191 states (and one regional economic integration organization) have ratified the Kyoto Protocol.
6   At the time of writing preparations were being made for COP21 to be held in Paris in December 2015. The Paris talks aim to develop a new, inclusive post-Kyoto global treaty.
7   See www.un.org/documents/ga/conf151/aconf15126–1annex1.htm, accessed 12 October 2014.
8   For example, the Fukushima nuclear disaster has amplified the efforts of the anti-nuclear movement and contributed to Germany's decision to bring forward the phasing out of nuclear power.

References

Abbott, K.W. 2011, 'The transnational regime complex for climate change', *Environment & Planning C: Government & Policy*, vol. 30, no. 4, pp. 571–90.

Agyeman, J., Evans, B. & Kates, R.W. 1998, 'Greenhouse gases special: thinking locally in science, practice and policy', *Local Environment: The International Journal of Justice and Sustainability*, vol. 3, no. 3, pp. 245–6.

Archibugi, D. & Held, D. 2011, 'Cosmopolitan democracy: paths and agents', paper presented to the *Global Governance: Political Authority in Transition*. ISA Annual Convention 2011, Montreal PQ Canada, 16–19 March 2011.

Beck, U. 1992, *Risk society: towards a new modernity*, trans. M. Ritter, Sage, London.

Beck, U. & Beck-Gernsheim, E. 2002, *Individualization: institutionalized individualism and its social and political consequences*, Sage, London.

Biermann, F. 2007, ' "Earth system governance" as a crosscutting theme of global change research', *Global Environmental Change*, vol. 17, pp. 326–37.

Biermann, F., Betsill, M.M., Gupta, J., Kanie, N., Lebel, L., Liverman, D., Schroeder, H. & Siebenhuner, B. 2009, *Earth system governance: people, places and the planet. Science and implementation plan of the Earth System Governance Project*, vol. ESG Report 1, IHDP: The Earth System Governance Project, Bonn.

Brown, V.A., Harriss, J.A. & Russell, J.Y. (eds) 2010, *Tackling wicked problems: through the transdisciplinary imagination*, Earthscan, London.

Bulkeley, H. 2005, 'Reconfiguring environmental governance: towards a politics of scales and networks', *Political Geography*, vol. 24, no. 8, pp. 875–902.

Bulkeley, H. & Newell, P. 2010, *Governing climate change*, Routledge, Abingdon, Oxon.

Bulkeley, H., Andonova, L., Backstrand, K., Betsill, M., Compagnon, D., Duffy, R., Kolk, A., Hoffman, M., Levy, D. & Newell, P. 2012, 'Governing climate change transnationally: assessing the evidence from a database of sixty initiatives', *Environment and planning C: government and policy*, vol. 30, no. 4, pp. 591–612.

Bulkeley, H., Castan Broto, V. & Edwards, G.A.S. 2015, *An urban politics of climate change. Experimentation and the governing of socio-technical transitions*, Routledge, London.

Butler, J.H. 2010, *The NOAA Annual Greenhouse Gas Index (AGGI)*, US Department of Commerce, National Oceanic & Atmospheric Administration (NOAA), Boulder, CO., accessed 20 August 2011, www.esrl.noaa.gov/gmd/aggi/.

Carew, A.L. & Wickson, F. 2010, 'The TD wheel: a heuristic to shape, support and evaluate transdisciplinary research', *Futures*, vol. 42, no. 10, pp. 1146–55.

Centola, D. & Macy, M. 2007, 'Complex contagion and the weakness of long ties', *American Journal of Sociology*, vol. 113, no. 3, pp. 702–34.

Civil Exchange 2012, *Whose society? The Big Society audit.* Published by Civil Exchange in association with DHA Communication, UK, accessed 4 June 2015, www.civilexchange.org.uk/wp-content/uploads/2015/01/Whose-Society_The-Final-Big-Society-Audit_final.pdf.

Climate Analytics Ecofys and PIK 2013, *Analysis of current greenhouse gas emission trends*, accessed 4 June 2015, http://climateactiontracker.org/publications/publication/154/Analysis-of-current-greenhouse-gas-emission-trends.html.

Crompton, T. 2008, *Weathercocks and signposts: the environment movement at a crossroads*, World Wildlife Fund, UK accessed 4 June 2015, http://assets.wwf.org.uk/downloads/weathercocks_report2.pdf.

Evans, D. & Abrahamse, W. 2009, 'Beyond rhetoric: the possibilities of and for "sustainable lifestyles"', *Environmental Politics*, vol. 18, no. 4, pp. 486–502.

Feola, G. & Nunes, R. 2014, 'Success and failure of grassroots innovations for addressing climate change: the case of the Transition Movement', *Global Environmental Change*, vol. 24, no. 0, pp. 232–50.

Fisher, D. 2010, 'COP-15 in Copenhagen: how the merging of movements left civil society out in the cold', *Global Environmental Politics*, vol. 10, no. 2, pp. 11–17.

Gardiner, S.M. 2006, 'A perfect moral storm: climate change, intergenerational ethics and the problem of moral corruption', *Environmental Values*, vol. 15, pp. 397–413.

Gardiner, S.M. 2011, *A perfect moral storm: the ethical tragedy of climate change*, Oxford University Press, New York.

Garnaut, R. 2008, *The Garnaut climate change review. Final report*, Cambridge University Press, Port Melbourne, Australia.

Giddens, A. 2009, *The politics of climate change*, Polity, Cambridge.

Grin, J., Rotmans, J., Schot, J. 2010, *Transitions to sustainable development: new directions in the study of long term transformative change*, Routledge, New York.

Gupta, J., Termeer, K., Klostermann, J., Meijerink, S., van den Brink, M., Jong, P. & Nooteboom, S. 2008, *Institutions for climate change: a method to assess the inherent characteristics of institutions to enable the adaptive capacity of society*, Glogov.org – The Global Governance Project, accessed 1 March 2010, www.glogov.org/images/doc/08-31_adaptive_capacity%20article%20final.pdf.

Hajer, M.A. 1995, *The politics of environmental discourse: ecological modernization and the policy process*, Clarendon Press, Oxford.

Hansen, J. (ed.) 2008, 'Tipping point: perspectives of a climatologist', in E. Fearn, ed., *State of the wild 2008-2009: a global portrait of wildlife, wildlands, and oceans.* Wildlife Conservation Society/Island Press, pp. 6–15.

Haxeltine, A., Whitmarsh, L., Bergman, N., Rotmans, J., Schilperoord, M. & Kohler, J. 2008, 'A conceptual framework for transition modelling', *International Journal of Innovation and Sustainable Development*, vol. 3, no. 1/2, pp. 93–114.

Held, D., Hervey, A. & Theros, M. (eds) 2011, *The governance of climate change. Science, economics, politics and ethics*, Polity, Cambridge.

Hoffmann, M. 2011, *Climate governance at the crossroads*, Oxford University Press, Oxford.

Howaldt, J., Schwarz, M., Henning, K. & Hees, F. 2010, *Social innovation: concepts, research fields and international trends*, accessed 4 April 2015, www.international monitoring.com/fileadmin/Downloads/Trendstudien/Trends_V2/IMO-MAG%20 Howaldt_final_mit_cover.pdf.

Hulme, M. 2009, *Why we disagree about climate change: Understanding controversy, inaction and opportunity*, Cambridge University Press, Cambridge.

Hulme, M. 2010, 'Mapping climate change knowledge: An editorial essay', *WIREs Climate change*, vol. 1, no. January/February, pp. 1–8.

IPCC 2007, 'IPCC fourth assessment report: climate change 2007', contribution of working group I to the *Fourth Assessment Report of the Intergovernmental Panel on Climate Change*, 2007, Cambridge University Press, Cambridge.

IPCC, 2014a, 'Climate change 2014, synthesis report', in [core writing team R.K. Pachauri and L.A. Meyer (eds)], contribution of working groups I, II and III to the *Fifth Assessment Report of the Intergovernmental Panel on Climate Change*, IPCC, Geneva, Switzerland, 151 pp.

IPCC 2014b, ' "Summary for policymakers" in climate change 2014: mitigation of climate change', in Edenhofer, O., R. Pichs-Madruga, Y. Sokona, E. Farahani, S. Kadner, K. Seyboth, A. Adler, I. Baum, S. Brumner, P. Eickemeier, B. Krieman, J. Savolainen, S. Schlömer, C. von Stechow, T. Zwickel and J.C. Minx (eds), contribution of working group III to the *Fifth Assessment Report of the Intergovernmental Panel on Climate Change*, Cambridge University Press, Cambridge.

Ki-moon, B. 2009, 'Forward' in P. McMullen (ed.), *Climate change science compendium*, United Nations Environment Program (UNEP), p. ii, accessed 26 January 2015, www.unep.org/compendium2009/.

Kirwan, J., Ilbery, B., Maye, D. & Carey, J. 2013, 'Grassroots social innovations and food localisation: an investigation of the local food programme in England', *Global Environmental Change*, vol. 23, no. 5, pp. 830–7.

Lacis, A. 2010, *CO2: The thermostat that control's earth's temperature*, National Aeronautics and Space Administration (NASA), Goddard Institute for Space Studies, accessed 20 August 2011, www.giss.nasa.gov/research/briefs/lacis_01.

Lawrence, R.J. 2010, 'Beyond disciplinary confinement to imaginative transdisciplinarity', in V.A. Brown, J.A. Harriss & J.Y. Russel (eds), *Tackling wicked problems: through the transdisciplinary imagination*, Earthscan, London, pp. 16–30.

Leach, M., Rokstrom, J., Raskin, P., Scoones, I.C., Stirling, A.C., Smith, A., Thompson, J., Millstone, E., Ely, A. & Arond, E. 2012, 'Transforming innovation for sustainability', *Ecology and Society*, vol. 17, no. 2, pp. 452–8.

Levin, K., Cashore, B., Bernstein, S. & Auld, G. 2012, 'Overcoming the tragedy of super wicked problems: constraining our future selves to ameliorate global climate change', *Policy Sciences*, vol. 45, pp. 123–52.

Lidskog, R. & Elander, I. 2010, 'Addressing climate change democratically. Multilevel governance, transnational networks and governmental structures', *Sustainable Development*, vol. 18, pp. 32–41.

McGaurr, L. & Lester, L. 2009, 'Complementary problems, competing risks: climate change, nuclear energy and the *Australian*', in T. Boyce & J. Lewis (eds), *Climate Change and the Media*, Peter Lang, New York, pp. 174–85.

McGlade, C. & Ekins, P. 2015, 'The geographical distribution of fossil fuels unused when limiting global warming to 2 °C', *Nature*, vol. 517, no. 7533, pp. 187–90.

Marsden, G., Mullen, C., Bache, I., Bartle, I. & Flinders, M. 2014, 'Carbon reduction and travel behaviour: discourses, disputes and contradictions in governance', *Transport Policy*, vol. 35, pp. 71–8.

Meadowcroft, J. 2009, *Climate change governance*. Policy Research Working Paper no. WPS 4941, Washington, DC: World Bank, accessed 3 December 2012, http://documents.worldbank.org/curated/en/2009/05/10575776/climate-change-governance.

Meadowcroft, J. 2011, 'Engaging with the *politics* of sustainability transitions', *Environmental Innovation and Societal Transitions*, vol. 1, no. 1, pp. 70–5.

Middlemiss, L. 2010, 'Reframing individual responsibility for sustainable consumption: lessons from environmental justice and ecological citizenship', *Environmental Values*, vol. 19, no. 2, pp. 147–67.

Mulgan, G., Ali, R., Halkett, R. & Sanders, B. 2007, *In and out of sync: the challenge of growing social innovations*, Research report. National Endowment for Science, Technology and the Arts (NESTA), London, accessed 4 June 2015, http://young foundation.org/wp-content/uploads/2013/03/In-and-out-of-sync-the-challenge-of-growing-social-innovations-Sept-2007.pdf.

Newell, P. 2008, 'The political economy of global environmental governance', *Review of International Studies*, vol. 34, pp. 507–29.

North, P. 2011, 'The politics of climate activism in the UK: a social movement analysis', *Environment and Planning A*, vol. 43, pp. 1581–98.

Parkinson, J. & Mansbridge, J. (eds) 2012, *Deliberative systems: deliberative democracy at the large scale*, Cambridge University Press, Cambridge.

Parks, B.C. & Roberts, J.T. 2010, 'Addressing inequality and building trust to secure a post-2012 global climate deal', in M.T. Boykoff (ed.), *The politics of climate change: a survey*, Routledge, London, pp. 111–35.

Paterson, M. & Stripple, J. 2010, 'My space: governing individuals' carbon emissions', *Environment and Planning D: Society and Space*, vol. 28, pp. 341–62.

Pearse, R., Goodman, J. & Rosewarne, S. 2010, 'Researching direct action against carbon emissions: A digital ethnography of climate agency', *Cosmopolitan Civil Societies Journal*, vol. 2, no. 3, pp. 76–103.

Pettenger, M.E. 2007a, 'Introduction: power, knowledge and the social construction of climate change', in M.E. Pettenger (ed.), *The social construction of climate change: power, knowledge, norms, discourses*, Ashgate, Hampshire, UK, pp. 1–19.

Pettenger, M.E. (ed.) 2007b, *The social construction of climate change: power, knowledge, norms, discourses*, Ashgate, Hampshire, UK.

Riedy, C. & Herriman, J. 2011, 'Deliberative mini-publics and the global deliberative system: insights from an evaluation of worldwide views on global warming in Australia', *Portal Journal of Multidisciplinary International Studies*, vol. 8, no. 3, pp. 1-29.

Rittel, H.W.J. & Webber, M.M. 1973, 'Dilemmas in a general theory of planning', *Policy Sciences*, vol. 4, no. 2, pp. 155–69.

Robinson, K., Steffen, W. & Liverman, D. 2011, *Climate change: Global risks, challenges and decisions*, Cambridge University Press, Cambridge.

Rootes, C., Zito, A. & Barry, J. 2012, 'Climate change, national politics and grassroots action: an introduction, environmental politics', *Environmental Politics*, vol. 21, no. 5, pp. 677–90.

Saward, M. 2008, 'Representation and democracy: revisions and possibilities', *Sociology Compass*, vol. 2, no. 3, pp. 1000-13.

Seyfang, G. & Haxeltine, A. 2012, 'Growing grassroots innovations: exploring the role of community-based initiatives in governing sustainable energy transitions', *Environment and Planning C: Government and Policy*, vol. 30, pp. 381–400.

Seyfang, G. & Smith, A. 2007, 'Grassroots innovations for sustainable development: towards a new research and policy agenda', *Environmental Politics*, vol. 16, pp. 584–603.

Shove, E. 2010, 'Beyond the ABC: climate change policy and theories of social change', *Environment and Planning A*, vol. 42, no. 6, pp. 1273–85.

Smith, A. & Seyfang, G. 2013, 'Constructing grassroots innovations for sustainability', *Global Environmental Change*, vol. 23, no. 5, pp. 827–9.

Stern, N. & Stern, N.H. 2007, *The economics of climate change: the Stern review*, Cambridge University Press, Cambridge.

Stevenson, H. & Dryzek, J.S. 2012, 'The discursive democratisation of global climate governance', *Environmental Politics*, vol. 21, no. 2, pp. 189–210.

Stevenson, H. & Dryzek, J.S. 2014, 'Democratizing global climate governance: a deliberative systems approach', paper presented to the 8th Pan-European Conference on International Relations, Warsaw, Poland, 18–21 September 2013.

UK Cabinet Office n.d., *Building the Big Society*, accessed 4 June 2015, www.gov.uk/government/uploads/system/uploads/attachment_data/file/78979/building-big-society_0.pdf.

UNEP 2014, *The Emissions Gap Report 2014*, United Nations Environment Program (UNEP), Nairobi.

Weber, E.U. 2010, 'What shapes perceptions of climate change?', *Wiley interdisciplinary reviews: climate change*, vol. 1, no. 3, pp. 332–42.

Whelan, J. & Stone, C. 2012, *Big society and Australia: how the UK government is dismantling the state and what it means for Australia*, Centre for Policy Development, accessed 4 June 2015, http://cpd.org.au/wp-content/uploads/2012/05/cpd_big_society-FINAL-WEB-VERSION.pdf.

World Bank 2014, *Turn down the heat: confronting the new climate normal*, World Bank, Washington, DC.

2 The social construction of climate change

Introduction

In Chapter 1 I briefly outlined the importance of applying the social sciences to the climate change 'problem'. Here I will expand on this to argue that how we *know* climate change is socially constructed[1] and that the following three propositions have a bearing on this fact.

First, I propose that the social sciences have traditionally played a limited role in relation to both our understanding of, and reaction to, climate change. In response, I argue for a balancing of the hegemonic techno-scientific and economic bias with a social perspective through adopting a social constructivist epistemological stance. Second, I propose that to understand climate change from a social constructivist perspective there is a need to appreciate the discourses that commonly contribute to differing social and political views and responses. Third, I propose that to understand the politico-economic and societal conditions under which climate change has become a core issue of global concern, there is a need to acknowledge the centrality of concepts of risk and responsibility. I therefore select a social theory that adopts risk and uncertainty as the central characteristics of a post-industrial world (Beck's risk theory) for revealing how climate change occupies its contemporary position in our individual and collective psyches and for illuminating potential pathways for social change.

Role of the social sciences in climate change

Climate change has been principally considered a scientific problem (Rosa & Dietz 1998, p. 239) and, as such, scientific discourse has sought to provide accurate knowledge of how the climate is changing (Crotty 1998) and it has privileged scientific expertise (Demeritt 2001; Victor 2015; Zehr 2015). As Lahsen (2007, p. 190) argues, 'the perceived material reality of climate change is defined in social settings by scientists and policymakers.... In other words "science ... *is* the politics of climate change"'.

Climate science continues to dominate knowledge of climate change, primarily through the IPCC. Established in 1988, the IPCC has produced five assessment reports over this 25-year period, drawing on the expertise of hundreds of scientists operating under the oversight of governments. How we have come to 'know' climate change has largely been mediated through the natural sciences with the IPCC playing a central role to our understanding. Victor (2015) portrays the IPCC's dual roles as independent scientific 'interpreter' and consensus-driven 'diplomat'. He notes that the IPCC is dominated by scientists with a significant lack of expertise in the social sciences, economics being the exception.

Constructivist critiques of the IPCC (Demeritt 2001, 2006; Miller 2004) – the pre-eminent source of scientific knowledge concerning climate change – argue that the IPCC has perpetuated a globalizing of positivist climate knowledge through removing climate from its local and regional contexts. Demeritt (2001) argues that this abstracts its impacts away from social and political contexts and universalizes both its causative and remedial actions. As Agrawala (1998, p. 312) puts it, the IPCC and related bodies 'have tried as much as possible to divorce the scientific study of the problem from the social and political contexts of both its material production and its cognitive understanding'.

These globalizing inclinations privilege objectivist knowledge and tend to trivialize uneven power relations and basic inequalities evident across human relations. They also exclude other kinds of knowledge about the natural world and places, and the values of cultural importance of particular peoples or communities.

According to Rosa and Dietz (1998, p. 440) this scientistic framing of climate change can be challenged on two main fronts: 'the first challenges the social authority of scientific knowledge by emphasizing the uncertainties that underpin scientific claims about climate change, and the second emphasizes the historical, social and political context of claims-making'.

As argued by Demeritt (2001, p. 329), the positivist framing of climate change promulgates scientific certainty as the rationale for uniting the world's citizens behind a global climate policy and 'continued scientific uncertainty has become the principal rationale for continued inaction'. This narrow scientific focus confines global climate change to

> an undifferentiated global 'we'and relies exclusively on the authority of science to create this sense of some other basis of appeal, 'we' are likely to act more as spectators than participants in the shaping of our related but different futures.

The positivist framing of climate change through scientific knowledge and claim-making can be illustrated through the historic treatment of the weather, which has more recently coalesced and collapsed into a globalized notion of climate change. Miller (2004), in tracking the historic rise of the global governance of climate, claims that the weather, historically of local and regional interest, has been aggregated to now form an issue of global politics (p. 51) and 'a common concern of humankind' (WCED 1987, p. 55). While this situation serves the creation of a common global order around climate change, Miller (2004) questions how this might be related back to individual lives and livelihoods (p. 63). The *globalizing* of climate has shifted the discourse away from local and tangible 'vagaries of the weather', recorded through 'our sense and memories' in 'the calendar or the gardeners' almanac' (Jasanoff 2010, p. 235). In the global order (Marshall 2011), the unpredictability of the weather is conflated to the 'chaotic climate' (Hulme 2009, p. 26) which must be stabilized as a public 'good'.

Climate change has attracted influential economic critiques (Garnaut 2008, 2011; Stern & Stern 2007) that monopolize climate change discourses. These economic critiques tend to align with neoclassical economics, which fits easily into the dominant discourse. Responses to climate change therefore focus on 'individualistic, market-based and calculative' human practices conveyed through technology and the development of markets (Szerszynski & Urry 2010, p. 3). Many academics have recently decried the limited purview of the social sciences in climate change discourse, restricted to these narrow economistic responses (Beck 2010; Hulme 2009; Lever-Tracy 2008, 2010; Shove 2010; Szerszynski & Urry 2010; Urry 2009, 2010). As Szerszynski and Urry (2010, p. 3) argue, 'in the developing analysis of this new global risk . . . the social is both central and pretty well invisible'.

Social constructivism and the study of climate change

In response, scholars interested in the social sciences have increasingly adopted social constructivism to investigate 'the social and cultural elements involved in producing environmental knowledge' (Jasanoff & Wynne 1998, p. 4) and, of particular interest here, knowledge of climate change.

Pettenger (2007, p. 7) argues that constructivism provides a new perspective on climate change that promises to uncover the various societal actors, structures and processes that have been obscured by the dominant technocratic and economistic framings. She outlines three principles of social constructivism which lie 'nested within the broad theme of power and knowledge': ideational/material factors; agent/structure duality; and process and change (Pettenger 2007, p. 6). The ideational/material factors of con-structivism engage both with ideas and with material factors or things and are concerned with how material and social realities co-evolve. This goes to the heart of how responses to climate change not only involve technological solutions (for example renewable energy and battery storage advances) but also the social realities of how people adopt and adapt to techno-logical change. In the process of arriving at their understandings of the climate change dilemma, constructivists have adopted and incorporated Giddens' theory of structuration (Jackson & Sorensen 2006, p. 163) in recognition of the duality of agents and structure. As Pettenger (2007, p. 7) points out, 'the social construction of actors' identities and interests and of structures, such as discourses and norms, is the heart of constructivism'. The third principle of constructivism, process and change, illuminates its capacity to understand change through focusing on processes (proceduralism) rather than objects (i.e. universalist and objective) (Miller 2013). Constructivism opens up reflexive space, allowing 'the construction of social structures by agents' as well as allowing 'those structures, in turn, [to] influence and reconstruct agents' (Pettenger 2007, p. 7 citing Finnemore 1996, p. 24).

Structuration theory

Structuration theory is particularly influential in constructivist thinking and has been drawn on substantially in the development of more recent interdisciplinary and transdisciplinary approaches to social and policy change (Buchs *et al.* 2011; Grin *et al.* 2010; Hargreaves *et al.* 2011). Some other examples of approaches that utilize structuration theory are: socio-technical transitions theory (Grin *et al.* 2010), social practice theory (Shove & Walker 2010) and related interdisciplinary theories that draw strongly from science and technology studies, such as strategic niche management (Kemp *et al.* 1998; Raven *et al.* 2010) and transition management (Loorbach & Rotmans 2010).

Structuration theory (Giddens 1984) is a social theory concerned with human action and behaviour within its societal context. As described above, it represents a key aspect of a social constructivist appreciation of climate change. Giddens developed structuration theory as a response to the 'positivistic view' of the natural sciences (Blaikie 1993, p. 90) and their dominance in the formulation of social scientific principles. As Giddens states, contrary to nature, there are no universal laws governing human conduct (Giddens 1984, p. xxviii).

Structuration theory is therefore described as 'an ontological framework for the study of human social activities' (Blaikie 1993, p. 69). It is concerned with the production and reproduction of society brought about through the mutual dependence of *agency* and *structure*. 'Agents' imply actors who can exert power, so agency refers not to the intention to act but the ability of humans to act (Giddens 1984, p. 9). Actors are embedded in structures, or rules and resources. This duality of structure is defined by Giddens to mean that 'social structures are both constituted *by* human agency, and yet at the same time are the very *medium* of this constitution' (Giddens 1976, p. 121; Held & Thompson 1989). Agents are embedded in social structure and therefore constantly reproduce societal conditions recursively. In this way, Giddens distinguishes human action from fatalistic and determinist understandings: agents not only intend but are capable of choosing to act rationally; however, correspondingly, there are both conditions and consequences of those actions.

Structure has the ability to both enable and constrain human action. It acts 'like the rules of grammar' (Held & Thompson 1989, pp. 3–4) as it not only allows action but also sets the boundaries of action. These rules are the 'cognitive, interpretive frames' and the 'cultural norms' (Grin *et al.* 2010, pp. 42–3), which are continuously instantiated and reproduced through everyday action. Structure is also supported by *resources*, which can be *allocative* (such as control over money or things) and *authoritative* (control over people) (Grin *et al.* 2010, pp. 42–3). Structuration theory therefore establishes that actors are not free agents in the neoliberalist sense of being able to enact individual choice and free will but that there are unconscious motives that underlie human action and with that, unintended or unknown consequences.

Giddens' theory has been criticized for its lack of inclusion of 'the role of technology in social life' (Grin *et al.* 2010, p. 45).[2] Another criticism is that Giddens overemphasizes social structures and individual actions 'and never considers the ghost of networked others that continually inform that action' (Thrift 1996, p. 54 cited in Grin *et al.* 2010, p. 45). The role of collectives and horizontal scale interactions between actors is therefore ignored in preference to the vertical interactions between actors and structures (Grin *et al.* 2010, p. 45). Finally, as Giddens' concern is with the everyday practices of daily life, agency is often understood in micro terms and structure in macro terms. In other words, agents could be considered in macro terms as collective groupings of actors such as organizations or social movements and structures could be considered at the micro level in the rules that structure local practices (Grin *et al.* 2010; Hargreaves *et al.* 2011; Shove 2003).

Role of discourse

In approaching the climate change 'problematique' (Max-Neef 2005) from a social constructivist perspective, the role of discourses comes to the fore.[3] Dryzek (2005, p. 9) defines a discourse as:

> a shared way of apprehending the world. Embedded in language, it enables those who subscribe to it to interpret bits of information and put them together into coherent stories or accounts. Discourses construct meanings and relationships, helping to define common sense and legitimate knowledge.

Discourses are essential to our contemporary understanding of environmental issues, as they both define and build on the different elements of understanding surrounding an issue. 'Each discourse rests on assumptions, judgments and contentions that provide the basic terms for analysis, debates, agreements and disagreements' (Dryzek 2005, p. 9). Discourses also manifest power. They can dominate or suppress other storylines (Foucault 1980) and can 'favor certain descriptions of reality and thereby empower certain actors while marginalizing others' (Bäckstrand & Lövbrand 2007, p. 125).

Discourses can create change by influencing institutions and inducing policy development (Bäckstrand & Lövbrand 2007).[4] This implies that actors need to influence and re-imagine culturally created narratives of climate change by 'redefin[ing] the chessboard' so that 'environmental problems are seen as opportunities rather than troubles' (Dryzek 1997, p. 13).

The discussion of climate change discourses below assists in revealing how our understanding of climate change extends beyond universally agreed scientific knowledge to incorporate thicker, contested and values-laden social conceptions. The focus of this section is on climate change discourses characterized in relation to responsibility and risk.

Discourses of climate change

The power of discourses in communicating climate change knowledge that can translate into social action can be understood from two broad perspectives. First, the scientific and economic storylines of climate change, prevalent in global politics and policy making, influence and create selective understandings of climate change, narrow its perception both in terms of 'problem' and 'solution' and serve to replicate hegemonic power. Second, on a more individual and psychological level, discourses can drive particular courses of action, potentially stimulating or stifling forms of climate change mitigation practice (this point is drawn out further in the next chapter).

The analysis of discourses 'assumes the existence of multiple, socially constructed realities' (Hajer & Versteeg 2005, p. 176) and it is therefore the analysis of *meaning* that becomes centrally important in climate change policy development. As Hajer and Versteeg (2005, p. 176) declare: 'for inter-pretative environmental policy research, it is not an environmental phe-nomenon in itself that is important, but the way in which society makes sense of this phenomenon'.

Matters of responsibility and lifestyle can therefore come to the fore in a discourse approach and they can be examined to determine their underlying meanings as well as their political and societal ramifications. In this way, 'policy making becomes a site of cultural politics, leading people to reflect on who they are and what they want' (Hajer & Versteeg 2005, p. 182). Analyses of environmental discourses commonly portray the polit-ical narratives of climate change that are revealed in contemporary climate governance arrangements (Bäckstrand & Lövbrand 2007; Dryzek 2012; Okereke 2006, 2008; Rutherford 1999). However, other analyses expose culturally created climate change storylines. For example, Hulme (2008) argues that contemporary climate change discourse can be conceived of as a 'climate change-as-catastrophe' storyline through a historic analysis of human response to climatic change over time. Marshall (2011), in a some-what similar vein, asserts that human responses to climate change can be read as a rendering of psycho-social disorder. The analysis of climate change discourses thereby enriches and diversifies understanding of climate change as a research subject. The discourses of climate change illustrate different cultural interpretations that underpin value sets related to climate change that are distinct from its positivist, scientific framing. In other words, understanding that climate change discourses represent different values and worldviews assists in appreciating why and how people respond differently to taking action on climate change.

The 2001 Working Group (WG) III report of the IPCC considers several pragmatic climate change narratives related to three discursive typologies of climate change, described as *hierarchical*, *market* and *egalitarian*. According to the IPCC, each can be used to classify the positions of different climate change actors, assist in resolving differences and understand how dialogues regarding climate change can evolve over time (IPCC 2001, p. 372). These three positions are derived from Cultural Theory, which outlines four main behavioural groupings or typologies – individualist (equivalent to market), egalitarian, hierarchist and fatalist – to explain human–nature interactions and risk perceptions (Jasanoff 2010). Cultural Theory is also described as grid-group theory (Douglas & Wildavsky 1983), where 'grid' refers to the spatial, hierarchical dimensions of authority or interest and 'group' refers to the extent of individualism or collectivity. Egalitarians, for example, display low 'grid' (that is, they are free to negotiate equally with others) and high 'group' (or collectivist) characteristics while hierarchists share high 'group' characteristics with egalitarians but are also high 'grid' (or 'imposed inequality'). Individualists are low grid and low group and fatalists display low group and high grid characteristics (Riedy 2008).

Each of these typologies has its own view of nature and conception of society. Fatalists perceive nature as a lottery and climate change outcomes as a function of chance (consequently, fatalists do not engage in climate policy discussions and are not identified with a specific climate policy discourse); individualists perceive nature as resilient and rely on markets to respond to climate change 'stimuli'; hierarchists perceive nature as manageable and prefer the use of regulation and technologically-based 'solutions'; and egalitarians perceive nature as fragile and regard the engagement of deliberative processes and civil society as critical in a climate change response (O'Riordan & Jordan 1999, pp. 86–7).

These three discursive typologies[5] – hierarchical, market (or individualist) and egalitarian – present as persistent themes in the climate change literature. Each discourse expresses different concepts of responsibility and thereby provides a means to expose and track constructs of responsibility within contemporary climate change debate. I will examine how each discourse constructs responsibility for climate change in the next section.

Responsibility discourses

Hierarchical discourses, also described as 'green governmentality', are 'top-down', 'science-driven and sovereign-based', 'embedded in expert-oriented and public inaccessible storylines that favor policy and research elites' (Bäckstrand & Lövbrand 2007, p. 128). Responsibility for climate change action within hierarchical discourses lies primarily with institutions (for example, the UNFCCC).

Individualist discourses emphasize neoliberalist, market-based processes and individualized responsibility (for example, emissions trading schemes). This discourse is often expressed as ecological modernization (Hajer 1995), which encompasses both economic growth and environmental protection.

Egalitarian discourses involve collaborative, multilateral, public–private processes and responsibility is shared across society and institutions (Michaelis 2003). Bäckstrand and Lövbrand (2007) use the term 'civic environmentalism' to describe the egalitarian discourse.

Contemporary discourses within the climate change policy setting are almost solely characterized by a market-driven (*individualist*) storyline (Bäckstrand & Lövbrand 2007; Michaelis 2003; Oels 2005). Bäckstrand and Lövbrand (2007) define the 'commodification of carbon' in the Kyoto Protocol mechanisms as symptomatic of the hegemonic ecological modernization discourse. Oels (2005, p. 199), applying Foucault's notion of advanced liberal government (which can be equated with neoliberalism), argues that market-based solutions dominate climate change institutional arrangements, which have been opened up to much broader participation. She states that:

> The Kyoto Protocol establishes markets for emissions trading in the form of Joint Implementation, Emission Trading and Clean Development Mechanism. These markets institutionalize the idea that who or where emission reductions should take place is a matter of costs, not an ethical or moral issue.
>
> (Oels 2005, p. 199)

Climate change policy options under advanced liberal government are no longer concerned with moral responsibility but become limited to market-prescribed solutions that shift responsibility in order 'to secure Western lifestyle[s]' (Oels 2005, p. 202). Both the discursive frameworks of green governmentality and advanced liberal government thereby incorporate notions of individualized responsibility, while their counter-narratives envision responsibility as shared and opened up to wider citizen participation. Responsibility and discourse therefore come to the fore in a discourse approach and a particular responsibility discourse could either promote or inhibit social action for climate change mitigation.

Risk discourses

The conceptualization of risk has gained prominence in the social sciences. Mythen (2004) proposes four paradigms of risk that have been approached through the social sciences. First, he refers to Mary Douglas's anthropological approach to Cultural Theory with differences in risk perception identified 'through particular patterns of social solidarity, worldviews and cultural values' (p. 4). (The four typologies set out in Cultural Theory are discussed above.) Second, there is a psychometric approach, which examines the psychological basis of human perception of risk and estimations of harm, popularized in the field of risk assessment. Third, he proposes discourse approaches as they 'have accentuated the role of social institutions in constructing understandings of risk which restrict and regiment human behaviour' (p. 5). Finally, there are the social theorists (Ulrich Beck and Anthony Giddens) who critique risk within the context of 'risk society'. Here I identify climate change discourses that apply notions of risk before honing in on Beck's risk theory, which I apply as an overarching framework to understand the social construction of risk in our contemporary climate challenged society.

Szersynski and Urry (2010, pp. 1–2) identify three climate change discourses: scepticism, gradualism and catastrophism, which resonate with contemporary social and political debates around climate change and risk. The discourse of scepticism considers climate change as natural, not human induced and non-threatening. The scepticism discourse has gained support from the increasing influence of ultra-conservative ('right wing') politics (exemplified by the Tea Party in the USA and the incumbent Liberal–National Party coalition in Australia) and a powerful fossil fuel ('carbon mafia') lobby (Hamilton & Downie 2007; Klein 2014) in climate change politics. It is apparent that scepticism is gaining traction within certain societies and can be aligned with particular political preferences. Tranter (2011), Moser (2009) and Leiserowitz *et al.* (2014) identify a positive relationship between political party preference and climate change beliefs, in Australia (Tranter) and the USA respectively (Moser & Leiserowitz *et al.*). Leviston *et al.* (2011) suggest that the increasing polarization of views around climate change beliefs is based on political alignment within Australia, the UK and the USA. They argue that this polarization is because of the move of some political parties towards a more conservative position (p. 8).

The gradualism discourse proposes that climate change is occurring gradually and while humans are contributing to it, it is a risk that can be managed. This discourse can be seen in the techno-managerial language of institutions such as the UNFCCC (Szerszynski & Urry 2010). The catastrophism discourse proposes that the climate system can experience abrupt and unpredictable change and that humans are throwing the system into disequilibrium. This discourse is reflected in the work of Lovelock (2009) and Hansen (2007) for example, but is increasingly penetrating the narratives of grassroots based community organizations such as Transition Towns and the Climate Emergency Network.

In summary, environmental discourses are important informants of individual attitudes and motivations towards environmental concerns. They help to reveal how people relate in their everyday lives to matters of global risk, such as climate change. Macnaghten and Urry (1998) suggest that 'the storyline of "global nature" in particular would lack the connection with concerns of everyday life and thereby have a disempowering effect' (cited in Hajer and Versteeg 2005, p. 180). The question of how action on climate change becomes personal but not disempowering has been the subject of considerable contention (Blake 1999; Hall *et al.* 2010; Wolf & Moser 2011). In the following section, I raise some differing perspectives on how climate change discourses are critical to how and why people choose to take responsibility for climate change through their voluntary actions – a theme that I address more fully in Chapter 3.

I turn now to consider Beck's risk theory as it brings together the important elements of structuration theory and discourse (discussed above) and proposes that in modern society there is a growing individualization of responsibility for global risks such as climate change.

A social theory of climate change: Beck's risk society

The notion of risk is central to the study of global environmental issues and risk theories often form the basis of scholarship on climate change (Dryzek 1997; Hajer 1995; Hulme 2008, 2009). The work of social theorist Ulrich Beck is fundamental to this erudition. Beck was a key commentator on the impact of industrialization on contemporary social conditions in the developed world. His work examines the role of science and technology in post-industrial society, the dual processes of individualization and globalization, and the growing inadequacies of what were once respected institutions of government, law, market and the media.

Beck, in common with other prominent risk theorists (especially Bauman and Giddens with whom he shares many common theoretical positions), adopts a social constructivist and transdisciplinary stance (Beck 2000). The relationship between agents and structure is central to his thesis as is reflexivity, discourse, participatory democracy and cosmopolitanism.

In asking: 'how do we wish to live?', Beck (1992) places ethical considerations at the foundation of his risk thesis and proposes that societal transformation will proceed through an 'ecological democracy [which] would democratize the politics of expertise by rolling back the industrial coalition's colonization of politics, law and the public sphere' (Dryzek *et al.* 2003, p. 170). Global risks or 'bads' unlock opportunities for large scale change by opening up depoliticized realms of decision-making, which are constrained by epistemological systems to democratic scrutiny (Beck 2000). The processes of individualization, globalization and attributing risk both delegitimize and destabilize the extant regime, creating potential for broad scale institutional change (Beck 2000).

Beck's work is often criticized for its lack of empirical integrity (Mythen 2004), yet his insight into how complex global crises grounded in science and technology are promulgated and responded to lends a rich conceptual understanding to social reactions to climate change. There are four core elements to Beck's risk thesis that I discuss in more detail below: risk society, individualization, reflexive modernity and sub-politics.

Risk society

In *Risk Society*, Beck argues that risks today escape perception and are often the by-product of technological advancement and overproduction. Risks are now global and intergenerational, superseding both time and place – 'in the risk society the unknown and unintended consequences come to be a dominant force in history and society' (Beck 1992, p. 22). Reflective of this environmental 'bent', 'Beck habitually refers to three "icons of destruction": nuclear power, environmental despoilation and genetic technology (1992: 39; 1995a: 4)' (Mythen 2004, p. 19). His primary interest is to demonstrate the catastrophic nature of risk and its anthropogenic causes.

Beck proposes that risks in postmodern society display particular characteristics. They are increasingly invisible and irreversible. Consider, for example, genetically modified organisms, the radiation risks posed by nuclear accidents and the impact of pesticides released into the environment on human and ecosystem health. These risks according to Beck (1992, p. 23)

> induce systematic and often irreversible harm, generally remain invisible, are based on causal interpretations, and thus initially only exist in terms of the (scientific or anti-scientific) knowledge about them. They can thus be changed, magnified, dramatized or minimized within knowledge, and to that extent they are particularly open to social definition and construction.

Risk distribution does not necessarily follow the assumed inequalities of class but can strike anyone (in what Beck describes as a *'boomerang effect'*) and this acts to break down these traditional societal divisions. According to Beck (1992, p. 23): 'ecological disaster and atomic fallout ignore the borders of nations', thus, 'risk society . . . is a world risk society.' Modernization risks create opportunity for economic exploitation within capitalist societies, so that 'with the economic exploitation of the risks it sets free, industrial society produces the hazards and the political potential of the risk society' (Beck 1992, p. 23). Risks therefore are reproduced rather than contained. Lastly, Beck outlines how the previously *'unpolitical'* is exposed to political scrutiny by a broader range of actors, in particular the public, under the conditions of the risk society (Beck 1992, p. 24):

> What thus emerges in risk society is the *political potential of catastrophes*. Averting and managing these can include a *reorganization of*

power and authority. Risk society is a *catastrophic* society. In it the exceptional condition threatens to become the norm.

(Beck 1992, p. 24 – emphasis in the original)

There are four categories of these risks in the risk society that 'no one saw and no one wanted' (Barry 2007, p. 245): ecological, health, economic and social; each one features as a recurring motif in Beck's work.

Beck describes how risk is mediated through knowledge and knowledge systems, and in particular, science. Risk is aligned with progress and indeed it is the tying of progress to technological development that creates a powerful legitimacy to risk in modern society. The growing 'risk industry' provides further evidence that rather than perceiving risks as problems that should be corrected at source, industry and science use risk problems as further sources of technological research and development to become '*self-producible* risk' (Beck 1992, p. 56).

Beck theorizes that science and technology, being non-reflexive, 'are *entirely incapable* of reacting adequately to civilizational risks, since they are prominently involved in the origin and growth of those risks' (Beck 1992, p. 59). In response, 'people themselves become small, private alternative experts in risks of modernization' (Beck 1992, p. 61). This becomes a persistent theme in Beck's work – the seeming paradox of individualization generated in response to the conditions of the risk society which for Beck becomes a 'double-edged sword' creating 'greater choice and autonomy' but also 'the burden of continual decision and responsibility' (Mythen 2004, p. 119).

Beck (1992) hypothesizes that in response to the conditions of the risk society, individualization develops but there is a paradoxical tension created between individuals and the state and other institutions. Beck proposes that as the conditions that create the risk society (primarily the processes of globalization and technological change) heighten, risks intensify and become increasingly uncontrollable. Beck describes the response of institutions to these conditions as 'organised irresponsibility'.[6] That is, organizations wish to create the impression of control and responsibility in light of these increased risks but instead reveal that the processes unleashed cannot be effectively controlled. Beck refers to genetically modified organisms and nuclear power as examples of the types of risks that fall into this category. With 'organised irresponsibility', the trust relations between people and institutions start to fail, again reinforcing the processes of individualization. In the case of the political institutions that represent and articulate democracy, the failure of trust between institutions and individuals leads to citizen apathy (Beck 1992, p. 137) and, as a result, traditional modes of democracy cease to operate effectively. Beck proposes that, as a response to the failure of institutional trust and 'organised irresponsibility', citizens may assert their constitutional rights through alternative democratic means:

If one conceives of this process of the realization of civil and constitutional rights in all its stages as a process of political modernization, then the following seemingly paradoxical statement becomes comprehensible: political modernization disempowers and unbinds politics and politicizes society.

(Beck 1992, p. 194)

Beck alludes here to his thesis that the processes of modernity and the freeing of individual agents from the strictures of state control will transition to a cosmopolitan society (Beck 2006). Beck's 'cosmopolitan vision' entails people acknowledging that they live in an 'endangered world' but are also part of their 'local histories and survival situations' (Beck 2010, pp. 258–9). According to Beck (2010, pp. 258–9)

climate change ... releases a 'cosmopolitan momentum'. Global risks entail being confronted with the global other. They tear down borders and mix the local with the foreign, not as consequence of migration, but rather as consequence of 'interconnectedness' (David Held) and risks. Everyday life becomes cosmopolitan: people have to conduct and understand their lives in an exchange with others and no longer exclusively in an interaction with their own kind.

For Beck then, the risk society provides the way for cosmopolitan social change to occur, created through the fracturing of institutional power and the rise of new forms of social movements. Everyday life becomes a response to global risk 'moments' and involves individuals coming together with others in order to create a new world order (a second modernity) based on a global, citizen-led deliberative democracy (Dryzek 2001, 2008, 2009).

Individualization

Individualization forms the second fundamental component of Beck's risk theory as individuals are cast free of their societal constraints and are required to forge their own biographical pathways (Beck 1992, p. 135). Here, Beck provides insight into his perception of the very deep psychological impacts of globalization and technological change on the individual. He reiterates the seeming paradox of the individual as both required to assume high levels of personal autonomy as traditional institutions withdraw or become meaningless, or '*zombies*' (Beck 2000, p. 80), and also as personally powerless in the face of global developments.

According to Beck (Beck 1992, p. 88), the conditions established in the risk society create '[a] tendency towards the emergence of individualized forms and conditions of existence, which compel people – for the sake of their own material survival – to make themselves the centre of their own planning and conduct of life'. Globalization, in other words, cultivates a higher degree of '*individual or agential reflexivity* than ever before' (Archer 2007, p. 32) and this fundamentally impacts on individual lifestyles and biographies. This brings together the dual aspects of globalization and individualization in relationship and requires the principles of modernity established within traditional institutions of the state, law and politics to be recast (Beck 2000, p. 83).

For Beck this individualizing process contributes to the removal of societal constrictions and opens up new possibilities. As individualization frees agents from structural restraints, the potential for individuals (as social agents) to actively engage with and change the prevailing social structure is created: 'In effect structural change forces social actors to become progressively more free from structure. And for modernization successfully to advance, these agents must release themselves from structural constraint and actively shape the modernization process' (Lash & Wynne, cited in Beck 1992, p. 2). Individualization is discussed in more detail in Chapter 3.

Reflexive modernity

A third element of Beck's theory that I wish to discuss here is *reflexive modernity*. Reflexive modernity describes the dual processes of globalization and individualization that create the conditions for solving the problems that modernity produces:

> As the term 'reflexive' implies, what Beck (in agreement with Giddens who also focuses on the 'reflexivity' of social institutions) suggests is that modernization should mean that society as a whole increasingly reflects upon its own development and the institutions which further and/or realize that development.
>
> (Barry 2007, p. 251)

Societal progress or evolution (in Beck's terms, *second modernity*) is dependent on reflexivity (Barry 2007; Lash & Wynne 1992 in Beck, 1992), and greater democratic control and public accountability lead to 'the democratic "redefinition" of what constitutes progress' (Barry 2007, p. 255). Reflexive modernization requires industrial society to look back upon itself in a process of self-confrontation (Dryzek *et al.* 2003, pp. 169–70) as the foundations of industrial modernity are undermined through the modernization processes themselves:

> Additionally and radically, what reflexive modernisation implies is that society democratically makes decisions on its development path; that is, democratically 'regulate' social progress. The politics of 'risk society' thus concerns both the *direction* and the *substance* of social progress, and thus of social organisation as a whole.
>
> (Barry 2007, p. 252)

Barry (2007) further argues that reflexive modernization can be seen to be a form of 'social learning' (p. 251), a means by which society, through greater 'democratic accountability and institutional innovation' (Barry 2007, p. 252), seeks to address or otherwise cope with the pervasive risks arising from industrial modernization.

Essential to Beck's reflexive modernization argument is that current ecological and other risks will only be resolved if we begin with the moral question, 'How do we wish to live?'

> New possibilities for social and political transformation arise from people's growing awareness that they are living in a society whose habits of production and consumption may be undermining the conditions for its future existence. Thus Beck believes that reflexive modernization is accompanied by waning influence of state structures compared to diverse 'sub-political' spaces of civil society.
>
> (Dryzek *et al.* 2003, pp. 169–70)

Sub-politics

The fourth element of Beck's theory concerns the sub-political regimes that develop under the conditions of risk which characterize the second modernity.

Reflexive modernization is the process, according to Beck, that will open up industrial democracy to alternative forms of democratic action and political and social systems. The stable industrial regime relies on a 'rules-based' politics (Beck 1997, p. 53) characterized by the goals of 'economic growth, full employment, social security, and the succession of power in the sense of a change of parties or personnel' (Beck 1997, p. 53). This form of politics serves to maintain the existing power arrangements and privileges of the political regime played according to an established set of 'democratic and economic rules of the game' (Beck 1997, p. 53): 'The political is comprehended and operated as a rule-directed, rule-applying, but not a rule-changing, much less a rule-inventing, politics: it is a variation in the execution of politics but not a politics of politics.' In counterpoint, *reflexive modernity* is an age of uncertainty distinguished by global risks, which combines the threat of catastrophe with the opportunity to 'reinvent our political institutions and invent new ways of conducting politics at social "sites" that we previously considered unpolitical' (Beck 1997, p. 53).

Post-industrial development takes on this form of a third intermediate entity, 'sub-politics', which sits between politics and non-politics (Beck 1992, p. 186). The new forms of 'sub-politics' that emerge in the context of risk engage citizens in the 'selection, allocation, distribution, and amelioration of risks' (Dryzek *et al.* 2003, p. 164) and for the first time link the environmental imperative to the state's legitimation imperative. Sub-politics, then, is consistent with the strong form of ecological modernization[7]

(Christoff 1996) and through opening political institutions and economic processes to an ecological rationality, the role of the state in politics declines as the role of sub-political spaces rises (Beck 1997; Dryzek *et al.* 2003). The new awareness of risk that permeates these sub-political spaces creates a centrality for trust: in sub-politics 'risk and trust intertwine' (Christoff 1996, p. 492).

In a rare show of empiricism, Beck (1997) employs the example of the Brent Spar oil rig controversy to illustrate his thesis. The proposal to sink the obsolete oil storage platform in the North Sea off the coast of Britain by the Shell Company sparked an international environmental controversy in the summer of 1995. Greenpeace launched an international campaign, which successfully stopped the disposal of the oil rig at sea. However, in Beck's analysis, the most damaging aspect of the campaign was to the UK government's and Shell's legitimacy (the UK government had approved Shell's proposal) through a consumer boycott that extended throughout Western Europe:

> Suddenly, everybody seemed to recognize the political moments in everyday life and acted upon them, in particular by refusing to fuel up at Shell gas stations. Quite improbable, really: car drivers united against the oil industry. In the end the legitimate state power is confronted with illegitimate international action and its organizers.[8] By so doing the means of state legitimacy precisely brought about the break away from these structures ... the anti-Shell coalition brought about a change in the political scenery: the politics of the first, industrial modernity made way for the new politics of the second, reflexive modernity.
>
> (Beck 1997, p. 62)

Beck is sanguine regarding the rendering of the contradictions in the result, acknowledging that the opening up of political institutions to sub-political forces will generate variable outcomes. A diversity of sub-political interests can attach to risk issues and expose the limits of social trust in politics and institutions. The 'Convoy of No Confidence'[9] for example demonstrated sub-political emotions around institutional distrust[10] and were harnessed against a government trying (at least) to strengthen its ecological modernisation credentials: 'These different partial arenas of cultural and social sub-politics – media publicity, judiciary, privacy, citizens' initiative groups and the new social movements – add up to forms of a new culture, some extra-institutional, some institutionally protected' (Beck 1992, p. 198).

Conclusion

In this chapter I established that the social sciences have been historically under-represented in climate change research and discourse. A social constructivist approach is put forward that incorporates three key instruments for examining complex social problems that arise from global conditions of risk: ideational/material factors, which I draw on in Chapter 4 in relation to the co-evolution of society and technology; agent/structure duality, which is exemplified in structuration theory and which underpins the essential relationship between actors and structures; and finally, understanding through this relationship how change occurs. Further, the critical role of discourses in a social constructivist climate change investigation is highlighted as they reveal how social and political responses to climate change have been constructed and enacted. Environmental discourses focused on responsibility and risk can reveal how individualized responsibility to a global risk issue can arise and infiltrate our collective psyches. Beck's social theory of risk accentuates key themes that provide a meta-theoretical frame and guide the content of the book. The four elements of Beck's thesis discussed – risk society, individualization, reflexive modernity, and sub-politics – all contribute to understanding the roles of individualization, responsibility, risk and social change when considering contemporary community-level responses to climate change.

Notes

1 According to Zehr (2015), there are four main areas of research that contribute to the sociological understanding of climate change: (1) the social causes of climate change, often expressed through theories of political economy and in particular sustainable consumption; (2) sociological understanding of the construction of climate change knowledge through 'public values, attitudes, and knowledge and social movement activity' (Zehr 2015, p. 129); (3) the relationship between climate change and social inequality; and (4) empirical studies of climate change mitigation and adaptation (Zehr 2015).

2 Although it should be noted that other contemporaries of Giddens, such as risk theorists Ulrich Beck and Zygmunt Bauman, engage critically with the social elements of science and technology.

3 The other key focus is media. There is a rich literature on the importance of media in influencing public understanding and concern about climate change (see, for example, Boyce & Lewis 2009 and Boykoff 2007, 2008, 2009), however, I do not discuss the role of the media here.

4 Bäckstrand & Lövbrand (2007) describe policies as the 'product of discursive struggles' (p. 125).

5 These are by no means the only discourse typologies that have been applied to climate change. See for example Stevenson & Dryzek 2012, 2014.

6 Giddens (1999) nicely summarizes Beck's concept of 'organised irresponsibility': 'By this he means that there are a diversity of humanly created risks for which people and organisations are certainly "responsible" in a sense that they are its authors but where no one is held specifically accountable' (p. 9).

7 Christoff (1996 p. 496) argues for an ecological modernization continuum that ranges from weak to strong to describe the efficacy of a state's enduring sustainable development transformations. He discusses strong ecological modernization in the following terms:

> strong ecological modernization therefore also points to the potential for developing a range of alternative ecological modernities, distinguished by

their diversity of local cultural and environmental conditions although still linked through their common recognition of human and environmental rights and a critical or reflexive relationship to certain common technologies, institutional forms and communicative practices which support the realisation of ecological rationality and values ahead of narrower instrumental forms.

8   Here Beck (1997) is referring to the Greenpeace action which worked against the sovereign and legal rights of the UK and Shell.
9   Wilson, L. 2011, 'A convoy of no confidence pulling to a halt in Canberra' *The Australian*, 22 August 2011, www.theaustralian.com.au/national-affairs/a-convoy-of-no-confidence-pulling-to-a-halt-in-canberra/story-fn59niix-1226119228798, accessed 3 June 2015.
10 In this case around perceptions that the Australian Prime Minister, Julia Gillard, gained office based on a lie regarding introducing a carbon tax.

References

Agrawala, S. 1998, 'Structural and process history of the intergovernmental panel on climate change', *Climatic change*, vol. 39, no. 4, pp. 621–42.
Archer, M.S. 2007, *Making our way through the world: human reflexivity and social mobility*, Cambridge University Press, Cambridge.
Bäckstrand, K. & Lövbrand, E. 2007, 'Climate governance beyond 2012: competing discourses of green governmentality, ecological modernization and civic environmentalism', in M.E. Pettenger (ed.), *The social construction of climate change: power, knowledge, norms, discourses*, Ashgate, Hampshire, UK, pp. 123–47.
Barry, J. 2007, *Environment and social theory*, 2nd edn, Routledge, London.
Beck, U. 1992, *Risk society: towards a new modernity*, trans. M. Ritter, Sage, London.
Beck, U. 1997, 'Subpolitics', *Organization & Environment*, vol. 10, no. 1, pp. 52–65.
Beck, U. 2000, 'The cosmopolitan perspective: sociology of the second age of modernity', *British Journal of Sociology*, vol. 51, no. 1, pp. 79–105.
Beck, U. 2006, *Cosmopolitan vision*, Polity, Cambridge, UK.
Beck, U. 2010, 'Climate for change, or how to create a green modernity?', *Theory, Culture and Society*, vol. 27, no. 2–3, pp. 254–66.
Blaikie, N. 1993, *Approaches to social enquiry*, Polity, Cambridge UK.
Blake, J. 1999, 'Overcoming the "value-action gap" in environmental policy: tensions between national policy and local experience', *Local Environment*, vol. 4, no. 3, pp. 257–78.
Boyce, T. and Lewis, J. (eds) 2009, *Climate change and the media*, Peter Lang, New York.
Boykoff, M.T. 2007, 'From convergence to contention: United States mass media representations of anthropogenic climate change science', *Transactions of the Institute of British Geographers*, vol. 32, no. 4, pp. 477–89.
Boykoff, M.T. 2008, 'The cultural politics of climate change discourses in UK tabloids', *Political Geography*, vol. 27, pp. 549–69.
Boykoff, M.T. (ed.) 2009, *The politics of climate change: a survey*, 2nd edn, Routledge, London.
Buchs, M., Smith, G. & Edwards, R. 2011, *Low carbon practices: a third sector research agenda*, Working Paper 59, Third Sector Research Centre, Birmingham, UK.

Christoff, P. 1996, 'Ecological modernisation, ecological modernities', *Environmental Politics*, vol. 5, no. 3, pp. 476–500.

Crotty, M. 1998, *The foundations of social research: meaning and perspective in the research process*, Allen & Unwin, St Leonards, Australia.

Demeritt, D. 2001, 'The construction of global warming and the politics of science', *Annals of the Association of American Geographers*, vol. 91, no. 2, pp. 307–37.

Demeritt, D. 2006, 'Science studies, climate change and the prospects for constructivist critique', *Economy and Society*, vol. 35, no. 3, pp. 453–79.

Douglas, M. & Wildavsky, A. 1983, *Risk and culture: an essay on the selection of technological and environmental dangers*, University of California Press, Berkeley, CA.

Dryzek, J.S. 1997, *The politics of the earth: environmental discourses*, Oxford University Press, Oxford.

Dryzek, J.S. 2001, 'Legitimacy and economy in deliberative democracy', *Political Theory*, vol. 29, no. 5, pp. 651–69.

Dryzek, J.S. 2005, *The politics of the earth: environmental discourses*, 2nd edn, Oxford University Press, Oxford.

Dryzek, J.S. 2008, 'Two paths to global democracy', *Ethical Perspectives*, vol. 15, no. 4, pp. 469–86.

Dryzek, J.S. 2009, 'Democratization as deliberative capacity building', *Comparative Political Studies*, vol. 42, no. 11, pp. 1379–402.

Dryzek, J.S. 2012, *The politics of the earth: environmental discourses*, 3rd edn, Oxford University Press, Oxford.

Dryzek, J.S., Downes, D., Hunold, C., Schlosberg, D. & Hernes, with H.-K. 2003, *Green states and social movements: environmentalism in the United States, United Kingdom, Germany and Norway*, Oxford University Press, Oxford.

Foucault, M. 1980, *Power/knowledge: selected interviews and other writings, 1972–1977*, Pantheon, New York.

Garnaut, R. 2008, *The Garnaut climate change review, Final report*, Cambridge University Press, Port Melbourne, Australia.

Garnaut, R. 2011, *The Garnaut review 2011. Australia in the global response to climate change*, Cambridge University Press, Port Melbourne, Australia.

Giddens, A. 1976, 'Classical social theory and the origins of modern sociology', *American Journal of Sociology*, pp. 703–29.

Giddens, A. 1984, *The constitution of society. Outline of the theory of structuration*, University of California Press, Berkeley, CA.

Giddens, A. 1999, 'Risk and responsibility', *The Modern Law Review*, vol. 62, no. 1, pp. 1–10.

Grin, J., Rotmans, J. & Schot, J. 2010, *Transitions to sustainable development: new directions in the study of long term transformative change*, Routledge, New York.

Hajer, M. & Versteeg, W. 2005, 'A decade of discourse analysis of environmental politics: achievements, challenges, perspectives', *Journal of Environmental Policy & Planning*, vol. 7, no. 3, pp. 175–84.

Hajer, M.A. 1995, *The politics of environmental discourse: ecological modernization and the policy process*, Clarendon Press, Oxford.

Hall, N.L., Taplin, R. & Goldstein, W. 2010, 'Empowerment of individuals and realization of community agency', *Action Research*, vol. 8, no. 1, pp. 71–91.

Hamilton, C. with research assistance from Downie, C. 2007, *Scorcher: the dirty politics of climate change*, Black Ink Agenda, Melbourne, Australia.

Hansen, J. 2007, 'Climate catastrophe', *New Scientist*, vol. 195, no. 2614, pp. 30–4.

Hansen, J. (ed.) 2008, 'Tipping point: perspectives of a climatologist', in E. Fearn, ed., *State of the wild 2008-2009: a global portrait of wildlife, wildlands, and oceans*. Wildlife Conservation Society/Island Press, 6–15.

Hargreaves, T., Hazeltine, A., Longhurst, N. & Seyfang, G. 2011, *Sustainability transitions from the bottom up: civil society, the multi-level perspective and practice theory*, Working Paper 2011-01, University of East Anglia, Norwich.

Held, D. & Thompson, J.B. 1989, *Social theory of modern societies: Anthony Giddens and his critics*, Cambridge University Press, Cambridge.

Hulme, M. 2008, 'The conquering of climate: discourses of fear and their dissolution', *Geographical Journal*, vol. 174, no. 1, pp. 5–16.

Hulme, M. 2009, *Why we disagree about climate change: understanding controversy, inaction and opportunity*, Cambridge University Press, Cambridge.

IPCC 2001, 'Climate change 2001: mitigation', contribution of working group III in the *Third Assessment Report of the Intergovernmental Panel for Climate Change*, Cambridge.

Jackson, R. & Sorensen, G. 2006, 'Social constructivism', *Introduction to international relations theories and approaches*, 3rd edn, Oxford University Press, Oxford, pp. 161–77.

Jasanoff, S. 2010, 'A new climate for society', *Theory, Culture and Society*, vol. 27, no. 2–3, pp. 233–53.

Jasanoff, S. & Wynne, B. 1998, 'Science and decisionmaking', in S. Rayner & E. Malone (eds), *Human Choice and Climate Change*, vol. 1, Battelle Press, Columbus, OH, pp. 1–87.

Kemp, R., Schot, J. & Hoogma, R. 1998, 'Regime shifts to sustainability through processes of niche formation: the approach of strategic niche management', *Technology Analysis & Strategic Management*, vol. 10, no. 2, pp. 175–98.

Klein, N. 2014, *This changes everything: capitalism vs. the climate*, Simon and Schuster, New York.

Lahsen, M. 2007, 'Trust through participation? Problems of knowledge in climate decision making', *The social construction of climate change*. Aldershot: Ashgate, pp. 173–96.

Leiserowitz, A., Maibach, E., Roser-Renouf, C., Feinberg, G. & Rosenthal, S. 2014, *Politics and global warming, spring 2014*, George Mason University, New Haven, CT.

Lever-Tracy, C. 2008, 'Global warming and sociology', *Current Sociology*, vol. 56, no. 3, pp. 445–66.

Lever-Tracy, C. 2010, 'Sociology still lagging on climate change', *Sociological Research Online*, vol. 15, no. 4, p. 15.

Leviston, Z., Leitch, A., Greenhill, M., Leonard, R. & Walker, I. 2011, *Australians' views of climate change*, CSIRO, Canberra, Australia.

Loorbach, D. & Rotmans, J. 2010, 'The practice of transition management: examples and lessons from four distinct cases', *Futures*, vol. 42, no. 3, pp. 237–46.

Lovelock, J. 2009, *The vanishing face of Gaia: a final warning*, Basic Books, New York.

Macnaghten, P. & Urry, J. 1998, *Contested natures*, Sage, London.

Marshall, J.P. 2011, 'Climate change, Copenhagen and psycho-social disorder', *PORTAL Journal of Multidisciplinary International Studies*, vol. 8, no. 3, pp. 1–23.

Max-Neef, M.A. 2005, 'Foundations of transdisciplinarity', *Ecological Economics*, vol. 53, pp. 5–16.

Michaelis, L. 2003, 'Sustainable consumption and greenhouse gas mitigation', *Climate Policy*, vol. 3, no. Supplement 1, pp. S135–S46.

Miller, C.A. 2004, 'Climate science and the making of a global political order', in S. Jasanoff (ed.), *States of knowledge: the co-production of science and the social order*, Routledge, London, pp. 46–66.

Miller, T.R. 2013, 'Constructing sustainability science: emerging perspectives and research trajectories', *Sustainability Science*, vol. 8, no. 2, pp. 279–93.

Moser, S.C. 2009, 'Costly knowledge – unaffordable denial: the politics of public understanding and engagement on climate change', in M.T. Boykoff (ed.), *The politics of climate change: a survey*, Routledge, London, pp. 155–81.

Mythen, G. 2004, *Ulrich Beck: a critical introduction to the risk society*, Pluto Press, London.

O'Riordan, T. & Jordan, A. 1999, 'Institutions, climate change and cultural theory: towards a common analytical framework', *Global Environmental Change Part A: Human & Policy Dimensions*, vol. 9, pp. 81–93.

Oels, A. 2005, 'Rendering climate change governable: from biopower to advanced liberal government?', *Journal of Environmental Policy and Planning*, vol. 7, no. 3, pp. 185–207.

Okereke, C. 2006, 'Global environmental sustainability: Intragenerational equity and conceptions of justice in multilateral environmental regimes', *Geoforum*, vol. 37, pp. 725–38.

Okereke, C. 2008, *Global justice and neoliberal environmental governance: ethics, sustainable development and international co-operation*, Routledge, London.

Pettenger, M.E. 2007, 'Introduction: power, knowledge and the social construction of climate change', in M.E. Pettenger (ed.), *The social construction of climate change: power, knowledge, norms, discourses*, Ashgate, Hampshire, UK, pp. 1–19.

Raven, R., Bosch, S.v.d. & Weterings, R. 2010, 'Transitions and strategic niche management: towards a competence kit for practitioners', *International Journal of Technology Management*, vol. 51, no. 1, pp. 57–74.

Riedy, C. 2008, *A developmental perspective on climate policy discourse*, Oxford University Press: Delhi, India.

Rosa, E.A. & Dietz, T. 1998, 'Climate change and society', *International Sociology*, vol. 13, no. 4, pp. 421–55.

Rutherford, P. 1999, 'Ecological modernization and environmental risk', in E. Darier (ed.), *Discourses of environment*, Blackwell, Oxford, pp. 95–118.

Shove, E. 2003, 'Converging conventions of comfort, cleanliness and convenience', *Journal of Consumer Policy*, vol. 26, no. 4, pp. 395–418.

Shove, E. 2010, 'Social theory and climate change', *Theory, Culture & Society*, vol. 27, no. 2–3, pp. 277–88.

Shove, E. & Walker, G. 2010, 'Governing transitions in the sustainability of everyday life', *Research Policy*, vol. 39, no. 4, pp. 471–6.

Stern, N. & Stern, N.H. 2007, *The economics of climate change: the Stern review*, Cambridge University Press.

Stevenson, H. & Dryzek, J.S. 2012, 'The discursive democratisation of global climate governance', *Environmental Politics*, vol. 21, no. 2, pp. 189–210.

Stevenson, H. & Dryzek, J.S. 2014, *Democratizing global climate governance*, Cambridge University Press, Cambridge, UK.

Szerszynski, B. & Urry, J. 2010, 'Changing climates: introduction', *Theory, Culture & Society*, vol. 27, no. 2–3, pp. 1–8.

Tranter, B. 2011, 'Political divisions over climate change and environmental issues in Australia', *Environmental Politics*, vol. 20, no. 1, pp. 78–96.

Urry, J. 2009, 'Sociology and climate change', *The Sociological Review*, vol. 57, pp. 84–100.

Urry, J. 2010, 'Sociology facing climate change', *Sociological Research Online*, vol. 15, no. 3, pp. 1–3.

Victor, D.G. 2015, 'Embed the social sciences in climate policy', *Nature*, vol. 520, pp. 27–9.

WCED, UN. 1987, *Our common future. Report of the World Commission on Environment and Development*, Oxford University, Oxford.

Wolf, J. & Moser, S.C. 2011, 'Individual understandings, perceptions, and engagement with climate change: insights from in-depth studies across the world', *Wiley Interdisciplinary Reviews: Climate Change*, vol. 2, no. 4, pp. 547–69.

Zehr, S. 2015, 'The sociology of global climate change', *Wiley Interdisciplinary Reviews: Climate Change*, vol. 6, no. 2, pp. 129–50.

3 Individualization of responsibility and the politics of behaviour change

Introduction

In Chapter 2 I discussed how environmental discourses on responsibility can inform and shape both institutions and individuals and may promote or inhibit social action. Discourses of risk underpin how we have come to know climate change as a global 'bad'. Beck's risk theory provides a theoretical frame that establishes the societal conditions of a global risk society faced with the threat of catastrophic climate change. The following elements of Beck's risk thesis were identified: *individualization* (which I take up in more detail in this chapter); *reflexive modernity*, arising out of modernity and the impacts of globalization as a result of the individualization of responsibility; and *sub-politics*, which opens the hegemonic politico-economic system to an ecological rationality, directly relevant to the subject of grassroots social innovations and their transformative potential.

I now turn to consider an apparent conundrum in Beck's theory in order to illuminate why and how individuals take responsibility for climate change through their voluntary actions. On the one hand, Beck suggests that in the progress of reflexive modernity individuals free themselves from structural constraints in order for modernity to progress. On the other hand, the conditions of global risk lead to a failure in trust between individuals and institutions. How then can action on climate change be personal but not disempowering; and can the individualization of responsibility create the conditions for social change on climate change? In this chapter I direct my attention to these and the following questions in order to develop a fuller explication of the relationship between individual responsibility, empowerment, collective agency and structural change: how do we understand responsibility for climate change? In what ways do individuals act responsibly to mitigate climate change? How do individual actors acquire agency through their voluntary actions?

The notion of responsibility, and more particularly the individualization of responsibility for taking action on climate change, is therefore an important preliminary for understanding how individuals come together in collectives in order to take political action. Prior to entering into a more detailed discussion on the individualization of responsibility for climate change, it is important at this juncture to develop a fuller understanding of responsibility, how it is represented across varying disciplines and within different theoretical contexts, and why it is critical to understanding climate change policy in general and political action in particular. However, before turning to consider these varying theoretical positions, I commence by providing an overview of the social research concerned with how people view climate change and what motivates individuals to take responsibility for climate change.

People's views, motivations and behaviours on climate change

There is a considerable body of social research that seeks to understand people's willingness to address climate change through a reduction in their GHG emissions. Research undertaken in the USA and UK found that 66% of consumers agreed that individuals need to take responsibility for their contribution to climate change (AccountAbility and Consumers International 2007). Similar work conducted in Australia found even higher levels – 81% of Australian consumers agreed that everyone needs to take more responsibility for their personal contribution to global warming (AccountAbility Net Balance and LRQA 2008). Survey respondents frequently stated they undertook actions such as turning off lights and appliances around the home and buying more energy efficient light bulbs and appliances. Actions requiring greater commitments of time and money, for example buying green energy for the home or using a carbon calculator to measure their GHG emissions, were the least likely to be adopted (Leviston *et al.* 2014). European studies have revealed similar outcomes with citizens stating they were most likely to undertake 'passive' actions in relation to the environment that fit in with their daily lives (European Commission 2008, 2014) rather than 'active' ones, such as using their car less and buying environmentally friendly or locally produced products.

Despite high levels of concern regarding climate change, when mapping levels of concern regarding climate change against level of action, large discrepancies are identified. The majority of people (75%) researched in the UK and USA expressed concern about global warming 'but [were] challenged to see how their action could make a difference' and only 9% indicated both concern and willingness to take action (AccountAbility and Consumers International 2007). In the Australian research, an equal number expressed concern but not willingness to act (75%), whereas a higher number expressed a willingness to take action (21%) (p. 20). Pidgeon *et al.* (2008, p. 73) argue that despite the increased interest and concern regarding climate change in the UK it 'remains a low priority for most people in relation to other personal and social issues' and 'while people indicate frequently that they are willing to recycle and save energy in the home, only a minority of people do take measures to reduce their energy consumption for environmental reasons'. These findings reflect what is described as the 'value–action' gap: the inconsistency between individuals' stated intentions and their actions (Blake 1999; Kollmus & Agyeman 2002; Macnaghten 2003).

In an Australian survey there was significant softening in climate change concern from its height in 2006 when 91.4% of Australians agreed that climate change is an important issue, with 61% strongly agreeing (Ashworth *et al.* 2011, p. 15). People stated several reasons for lacking concern for climate change, perhaps most notably though was that they 'perceive that climate change will have a significant impact globally, nationally and on future generations, and a lesser impact on a local and personal level'. A similar decline in concern has been noted in other Western countries (European Commission 2014; Leviston *et al.* 2014). Leviston *et al.* (2011) found reduced levels of concern regarding climate change aligned with: the Global Financial Crisis (GFC) of 2008; the failure of the UNFCCC in Copenhagen in 2009 to reach a binding and ambitious agreement on action to address climate change; and the leaking of emails prior to the Copenhagen conference (known as 'Climategate'), which raised questions about the accuracy and impartiality of scientific knowledge contributing to the IPCC's work.

More recent surveys related to public views on climate change demonstrate that citizens maintain high levels of concern regarding global warming (European Commission 2014; Leiserowitz *et al.* 2014; Leviston *et al.* 2014). However, they also track reduced levels of concern over recent years in association with heightened political distrust and increased economic concerns, although there are recent indications that public concern may again be rising (Capstick *et al.* 2015). Support for national action remains strong; people consistently state that they believe governments hold the greatest responsibility for tackling climate change, followed by businesses and that individuals need to play their part (European Commission 2014; Leviston *et al.* 2014; The Climate Institute 2014).

Another significant barrier to people taking responsibility for their climate change mitigation actions relates to potential conflicts with current lifestyles. Programme measures that ask people to take 'simple and painless steps' (Crompton 2008) without concomitant changes away from unsustainable lifestyle behaviours are likely to fail. There is also the somewhat problematic expectation from governments that people will take on personal action without concomitant state action, as put here:

> The dominant framing of the issue [climate change] in the UK in recent years has juxtaposed an alarming global problem with small lifestyle change actions (e.g. recycling and switching off lights), leading to incredulity amongst many people who see this scale of response as insufficient.
>
> (Reeves, Lemon & Cook 2014, p. 119)

In the social research results presented here there are several important factors worth considering.[1] First, since the height of concern noted in 2007, there has been an apparent decline in belief in and concern about climate change internationally (this trend has been noted within the UK, Europe, USA and Australia), which may lead to fewer people taking personal responsibility for action on climate change.[2] Second, the increase in polarization in people's beliefs about climate change, along with the erosion in public trust in politicians and political institutions, is another concerning trend. These factors suggest that finding ways to address the decline in public engagement with climate change under conditions of increasing distrust and scepticism will be needed in order to develop the extensive response required to address this complex global problem. Theoretical perspectives on individual agency for climate change action may therefore be useful here. The next section provides an overview of five theoretical perspectives on how individuals express their responsibility for climate change.

Theories of responsibility

Responsibility is an expansive concept that communicates ideas of accountability, blame, duty and dependability (Bickerstaff & Walker 2002) – ideas that sit comfortably as broad moral principles for human action. The concept of responsibility can be considered to involve two broad dimensions. Responsibility, as it relates to justice and law, implies duties and obligations and is often expressed as being complementary to rights (so where rights exist, responsibilities are created) (Bickerstaff & Walker 2002; Caney 2005; Dobson 2006; Singer 2002, 2006). Second, responsibility is also a psychological phenomenon. which works both at the personal level (as self-control and free will), but is also relevant at a societal level where apart from the creation of obligations or duties, it also implies caring or moral values (Bierhoff & Auhagen 2000). Responsibility is a core tenet of international climate change policy. Diverse disciplines consider responsibility and its application varies across climate change discourses.

There are several ways that the individualization of responsibility is represented in the academic literature that are pertinent to understanding how and why people take responsibility for climate change through their voluntary actions. Here I briefly draw on a few that resonate with the question of how individuals' responsibility for climate change action is understood: individual responsibility as an attribute of neoliberalism, as a process of individualization and as an aspect of human behaviour. I also draw from a Cultural Theory discourse perspective to consider typologies of individual responsibility and discuss responsibility as it relates to ethics and citizen rights.

Neoliberalism and the rise of individualism

Neoliberalism, defined by Harvey (2006, p. 145) as 'the maximization of entrepreneurial freedoms within an institutional framework characterized by private property rights, individual liberty, free markets and free trade', is well engrained in Western states. The politico-economic ideology of neoliberalism is enacted through the dismantling of the social security net and 'the passing of all responsibility for their wellbeing to individuals and their families' (Harvey 2006, p. 151). Neoliberalist ideals have been embraced globally and have now been incorporated into the political centre-left, in addition to their traditional association with parties of the political right (Matravers 2007).

According to Jackson (2005, p. 38): 'The concept of individual choice, the rights of the individual and the supremacy of individual preference occupy a central role both in the structure of market economies and in the culture of Western society.' Calls for the recognition of individual responsibility have therefore become universally appealing – at least within Western democratic society. Governments increasingly call on their citizens to take greater responsibility across a broad spectrum of societal concerns, including obesity, employment, education, crime, terrorism and environmental harm. Indeed this supports Harvey's case that neoliberalism has 'become hegemonic as a mode of discourse' and 'become incorporated into the common-sense way we interpret, live in and understand the world' (2006, p. 145). Individual responsibility, drawn from this neoliberalist tradition, now resonates widely across matters of sustainability (such as climate change) where it has gained equal support from politicians, bureaucrats and ENGOs (Middlemiss 2014).

Several authors set forth the idea that the 'individualization of responsibility' threatens to seriously undermine effective action to curtail life-threatening environmental concerns (Maniates 2002; Maniates 2012; Middlemiss 2014; Scerri 2009; Scerri & Magee 2012). Commonly, the individualization of responsibility focuses on the 'low hanging fruit' (Maniates 2012) such as the 'ten simple things you can do' approach. This diverts people from more important environmental and citizen-led democratic action and hides the power disparity between citizens, governments and corporations. As Maniates (2012, p. 122) argues: 'Advocates of green consumption unwittingly propagate the myth that social change occurs only, or best, when super-majorities unite around small changes in everyday life.'

Maniates further proposes that the individualization of responsibility reduces democratic processes as citizens are conceived as consumers rather than joint participants with governments and corporations in addressing environmental problems, and by those same actors suggesting that sustainability can be achieved through 'private, individual, well-intentioned consumer choice' (Maniates 2002, p. 58). This leads Maniates (2002, pp. 58–9) to conclude that 'It is more than coincidental that as our collective perception of environmental problems has become more global, our prevailing way of framing environmental problem solving has become more individualized.'

Individualization as a response to risk society

Another theoretical approach to individual responsibility can be found in the social risk theories of Bauman, Beck (discussed in Chapter 2) and Giddens, who all draw on the notion of individualization as a defining feature of postmodern society. According to Beck, the breakdown in social classes, greater competition for jobs and the collapse of traditional family structures contributes to the growing liberation of individuals as the agents of their own life courses: 'The tendency is towards the emergence of individualized forms and conditions of existence which compel people – for the sake of their own material survival – to make themselves the centre of their own planning and conduct of life' (Beck 1992, p. 88).

This conception of individualization has been promoted through a neoliberal economic model, 'which rests upon an image of the autarkic human self' (Beck & Beck-Gernsheim 2002, p. xxi). Individuals are characterized not only as 'masters of their lives' but as self-sufficient 'monads', divorced from social networks and possessing no sense of mutual obligation. The type of individualization of responsibility that Beck and Beck-Gernsheim identify is distinct from this neoliberal interpretation, rooted as it is, according to the authors, in a historic line of 'social scientific' thought that places individualization as 'a product of complex, contingent and thus high level socialization' (Beck & Beck-Gernsheim 2002, p. xxi). Rather than atomistic beings, individuals exist within the context of developed modernity where 'human mutuality and community rest no longer on solidly established traditions, but, rather, on a paradoxical collectivity of reciprocal individualization' (Beck & Beck-Gernsheim 2002, p. xxi).

Institutions also play a role in establishing greater responsibility for individuals, as there are now many more expectations placed by governments on their citizenry to take responsibility for areas which previously would have been more acceptably under state control. A commonly cited example is the UK's Big Society policy, which Fudge and Peters (2011, p. 791) assert 'suggests that it is individuals, as agents of change, who are going to have to be the driving force behind reductions in greenhouse gas emissions' thus establishing an acceptance of less state intervention and greater responsibility for the individual.

According to Beck, individualization, which 'is imposed on the individual by modern institutions' (2007, p. 681), is a by-product of society that formulates around conditions of risk. So post-industrial society, which held the promise of wealth and wellbeing as a by-product of techno-scientific development, paradoxically has given rise to risks that are pervasive and deadly. These risks are not limited within state borders, are often invisible and can impact across generations. Beck and Beck-Gernsheim (2002, p. xxiii) hope for a form of 'cooperative individualism' where there is continuous negotiation and renegotiation of areas of collective concern, which opens up the potential for new forms of democratic organization. They argue that the invention of these 'new, politically open, creative forms of bond and alliance' (Beck & Beck-Gernsheim 2002, p. 18) is the 'life or death' challenge for democracy.[3]

Individual responsibility, action and behaviour change

The third body of literature that places individual responsibility central to climate change response is concerned with the psychology of human action and behaviour change. One form of psychological model that focuses on the individual is rational choice theory (RCT), which remains dominant in government policy and practice (Shove 2010). According to Jackson (2005, p. 35) there are three assumptions that underlie RCT: '1) that choices are rational, 2) that the individual is the appropriate unit of analysis in social action, and 3) that choices are made in the pursuit of individual self-interest.' This section therefore needs to be read within the context of the extensive body of social research (see above) which seeks to understand what motivates individuals to act (or not) on climate change.

Voluntary action as behaviour

Voluntary individual and/or household action to reduce carbon emissions is of particular interest to Western governments, as, reluctant to prescribe regulatory provisions for their citizens' behaviours and lifestyles, they expect their climate policy objectives (such as GHG emission reduction targets) will be voluntarily fulfilled through personal and household-level behaviour change (Lorenzoni *et al.* 2007). Examples of climate change information campaigns targeted by governments at individual lifestyle and behaviour change include: 'Be Climate Clever: I can do that' in Australia; in the UK, DEFRA's 'Are you doing your bit?' and the European Commission's 'You Control Climate Change'. Perhaps not surprisingly then, the voluntary action that people take around their lifestyles and homes, with particular emphasis on how an individual's behaviour is motivated by their concern about climate change, has been the focus of much empirical research (Norgaard 2011; Whitmarsh 2009; Wolf & Moser 2011).

Whitmarsh (2009) sets out a useful tripartite framework. She describes individual voluntary action as behaviour with *intention* that sits within a broader range of co-dependent influences (namely, cognition and affect). Voluntary action on climate change focuses on one aspect of this account – the behavioural – but with the understanding that in order to act people need 'to know about climate change in order to be engaged; they also need to care about it, be motivated and able to take action' (Lorenzoni, *et al.* 2007, p. 446). This action is dependent on a wide range of influences as individual behaviour is a 'product of social and institutional contexts' (Lorenzoni *et al.* 2007, p. 446) that create complex motivations and constraints on voluntary action, which have received little normative attention in relation to climate change. Whitmarsh makes a further distinction between intention and impact, arguing that most research has focused on the *impact* of action (for example, by measuring how much a household's energy costs have been reduced) rather than the *intent*. She captures the relevance of this distinction in three ways: first, she points out that people may undertake actions with the *intention* of mitigating carbon emissions but that these may be ineffective or 'futile'; second, she points out that intention can reveal the motivations underlying action; and third, that intention uncovers the harder-to-conceptualize range of values, beliefs and virtues that underscore pro-environmental behaviours.

Behavioural intention to mitigate climate change draws attention to the academic literature concerned with why people are failing to respond to the climate change threat through changes to their individual lifestyles (Norgaard 2009, p. 14). There is now widespread agreement that rationalist information deficit approaches (that is, approaches which assume that when information about climate change is provided, voluntary changes in behaviour will follow) have proven largely ineffective or unsustainable, and fail to acknowledge the complex mix of attitudes, values and social norms that undergird behavioural change. 'The widespread lack of public reaction to scientific information regarding climate change' (Norgaard 2009, p. 3) and the 'failure to integrate this knowledge into everyday life or transform it into social action' (Norgaard 2009, p. 29) become even more perplexing when considered within the context of people's stated high levels of concern regarding the effects of climate change.

Norgaard notes the disparity between people's concerns regarding climate change and their adoption of low carbon behaviours. This discrepancy between individuals' stated intentions and their actions has been widely described in the literature as the 'value–action' gap (as noted previously). There is a range of barriers proposed that contribute to the gap; however, of most relevance here is that people feel they lack the sense of empowerment to undertake actions that will lead to a less carbon-intensive lifestyle (Norgaard 2009; Räthzel & Uzzell 2009).

As demonstrated above, there is evidence that people are undertaking the 'easy-to-do' actions within their homes and lifestyles to reduce their carbon emissions but they are also demanding that governments play a greater role (Bickerstaff *et al.* 2008; Lorenzoni & Pidgeon 2006; Pidgeon *et al.* 2008). Not only do individuals believe the level of action from governments on climate change mitigation is unacceptably low, but they also doubt whether governments are serious about climate change as climate change responses are perceived to be against nations' economic interests. Declining levels of public trust in governments are particularly evident around responses to climate change (Hoppner & Whitmarsh 2010; O'Brien *et al.* 2009). This establishes both a tension between government and the individual on the acceptance of a personal responsibility model for climate change mitigation but also the possibility for greater action if governments can demonstrate to the community that they are prepared to take a bigger role in preventing serious climate change (Pidgeon *et al.* 2008).

In summary, the individualization of responsibility for climate change mitigation is based on a model of individual behaviour change now largely discredited (Bulkeley & Newell 2010; Marsden *et al.* 2014; Moloney *et al.* 2010). Such an approach relies on individuals changing their behaviour within their households and personal lifestyles, assuming that sufficiently armed, actors will make rational choices on how they act, what they use and buy, and the lifestyle choices they pursue (Moloney *et al.* 2010). There is now widespread agreement that rational choice-centred approaches (Jackson 2005) have been largely unsuccessful. They fail to acknowledge the complex mix of human behaviours, attitudes, values and social norms that underpin behavioural change and there is an 'assumed primacy of individual over collective behaviour change' (Moloney *et al.* 2010, p. 7616). The public desire for institutions to take responsibility for climate change mitigation among calls for individual responsibility by governments and other institutions raise issues for the public of institutional trust, capability and duty of care (Bickerstaff *et al.* 2008; O'Brien *et al.* 2009). The clash between these desires also alerts the individual to the uneven power relationships that operate between the individual and the state and other institutions (Maniates 2002; Marsden *et al.* 2014). Further, this draws attention to the way that people's actions are constrained by the structural components of, say, their energy supply. Consequently, an ambivalence to personal action might be created, where people 'choose not to choose' as they feel disempowered and ineffective in the face of the global climate challenge (Macnaghten 2003, p. 77).

Cultural theory: a discourse classification for individual responsibility

A fourth body of theory that relates to climate change and responsibility is Cultural Theory. Earlier (Chapter 2), I described the discursive typologies within Cultural Theory, which have been influential in classifying different actor worldviews on climate change, and which I will briefly recap here.

Cultural Theory's four distinct discourses describe people's different views of nature and society. Each discourse expresses different concepts of responsibility so that fatalists perceive nature as a lottery and climate change outcomes as a function of chance rather than a focus for human intervention; individualists perceive nature as resilient and rely on markets to respond to climate change; hierarchists perceive nature as manageable and prefer the use of regulation and technological solutions; and egalitarians perceive nature as fragile and regard the engagement of deliberative processes and civil society as critical in a climate change response (O'Riordan & Jordan 1999, pp. 86–7). There are, then, a myriad of ways that individual actors express their responsibility for climate change through voluntary actions aimed at reducing their carbon footprints. Elsewhere (Kent 2011) I have presented a simple typology of individual actions based on these Cultural Theory classifications to illustrate the types of action choices individuals are presented in contemporary, developed Western societies. The typology offers a distinction between the types of voluntary actions available to individual actors based on their cultural preferences.[4] In brief, in a top-down hierarchical approach to climate change mitigation, for example, global agreements are incorporated into national policy, which could be prescribed to the individual through compulsory personal carbon trading. Personal Carbon Allowance (PCA) schemes are a particular example of personal carbon trading,[5] which have been a focus of research and policy deliberation in the UK, where the government has considered a compulsory scheme (Seyfang & Paavola 2008). Individualist discourses tend to promote consumer action. Consumer-based actions have been widely considered in relation to pro-environmental behaviours, particularly climate change (Maniates 2002; Scerri 2009; Spaargaren & Mol 2008). Voluntary consumer actions are diverse and include: buying carbon offsets to offset a lifestyle choice such as an overseas holiday; paying a premium to encourage renewable energy uptake (e.g. Greenpower);[6] and investing in less GHG-intensive appliances (from washing machines to solar panels). Voluntary actions that fall within the egalitarian typology involve engagement with civil society. Again these are diverse and could include participating in online advocacy (through groups such as AVAAZ, see endnote 3) or taking part in voluntary activities through membership of an environmental organization or a climate action group.

The politics of behaviour change

Critical to this discussion is the role of individualistic responses to climate change abatement, which fall within the purview of consumer-based action in the above typology. According to my argument thus far, governments and other institutions emphasize voluntary individualistic forms of responsibility for climate change mitigation. However, individuals in perceiving the complexity and extent of the climate threat, and sensing their lack of power to enact global-level change, instead either choose not to take action or otherwise apply their agency through a limited and possibly ineffective range of personal- and private-sphere behaviours. This leads to two potential pathways for individualistic action. The first pathway positions consumer-based action as responsive to the prevailing forces of economic rationalism where the only pathway currently open to actors for pro-environmental behaviour is through their consumer acts. However this action, while appearing to empower actors within their personal spheres of authority (in other words, their homes and lifestyles), diverts individual attention away from challenging the 'knotty issues of consumption, consumerism, power and responsibility' (Maniates 2002, p. 45). Individualization, for Maniates (2002, p. 65), is symbolic of the wholesale decline in public engagement in democratic processes in the West, which can only be 'remade through collective citizen action as opposed to individual consumer behaviour'. In the same way, Scerri argues that personal actions deflect individuals from considering how these practices, when shared with other members of society, have the potential to challenge or support societal values; 'personal acts of consumption stand-in for citizen's ethico-political commitments. In the place of engaging in a regulating body-politic, individual citizens are called upon to take initiatives and shoulder responsibilities themselves' (Scerri 2009, p. 477). These contrasting perspectives on individualist worldviews (illustrated above) foreshadow the tensions between: a model of individualization of responsibility for climate change action that exists within an established hegemony which is essentially unable to assure a sustainable future; and the potential laid out by Beck and Giddens, for example (along with Spaargaren and Mol), for the progress of a reflexive modernity where individuals reflect on their everyday life and take 'citizen-consumer' action with global change potential.

At this point I turn to consider the critical moral dimension of responsibility. In the following section, I take up how responsibility is understood within ethical theories and approaches to climate change and how these relate to the individualization of responsibility for action on climate change.

The ethics of climate change

Ethical considerations are central to global climate change governance. Important ethical principles such as *polluter pays* and *common but differentiated responsibility* are fundamental to the UN Framework Convention on Climate Change and remain embedded in the Kyoto Protocol. However, these elements are often overshadowed by the scientific and economic rationales for action, diverting attention from climate change as fundamentally a collective action problem (IPCC 2014).

Principles of responsibility in climate change policy

Responsibility for climate change is one of the defining tenets of international climate change policy (UNFCCC 1992), as well as contestation, as the questions of who bears responsibility for the creation of GHG emissions and how responsibility is shared for their abatement are at the core of the climate issue (Baer *et al.* 2000; Garvey 2008; Parks & Roberts 2010). International climate change policy has been formulated around the principles of sustainable development established at the United Nations Conference on Environment and Development (UNCED) held in Rio de Janeiro, Brazil in 1992. These include important equity principles such as: inter- and intra-generational equity and the polluter pays principle (PPP). As Bulkeley (2001, p. 435) observes, 'the most long running and divisive debate' within climate change policy negotiations centres on concerns over equity and the 'respective responsibilities of nation states for reducing emissions of greenhouse gases'.

The key principle that structures how responsibility is conceived within the UNFCCC is the principle of Common but Differentiated Responsibility (CBDR) which sits at the heart of international climate change policy:

> In view of the different contributions to global environmental degradation, States have common but differentiated responsibilities. The developed countries acknowledge the responsibility that they bear in the international pursuit of sustainable development in view of the pressures their societies place on the global environment and of the technologies and financial resources they command.
>
> (Principle 7 of the Rio Declaration)

The CBDR principle is, therefore, a statement that binds notions of fairness and equity in relation to access to the global commons by developed countries and acknowledges the disparities between developed and developing nations in wealth, resources and access to technology. Unsurprisingly, the application of CBDR within the UNFCCC negotiations is hotly contested. The rapid development of transition economies (in particular Brazil, South Africa, India and China), which are fast increasing their emissions, is shifting the debate on CBDR. Progressively there are calls from the developed nations for developing countries to adopt mandatory emission targets.[7] This has been reinforced at recent United Nations meetings as agreement was established to incorporate all parties to the Convention within a future single legally binding agreement.

Risks, rights and responsibility

The notion of responsibility brings together both risks and rights and implies that moral principles are the basis for human response to global 'bads'. An ethical response to climate change that incorporates individualism is cosmopolitanism. Cosmopolitanism is described as consisting of three key elements: *individualism, universality* and *generality. Individualism* places human beings as the central units of concern of a cosmopolitan framework for climate change, and so climate change is primarily a matter of social and cultural concern rather than a response to ecological degradation. *Universality* applies the ethic of equality to each unit of concern, so that each person has the *right* to an equal share in the global atmospheric commons (Singer

2002). *Generality* implies that each individual unit of concern has a moral *responsibility* for everyone, not just some subset: family, fellow citizens or members of their cultural group (Pogge 2002; Singer 2011).

In Beck's risk thesis, the individualization of responsibility that arises under the conditions of a second modernity leads to a cosmopolitan paradigm. As Beck (2000, p. 83) states:

> The categorical principles of the first age of modernity – collectivity, territoriality, boundary – are replaced by a co-ordinate system in which individualization and globalization are directly related to each other and establish the conceptual frame for the concepts of state, law, politics and individuals which have to be redefined. The bearers of human rights are individuals and not collective subjects such as 'nation' or 'state'.

Beck suggests that globalization and the rise of international law could create 'a paradigm shift from nation-state societies to cosmopolitan society in so far as international law goes over the heads of nations and states and addresses individuals directly, thereby positing a *legally binding world society of individuals*' (2000, p. 84). Dobson (2006, pp. 168–9) points to a contrast between thin cosmopolitanism, where 'common humanity is a thin type of bind', to thick cosmopolitanism, which requires recognition of ourselves in all other humans. Thick cosmopolitanism, accordingly, requires us to not only adopt cosmopolitan principles but to also undertake political action. As Linklater (1998, p. 261) puts it: 'Thin conceptions of cosmopolitan citizenship revolve around compassion for the vulnerable but leave asymmetries of power and wealth intact; thick conceptions of cosmopolitan citizenship attempt to influence the structural conditions faced by vulnerable groups.'

Dobson proposes that such ties can be created when we feel responsible for the others' situation – 'if there is some identifiable causal relationship between what we do, or what we have done, and how they are'. When such responsibility is felt, matters of unequal power where a particular rationality becomes privileged (Okereke *et al.* 2009) can be addressed through a cosmopolitan obligation, which influences the prevailing structural conditions. Further a 'cosmopolitan obligation' (Harris 2008) implies that individuals should undertake action on climate change *irrespective* of a State's inaction (for example, where a developed nation fails to act through pursuing progressive climate change mitigation policies). As climate change is a problem of globalization, this obligation would feasibly extend from the local (individual) to the global (collective).

Conclusion

Normative understandings of responsibility can be understood to fall within two broad definitions: responsibility as a legally defined obligation or duty, represented for example in the UNFCCC's principle of CBDR, or otherwise as a core moral value, expressed through 'thick cosmopolitanism'. In examining these conceptions of responsibility through a transdisciplinary lens, five distinct aspects are revealed: spatial; temporal; moral/ethical; relational; and behavioural.

Responsibility for climate change can be located at a range of spatial scales from the personal to the global. Moreover, responsibility applies across the public and private spheres and thereby engages the breadth of actors involved in climate change policy development and deliberation. Responsibility for climate change mitigation can be reflected in the 'personal, private-sphere' (Stern 2005) behaviours of individuals and householders through to the global negotiating processes undertaken through, for example, the auspices of the UNFCCC. The spatial aspect of responsibility can inform how local- and personal-scale action relates to global-scale action. The temporal scale of responsibility is reflected in both the intergenerational impact of climate change (Gardiner 2006) and historic responsibility for GHG emissions (Friman & Linnér 2008). Both these issues have formed an important distinction within climate change negotiations and should inform humanity's moral response. Responsibility encompasses a philosophical dimension and allows exploration of the ethics of climate change (Singer 2002, 2006). Matters of fairness, equity and justice feature prominently within climate change discourse. An important consideration is how far the circle of care extends both temporally and spatially (Dobson 2006; Singer 2011) and whether we can incorporate all of humanity (now and in the future) through a *cosmopolitan obligation* to taking action on climate change. Theoretical understandings of responsibility are relational. That is, responsibility is commonly argued in relation to social theories of risk (Bauman, Giddens, Beck) and rights (Caney, Dobson). These relationships are complex and contested and continue to form one of the central platforms of disagreement within international negotiations on climate change. Responsibility has a behavioural dimension as it is a widely recognized attitudinal attribute examined in environmental psycho-social research (Bickerstaff *et al.* 2008; Pidgeon *et al.* 2008). Values of responsibility have been identified as significant motivators towards individual and collective behaviour change (Jackson 2005; Kaiser & Shimoda 1999). Understanding the behavioural aspect of individual and collective responsibility for climate change action is a particularly important consideration.

I contend that climate change as a global risk issue, characterized by its inherent complexities, multiplicities and disordered ways of knowing, has been positioned as the subject of individual responsibility. If we are to accept that this is the case then in what ways are individuals equipped to enact their responsibility towards climate change? What forms of agency do actors require and in what ways are these individual agencies responsive to the structural enablements and constraints of our presently unsustainable society?

Individual responsibility, agency and structure

> The self is not a passive entity, determined by external forces; in forging their self-identities, no matter how local their specific contexts of action individuals contribute to and directly promote social influences that are global in their consequences and implications.
>
> (Giddens 1991, p. 2)

Taking individual responsibility for climate change implies that actors are able (and willing) to take mitigation actions, and possess the power to engage in practices that will effectively reduce carbon emissions. Individual agency in this sense should be distinguished from the 'unintended consequences of everyday activities' (Pattberg & Stripple 2008, p. 8), such as the 'low hanging fruit' of changing light bulbs and purchasing energy efficient appliances.

Agents, or specifically 'active agents' (Rosewarne *et al.* 2014), can be distinguished by their capacity to take responsibility for climate change through their personal actions and not by their intentions alone (Whitmarsh 2009). Many people are motivated and able to take simple steps around their lifestyles and households; in other words, they display the *intention* to act in a fashion that may lead them to lower their carbon emissions. Agents, on the other hand, must demonstrate 'their capability of doing those things in the first place' (Giddens 1984, p. 9). Agency according to Giddens implies power in the sense of the Oxford English Dictionary definition, 'one who exerts power or produces an effect' and in Biermann and colleagues' terms, agency involves actors with 'the legitimacy and capacity to influence outcomes' (Biermann *et al.* 2009, p. 32).

This implies a logic of agency that extends beyond personal- and private-sphere behaviours, such as changing light bulbs, turning off electronic equipment at the switch and purchasing energy efficient equipment – in other words, actions that might contribute to a reduced personal or household carbon footprint but do not have an impact on the prevailing societal, political or economic systems that embed high levels of GHG emissions. Rather, agency should be read as those actions undertaken within the public sphere by empowered individuals who are able to reflect on the nature and consequences of their doing within a wider societal context. The capacity for individual actors to undertake effective action is, moreover, constrained by the extent of their ability to act and by 'the capability of the individual to "make a difference" to a pre-existing state of affairs or course of events' (Giddens 1984, p. 14). The role of individual agency therefore needs to be understood as being both enabled and constrained by the *status quo*, the extant social and cultural norms that support contemporary societal institutions and the 'rules' of behaviour (Beck 1992; Giddens 1991).

The implication is that active agency requires reflexivity. According to Held (2005), 'active agents' have the capacity to be self-reflexive and self-determining, and are bestowed with 'both opportunities and duties' (p. 12). They create opportunities to take action but also, concomitantly, they have a duty that this action 'does not curtail and infringe on the life chances and opportunities of others' (Held 2005, p. 13). Agency therefore implies a moral duty not only to act but to act without infringing the rights of others, thus expanding the notion of agency to incorporate a fundamental moral dimension. Moreover this moral obligation on the part of the individual to act exists even where governments fail to take action (Garvey 2008), conferring a 'thick cosmopolitan' obligation (Dobson 2006) on the individual that requires political action to address the structural/root causes of climate change.

Therefore the role of individual agency needs to be understood as being embedded in association with structure (Beck 1992; Biermann *et al.* 2009; Giddens 1991) so that:

> Modernization involves not only structural change, but a changing relationship between social structures and social agents. When modernization reaches a certain level agents tend to become more individualized, that is, decreasingly constrained by structures. In effect structural change forces social actors to become progressively more free from structure. And for modernization successfully to advance, these agents must release themselves from structural constraint and actively shape the modernization process.
>
> (Lash & Wynne 1992, p. 2 quoted in Beck 1992)

The ability for individual actors to effect social change is thereby contained within the understanding of the agent–structure relationship (see section on Structuration in Chapter 2). Reflexive individuals are not simply conceived of as reactive to social conditions; they can also actively intervene to change prevailing structures. However, while reflexive social actors are free to act, their actions can still be curtailed through institutional restraints. Moreover, as Pattberg and Stripple (2008) imply, individual action without critical reflection (such as 'small and painless steps') can simply reinforce the prevailing social norm of structural unsustainability (Gregory 2000; Middlemiss 2014; Scerri & Magee 2012).

As individualized responsibility shifts from being a reflexive moral imperative to a set of personal lifestyle practices divorced from their social moorings that 'neither sustain [n]or challenge the structuring of criteria for value in society' (Scerri 2009, p. 478), it becomes harder to imagine how atomized and disempowered individuals will be equipped to respond to climate change.

Constraints to individual agency

I outlined above three ways that individuals can display their agency in reducing their global warming impact: (1) as an agent of the state (*hierarchical*),

(2) as an economic agent (*individualistic*), or (3) as a moral agent (*egalitarian*). But in what ways are the conditions for individual agency being constrained in modern society? I propose that individual agency for voluntary action on climate change abatement can be limited in a number of distinct ways.

First, actors may not be empowered to take action, or in other words, *actors lack authority*. Agency derives from a sense of personal empowerment, which becomes the basis upon which people are able to take action within their spheres of authority. Norgaard's (2009) meta-analysis of psycho-social research on individual action in relation to climate change draws on several lines of empirical evidence to support the supposition that individuals, in fact, feel disempowered and ineffective. She makes the following observations: as there is no easy solution to climate change people no longer take it seriously (Norgaard 2009, p. 14); people lack a sense of efficacy which acts as a barrier to action (Norgaard 2009, p. 21); providing people with increased knowledge regarding the issue of global warming reduces their sense of personal responsibility (Norgaard 2009, p. 22), thus supporting Räthzel and Uzzell's (2009) contention that people perceive less responsibility for matters that are least under their personal control. Actors, in effect, are 'choosing not to choose' (Macnaghten 2003) to engage with issues, such as climate change. The global scale of the problem and the enormous power inequities evident at a personal level (compared to governments and corporations) overwhelm their ability to see themselves as 'authoritative actors' (Biermann *et al.* 2009, p. 32).

Second, *actors lack trust* in the very institutions (namely, governments) that they turn to for action on issues of global complexity and risk, such as climate change. Whereas governments place confidence in their citizens to respond to the climate crisis through their individual behaviours, the public displace their personal sense of disempowerment through the desire for institutional accountability. The result is a type of 'organised irresponsibility' (Beck 1992) where climate change becomes another 'risk' that people and organizations are responsible for, yet for which no one is held especially accountable (Giddens 1999).

Calls for individual responsibility by governments and other institutions raise issues for the public of institutional trust, capability and duty of care (Bickerstaff & Walker 2002; Bickerstaff *et al.* 2008; Macnaghten 2003; Pidgeon *et al.* 2008). In effect no social contract has been drawn up between individuals and governments to agree on the respective distribution of climate change risks and responsibilities (O'Brien *et al.* 2009). People perceive that governments are not taking acceptable levels of action to mitigate the threat of dangerous climate change. They also doubt whether governments are willing to take action on climate change as they perceive that such action is contrary to governments' economic interests (Darnton 2004, p. 24). People are also alert to the unequal power relationships that operate between the individual and the state and other institutions (Bickerstaff *et al.* 2008; Maniates 2002).

Third, *actors lack reflexivity*. The essential nature of reflexivity can be portrayed as breaking structural bonds in order to unleash individuals' agency (Beck 1992; Gregory 2000). If, on the other hand, individuals act '*without* questioning the norms of the wider society, the possibilities of change will be constrained by certain norms which are taken for granted' (Gregory 2000, p. 485). This sets up a 'vicious circle' where actors, in conducting their daily lives, reinforce the social norms that in turn 'circumscribe individual choice' (Gregory 2000, p. 485). Scerri (2009) argues that actors in Western society display their individualism as 'elemental particles of society' (citing Supiot 2007, p. 14) whose actions are merely 'an instrument of economic development' (p. 473). The 'individualization of responsibility' (Maniates 2002) has shifted the emphasis of voluntary pro-environmental behaviour to the domain of the consumer. Any ethical considerations are thereby subverted into expressions of green consumerism, which Scerri describes as a type of 'ethics-lite'. The linkages between morality and reasons for acting (Scerri 2009, p. 470) are severed in this atomistic interpretation as actors no longer reflect on their private behaviours in relation to broader societal values (p. 478). So in the same way as Räthzel and Uzzell (2009) propose a 'psycho-social dislocation', Scerri (2009, p. 479) argues that individualization creates a politico-ethical dislocation:

> In the contemporary West, possibilities for achieving sustainability fall foul of a way of life that, while free to exercise sovereign choices over a plethora of opportunities, is increasingly cut-off from political – that is, value- and so power-laden – commitments to inhabiting the ecosphere on ethical terms.

Activating agency

This chapter has specifically sought to determine why and how individuals take responsibility for climate change. I have initially established through an overview of social research into peoples' views, motivations and be-haviours on climate change that while people perceive that they are individually responsible for climate change, this is a responsibility shared with others, primarily governments. Also, despite peoples' stated concerns regarding climate change as an important global issue, individuals are failing to take significant action to address it. In response to the question, 'How do we understand responsibility for climate change?' I took from a transdisciplinary review of the literature concerned with responsibility for climate change action five aspects. Responsibility for climate change can be considered from the following dimensions: spatial, temporal, moral/ ethical, relational and behavioural. In considering in what ways individuals act responsibly to mitigate climate change, I distinguished between the personal and private-sphere behaviours that individuals enact within their homes and lifestyles, and political action in the public sphere. Utilizing a discourse classification approach from Cultural Theory I established a typology of individual action to distinguish the types of voluntary actions available to individuals based on their cultural preferences. The third question I considered was: 'How do individual actors acquire agency through voluntary action?' In reply to this question I established a definition of individual agency that requires actors to be authoritative (Biermann *et al.* 2009). In other words, in order for actors to display agency they need to possess the legitimacy and capacity to undertake voluntary action on climate change.

This exposed the conundrum in Beck's theses on risk and individualization, that is, whether the individualization of responsibility can create the conditions for social change on climate change. As stated in the introduction to this chapter, the root of this challenge lies in whether action on climate change can be personal but not disempowering. To attempt to understand this conundrum I needed to consider the role of individual agents in relation to structural enablements and constraints. I drew on three key constraints to the uptake of effective voluntary action on climate change at the individual scale to illustrate this point. First actors, while acknowledging individual responsibility for climate change abatement, feel disempowered in the face of the complexity and enormity of climate change risk. Second, in acknowledging their essential powerlessness, citizens turn to their governments to take responsibility for climate change mitigation. However, governments are seen by their citizens to be equally incapable, ineffective or uncommitted to rise to the climate challenge. Moreover, governments increasingly expect that individuals will take voluntary action in their personal lifestyles but outside of a social contract that sets up the provisions for sharing responsibility – thus creating a sense of distrust. Third, the structural conditions of modernity inhibit the ability for self-reflexive individuals to generate social change as much of their individual action operates to reinforce social norms, or worse, in the absence of reflexivity, the moral bases for voluntary action are subverted through consumerism.

These three constraints are embedded within two 'dislocations'. The first is a psycho-social dislocation that creates an artificial dichotomy between the individual and society, and between the local and the global, resulting in a type of hiatus in action through people 'choosing not to choose'. The second is the politico-ethical dislocation that separates individuals' moral reasoning for taking voluntary action from broader social values. Both dislocations imply the need for deep reflection on the climate change *problematique* at both the personal and societal scales (Gregory 2000), and suggest the necessity for a shift from individual responsibility to a shared one (Scerri 2009) along with a shift in power from governments and global institutions to civil society.

Finally, as climate change is a problem of increasing moral complexity (Gardiner 2006) situated within a socio-political context of increasing individualization, the individual and collective may diverge rather than converge on action for climate change mitigation. Enacting a cosmopolitan obligation within global climate governance provides one potential counter for this course, as it would establish the elements of a common moral platform from which to address the problem of climate change. Such a cosmopolitan obligation would require that individuals 'create collectivities with the relevant capabilities . . . [to form] individual-duty-fulfilling institutions' (Jones 2002, pp. 68–9 in Dobson 2006, p. 181) and that confer rights and responsibilities for climate change mitigation at both the local and global scale. These collectivities could act as a foil to the structural constraints on individual agency.

Notes

1   These social research findings around people's concerns about, and motivations for, taking action on climate change are seldom brought together into meta-analyses (Leviston *et al.* 2011 and Wolf & Moser 2011 are two notable exceptions). While the surveys discussed here identify some broad trends, care needs to be taken in drawing specific conclusions from studies, which have been conducted with a variety of surveying, sampling and analytical methods (Leviston *et al.* 2011).
2   Recent findings indicate that levels of concern may now be increasing. See Capstick *et al.* 2015.
3   The rise of global online organizations such as AVAAZ (www.avaaz.org, accessed 3 June 2015), which now has more than 40 million members, is perhaps indicative of this type of collective individualism at work.
4   Contrary to its depiction here, the Cultural Theory typology does not imply that individuals always act consistently with one of the four types.
5   In such a scheme, individual and household-level carbon emissions would be budgeted to fulfil national targets. A PCA scheme would operate in a similar way to an emissions cap and trade scheme. That is, a cap or limit is initially established and carbon trading on an individual level can occur up to the limit of the cap. Over time the cap is reduced so that the total amount of carbon allowed to be emitted is reduced.
6   Australian consumers can purchase Greenpower, which is charged at a premium to allow the energy retailer to purchase power from renewable sources. See www.greenpower.gov.au, accessed 3 June 2015.
7   For example, Garnaut (2008) states: 'All developing countries continue to reject containment of their emission growth through the adoption of mandatory targets' (p. 179).

References

AccountAbility and Consumers International 2007, *What assures consumers on climate change? Switching on citizen power*, accessed 22 August 2015, www.accountability.org/images/content/2/1/211/What%20Assures%20Consumers%20on%20Climate%20Change.pdf

AccountAbility Net Balance and LRQA 2008, *What assures consumers in Australia on climate change? Switching on citizen power.* 2008 Update – Australian Survey, accessed 22 August 2015, www.accountability21.net.

Ashworth, P., Jeanneret, T., Gardner, J. & Shaw, H. 2011, *Communication and climate change: what the Australian public thinks*, CSIRO Report, Canberra, Australia.

Baer, P., Harte, J., Haya, B., Herzog, A.V., Holdren, J., Hultman, N.E., Kammen, D.M., Norgaard, R.B. & Raymond, L. 2000, 'Climate change: equity and greenhouse gas responsibility', *Science*, vol. 289, no. 5488, p. 2287.

Beck, U. 1992, *Risk society: towards a new modernity*, trans. M. Ritter, Sage, London.

Beck, U. 2000, 'The cosmopolitan perspective: sociology of the second age of modernity', *British Journal of Sociology*, vol. 51, no. 1, pp. 79–105.

Beck, U. 2007, 'Beyond class and nation: reframing social inequalities in a globalizing world', *The British Journal of Sociology*, vol. 58, no. 4, pp. 679–705.

Beck, U. & Beck-Gernsheim, E. 2002, *Individualization: institutionalized individualism and its social and political consequences*, Sage, London.

Bickerstaff, K., Simmons, P. & Pidgeon, N. 2008, 'Constructing responsibilities for risk: negotiating citizen–state relationships', *Environment and Planning A*, vol. 40, pp. 1312–30.

Bickerstaff, K. & Walker, G. 2002, 'Risk, responsibility and blame: an analysis of vocabularies of motive in air-pollution(ing) discourses', *Environment and Planning A*, vol. 34, pp. 2175–92.

Bierhoff, H.-W. & Auhagen, A.E. 2000, 'Responsibility as a fundamental human phenomenon', in A.E. Auhagen & H.-W. Bierhoff (eds), *Responsibility: the many faces of a social phenomenon*, Routledge, London.

Biermann, F., Betsill, M.M., Gupta, J., Kanie, N., Lebel, L., Liverman, D., Schroeder, H. & Siebenhuner, B. 2009, *Earth System Governance: people, places and the planet. Science and implementation plan of the Earth System Governance Project*, vol. ESG Report 1, IHDP: The Earth System Governance Project, Bonn.

Blake, J. 1999, 'Overcoming the "value-action gap" in environmental policy: tensions between national policy and local experience', *Local Environment*, vol. 4, no. 3, pp. 257–78.

Bulkeley, H. 2001, 'Governing climate change: the politics of risk society?', *Transactions of the Institute of British Geographers*, pp. 430–47.

Bulkeley, H. & Newell, P. 2010, *Governing climate change*, Routledge, London.

Caney, S. 2005, 'Cosmopolitan justice, responsibility, and climate change,' *Leiden Journal of International Law*, vol. 18, no. 4, pp. 747–75.

Capstick, S., Whitmarsh, L., Poortinga, W., Pidgeon, N. & Upham, P. 2015, 'International trends in public perceptions of climate change over the past quarter century', *Wiley Interdisciplinary Reviews: Climate Change*, vol. 6, no. 1, pp. 35–61.

Crompton, T. 2008, 'Weathercocks and signposts: the environment movement at a crossroads', *World Wildlife Fund, UK*.

Darnton, A. 2004, *Driving public behaviours for sustainable lifestyles*. Report 2 commissioned by COI on behalf of Department of the Environment, Food and Rural Affairs (DEFRA), UK.

Dobson, A. 2006, 'Thick cosmopolitanism', *Political Studies*, vol. 54, pp. 165–84.

European Commission 2008, *Attitudes of European citizens towards the environment, Special Eurobarometer 295*, European Commission, accessed 30 March 2008, http://ec.europa.eu/public_opinion/archives/ebs/ebs_295_sum_en.pdf.

European Commission 2014, *Special Eurobarometer 409 - Climate change*, European Commission, accessed 22 August 2015, http://ec.europa.eu/public_opinion/index_en.htm.

Friman, M. & Linnér, B.-o. 2008, 'Technology obscuring equity: historical responsibility in UNFCCC negotiations', *Climate Policy*, vol. 8, no. 4, pp. 339–54.

Fudge, S. & Peters, M. 2011, 'Behaviour change in the UK climate debate: an assessment of responsibility, agency and political dimensions', *Sustainability*, vol. 3, no. 6, pp. 789–808.

Gardiner, S.M. 2006, 'A perfect moral storm: climate change, intergenerational ethics and the problem of moral corruption', *Environmental Values*, vol. 15, pp. 397–413.

Garvey, J. 2008, *The ethics of climate change*, Continuum International, London.

Giddens, A. 1984, *The constitution of society. Outline of the theory of structuration*, University of California Press, Berkeley, CA.

Giddens, A. 1991, *Modernity and self-identity: Self and society in the late modern age*, Polity, Cambridge.

Giddens, A. 1999, 'Risk and responsibility', *The Modern Law Review*, vol. 62, no. 1, pp.1–10.

Gregory, W.J. 2000, 'Transforming self and society: a "critical appreciation" model', *Systemic Practice and Action Research*, vol. 13, no. 4, pp. 475–501.

Harris, P.G. 2008, 'Climate change and global citizenship', *Law & Policy*, vol. 30, no. 4, pp. 481–501.

Harvey, D. 2006, 'Neo-liberalism as creative destruction', *Geografiska Annaler*, vol. 88B, no. 2, pp. 145–58.

Held, D. 2005, 'Principles of the cosmopolitan order', in G. Bock & H. Brighouse (eds), *The political philosophy of cosmopolitanism*, Cambridge University Press, Cambridge, pp. 10–27.

Hoppner, C. & Whitmarsh, L. 2010, 'Public engagement in climate action: policy and public expectations', in L. O'Neill, S. Whitmarsh & I. Lorenzoni (eds), *Engaging the public with climate change: behaviour change and communication*, Earthscan, London, pp. 47–65.

IPCC, 2014 'Climate change 2014: synthesis report', [in core writing team, R.K. Pachauri and L.A. Meyer (eds)], contribution of working group I, II and III to the *Fifth Assessment Report of the Intergovernmental Panel on Climate Change*. IPCC, Geneva, Switzerland, p. 151.

Jackson, T. 2005, *Motivating sustainable consumption: a review of evidence on consumer behaviour and behavioural change*, Sustainable Development Research Network, Surrey, UK.

Kaiser, F.G. & Shimoda, T.A. 1999, 'Responsibility as a predictor of ecological behaviour', *Environmental Psychology*, vol. 19, pp. 243–53.

Kent, J. 2011, 'Individual responsibility and voluntary action on climate change: activating agency', in P.G. Harris (ed.), *Ethics and global environmental policy: cosmopolitan conceptions of climate change*, Edward Elgar, Cheltenham, UK, pp. 66–88.

Kollmus, A. & Agyeman, J. 2002, 'Mind the gap: why do people act environmentally and what are the barriers to pro-environmental behaviour?', *Environmental Education Research*, vol. 8, no. 3, pp. 239–59.

Leiserowitz, A., Maibach, E., Roser-Renouf, C., Feinberg, G. & Rosenthal, S. 2014, *Politics and global warming, spring 2014*, George Mason University, New Haven, CT.

Leviston, Z., Leitch, A., Greenhill, M., Leonard, R. & Walker, I. 2011, *Australians' views of climate change*, CSIRO, Canberra, Australia.

Leviston, Z., Price, J., Malkin, S. & McCrea, R. 2014, *Fourth annual survey of Australian attitudes to climate change: interim report*, CSIRO, Perth, Australia.

Linklater, A. 1998, *The transformation of political community: ethical foundations of the post-Westphalian era*, University of South Carolina Press, Columbia, SC.

Lorenzoni, I., Nicholson-Cole, S. & Whitmarsh, L. 2007, 'Barriers perceived to engaging with climate change among the UK public and their policy implications', *Global Environmental Change*, vol. 17, no. 3-4, pp. 445–59.

Lorenzoni, I. & Pidgeon, N.F. 2006, 'Public views on climate change: European and USA perspectives', *Climatic Change*, vol. 77, no. 1/2, pp. 73–95.

Macnaghten, P. 2003, 'Embodying the environment in everyday life practices 1', *The Sociological Review*, vol. 51, no. 1, pp. 63–84.

Maniates, M.F. 2002, 'Individualization: plant a tree, buy a bike, save the world?', in T.M. Princen, M. Maniates & K. Conca (eds), *Confronting consumption*, MIT, Cambridge, MA.

Maniates, M.F. 2012, 'Everyday possibilities', *Global Environmental Politics*, vol. 12, no. 1, pp. 121–5.

Marsden, G., Mullen, C., Bache, I., Bartle, I. & Flinders, M. 2014, 'Carbon reduction and travel behaviour: discourses, disputes and contradictions in governance', *Transport Policy*, vol. 35, no. 0, pp. 71–8.

Matravers, M. 2007, *Responsibility and justice*, Polity, Cambridge, UK.

Middlemiss, L. 2014, 'Individualised or participatory? Exploring late-modern identity and sustainable development', *Environmental Politics*, vol. 23, no. 6, pp. 929–46.

Moloney, S., Horne, R.E. & Fien, J. 2010, 'Transitioning to low carbon communities – from behaviour change to systemic change: lessons from Australia', *Energy Policy*, vol. 38, no. 12, pp. 7614–23.

Norgaard, K.M. 2009, *Cognitive and behavioural challenges in responding to climate change: background paper to the 2010 World Development Report*, Policy Research Working Paper 4940, The World Bank, Geneva, Switzerland.

Norgaard, K.M. 2011, *Living in denial: climate change, emotions, and everyday life*, The MIT Press, London.

O'Brien, K., Hayward, B. & Berkes, F. 2009, 'Rethinking social contracts: building resilience in a changing climate', *Ecology and Society*, vol. 14, no. 2, pp. 12–28.

O'Riordan, T. & Jordan, A. 1999, 'Institutions, climate change and cultural theory: towards a common analytical framework', *Global Environmental Change Part A: Human & Policy Dimensions*, vol. 9, pp. 81–93.

Okereke, C., Bulkeley, H. & Schroeder, H. 2009, 'Conceptualizing climate governance beyond the international regime', *Global Environmental Politics*, vol. 9, no. 1, pp. 58–78.

Parks, B.C. & Roberts, J.T. 2010, 'Addressing inequality and building trust to secure a post-2012 global climate deal', in M.T. Boykoff (ed.), *The politics of climate change: a survey*, Routledge, London, pp. 111–35.

Pattberg, P. & Stripple, J. 2008, 'Beyond the public and private divide: remapping transnational climate governance in the 21st century', *International Environmental Agreements: Politics, Law and Economics*, vol. 8, no. 4, pp. 367–88.

Pidgeon, N.F., Lorenzoni, I. & Poortinga, W. 2008, 'Climate change or nuclear power – no thanks! A quantitative study of public perceptions and risk framing in Britain', *Global Environmental Change*, vol. 18, no. 1, pp. 69–85.

Pogge, T. 2002, 'Human rights and human responsibilities', *Global Justice & Transnational Politics*, pp. 151–95.

Räthzel, N. & Uzzell, D. 2009, 'Changing relations in global environmental change', *Global Environmental Change*, vol. 19, no. 3, pp. 326–35.

Reeves, A., Lemon, M. & Cook, D. 2014, 'Jump-starting transition? Catalysing grassroots action on climate change', *Energy Efficiency*, vol. 7, no. 1, pp. 115–32.

Rosewarne, S., Goodman, J. & Pearse, R. 2014, *Climate action upsurge. The ethnography of climate movement politics*, Routledge, London.

Scerri, A. 2009, 'Paradoxes of increased individuation and public awareness of environmental issues', *Environmental Politics*, vol. 18, no. 4, pp. 467–85.

Scerri, A. & Magee, L. 2012, 'Green householders, stakeholder citizenship and sustainability', *Environmental Politics*, vol. 21, no. 3, pp. 387–411.

Seyfang, G. & Paavola, J. 2008, 'Inequality and sustainable consumption: bridging the gaps', *Local Environment*, vol. 13, no. 8, pp. 669–84.

Shove, E. 2010, 'Beyond the ABC: climate change policy and theories of social change', *Environment and Planning A*, vol. 42, no. 6, pp. 1273–85.

Singer, P. 2002, *One world: the ethics of globalization*, Yale University Press, New Haven, CT.

Singer, P. 2006, 'Ethics and climate change: a commentary on MacCracken, Toman and Gardiner', *Environmental Values*, vol. 15, no. 3, pp. 415–22.

Singer, P. 2011, *The expanding circle: ethics, evolution and moral progress*, Princeton University Press, Princeton, NJ.

Spaargaren, G. & Mol, A.P.J. 2008, 'Greening global consumption: redefining politics and authority', *Global Environmental Change*, vol. 18, pp. 350–9.

Stern, P.C. 2005, 'Understanding individuals' environmentally significant behavior', *Environmental Law Reporter News and Analysis*, vol. 35, no. 11, p. 10785.

The Climate Institute 2014, *Climate of the nation 2014. Australian attitudes on climate change: are Australians climate dinosaurs?* The Climate Institute, Sydney, Australia.

Whitmarsh, L. 2009, 'Behavioural responses to climate change: asymmetry of intentions and impacts', *Journal of Environmental Psychology*, vol. 29, pp. 13–23.

Wolf, J. & Moser, S.C. 2011, 'Individual understandings, perceptions, and engagement with climate change: insights from in-depth studies across the world', *Wiley Interdisciplinary Reviews: Climate Change*, vol. 2, no. 4, pp. 547–69.

4   Rise of the grassroots

Introduction

The period 2006 to 2007 was a defining moment in the rise of community-based climate action, coinciding with heightened national and international public concern regarding climate change (Hanson 2010; Neilsen and Environmental Change Institute 2007). This period saw: the release of the IPCC's fourth report; the *Stern Review on the Economics of Climate Change*; and significant weather events, such as the aftermath of Hurricane Katrina and the severe drought that gripped Australia. People were mobilized at this time to take part in direct action on climate change. In Australia in November 2006 100,000 people marched in the Walk Against Warming[1] held in cities and regional towns (Hall *et al.* 2010). This mass demonstration in support of action on climate change would only be matched again in 2009 during the Copenhagen Climate Conference.

An Inconvenient Truth created a media surge around climate change (Boykoff 2007, p. 481) and has been credited with widespread elevated levels of awareness of the scientific basis for human induced global warming as well as with motivating people to moderate their carbon producing behaviours (Neilsen and Environmental Change Institute 2007). The film was an inspiration for many and acted as a strong incentive to seek out others taking climate action. By June 2007, 75 community-based CAGs existed across all states in Australia (Hall *et al.* 2010), coinciding with a flowering of grassroots groups internationally.[2] The first Camp for Climate Action was held in the UK in 2006 and the Transition Towns movement was established in Totnes in the same year. This coalescence of events gave climate change 'significance, a sense of urgency, a symbolic power that helped it emerge from the murkiness in which it had remained engulfed for two decades' (McGaurr & Lester 2009, p. 175).

The politics of moral failure

Climate change as a political issue has probably had a greater effect in Australia than any other nation (Jones 2010, p. 4). The Australian situation, characterized by its volatile climate politics, provides a pertinent example of the political conditions underlying the emergence of grassroots climate action. The development of local and community-based groups occurred within an environment of 'moral failure' within Australian politics (Jones 2010), which came to a head in late 2007 with the defeat of the incumbent Liberal–National coalition party following 12 years of conservative government. The number of CAGs increased rapidly at this time, primed by the perception of government inaction on climate change and as a foil to displacement of ENGOs in the formation of public policy. With public concern regarding climate change at its highest, the incoming Australian Labor Party (ALP) government prioritized climate change as a key policy platform (Rootes 2008). On election in 2007, the new Prime Minister Kevin Rudd moved to ratify the Kyoto Protocol, something which the previous government had failed to do. The release of the Garnaut Review (Garnaut 2008) recommending concerted Australian action to reduce GHG emissions and the subsequent development of the Carbon Pollution Reduction Scheme (CPRS) heralded a new era within Australian climate politics. After 12 years of conservative government and relative inaction on climate change, this period saw the Australian government taking climate change seriously and it became an issue of hot political debate.

The CPRS legislation, which would have established an Australian emissions trading scheme, was a key plank of Labor's policy platform but failed to win parliamentary support. The CPRS legislation was rejected twice in the Australian Senate.[3] Opposition to the CPRS came from a hostile, sceptical and industry-supporting Coalition, which argued that the legislation went too far (Jones 2010), and from the Australian Greens who decided not to support the legislation because it did not go far enough. The Senate's failure to pass the legislation gave the Labor government under Kevin Rudd a trigger for a double dissolution[4] and a new election around the issue (Rootes 2011). Instead, in what was perceived as a betrayal of public trust on the 'great moral, economic and social challenge of our time' (Jones 2010, p. 9), Rudd deferred the CPRS until 2013.

Stepping back from this election commitment was seen as a huge betrayal of trust by Labor supporters concerned about climate change. *'I'm an old Labor voter and they promised this was, this is the issue of our times and they promised and they lied and I'm furious at the Labor Party, absolutely furious, so I'm compelled by that'* (David, 63, VIC4).[5] This led to a critical juncture in Australian climate politics that according to Stewart (2013) 'released' sceptics and deniers as a powerful countermovement. The deferral of the CPRS, considered Rudd's 'worst mistake' (Rootes 2011, p. 412), contributed to a haemorrhaging of electoral support for the incumbent Prime Minister, largely to the Australian Greens. With an election looming, Rudd was dumped from the leadership to be replaced by Julia Gillard in June 2010.

Climate change rated barely a mention in the 2010 election (Jones 2010). Labor's major climate change policy proposal centred on the creation of a 'much-derided citizen's assembly to generate consensus on measures to address climate change' (Rootes 2011, p. 412), indicative of the 'near-pathological risk-aversion' evident in government policymaking around climate change at this time. The election resulted in a hung parliament[6] with Labor managing to remain in government only by gaining the support of the Australian Greens and three independents. One of the conditions for their support was the implementation of a climate change policy that included a price on carbon. In October 2010, the government established the Multi-Party Climate Change Committee (MPCCC) to investigate options for establishing a carbon price and to build community understanding and support (Jones 2010).

From 1 July 2011, the Senate gained additional Green parliamentarians, who together with key independents established a more favourable environment for progressive climate change policy. The Clean Energy Legislative Package passed into law on 8 November 2011.[7] The main features of the Package[8] were: the Clean Energy Act 2011, which established a carbon pricing mechanism from 1 July 2012; the establishment of the Climate Change Authority, which remains responsible for setting carbon pollution caps and reviewing the carbon price mechanisms and other climate change laws; and the establishment of the Clean Energy Regulator. However, this signal of a progressive climate politics within Australia was short-lived as a strong Opposition campaign was mounted to repeal the carbon tax, fervently supported by climate change sceptics and deniers. In 2013, a little over 12 months from the time the carbon pricing mechanism came into effect (on 1 July 2012), the Liberal–National Party coalition was elected with Tony Abbott as Prime Minister and the carbon tax legislation repealed.

Copenhagen climate conference

If 2006 marked the rapid transcendence of a climate action movement, the period following the 2009 Copenhagen Climate Conference marked its decline (Rosewarne *et al.* 2014). Following increasingly dire warnings of catastrophic climate disruption from the scientific community (IPCC 2007), the United Nations Climate Change Conference in Copenhagen (COP15) in December 2009 represented the pinnacle of hopes for action on climate change, particularly for ENGOs and concerned sectors of civil society (Fisher 2010). For many, Copenhagen offered the promise of tangible emission reduction commitments from the major carbon polluting nations (Dimitrov 2010; Doelle 2010).

The unprecedented level of interest in the Copenhagen talks led to high numbers of registrants. Fisher (2010), for example, notes that for the first time in Copenhagen 'more than two-thirds of those registered (20,611 individuals) were NGO observers' (p. 12). However, the venue was capable of holding only 15,000 delegates, and further restrictions put in place in the final days meant that a mere 300 representatives from NGOs attended

(McGregor 2011). Direct actions by some NGOs within the conference venue, the Bella Center, resulted in the revocation of accreditation of several high profile international NGOs (Fisher 2010). According to Fisher, the heightened presence of an international, coordinated, climate justice movement (Doherty & Doyle 2008; Jamison 2010) in organized protests, direct actions and civil disobedience outside the venue and in the city of Copenhagen more broadly, created 'disenfranchisement'. Fisher defines disenfranchisement as 'being deprived of the capability to participate and to influence agenda-setting and decision-making (Fisher & Green 2004: 69)'. Fisher asserts that this would trigger diminished participation in future UNFCCC negotiations,[9] a harbinger of the future role of civil society both 'inside' and 'outside' the formal United Nations processes.

Midway through the climate talks on 12 December 2009, an international day of climate action saw civil society actions across the world – 100,000 people marched in Copenhagen while hundreds of thousands gathered at events held in capital cities and major towns around the world.[10] The hopes of many within civil society rested on achieving an international agreement that would lock in action to limit global temperature rise below two degrees.

However, the outcome of the Copenhagen Climate Conference was a disappointment to ENGOs and civil society organizations campaigning for an ambitious and binding global treaty. Despite the unprecedented attendance of 120 political leaders (McGregor 2011) in the final days of the conference, the majority of commentators described the conference as a failure (Christoff 2010; Dimitrov 2010; Rogelj *et al.* 2010). The outcome of the Copenhagen Climate Conference was the non-binding Copenhagen Accord. It had been hoped that COP15 would secure binding commitments to GHG reductions which would ensure that global warming in the twenty-first century did not exceed two degrees (den Elzen 2010). The Copenhagen Accord failed to deliver this outcome.

The final days of the Copenhagen climate talks, and in particular the final negotiation of the Copenhagen Accord where the majority of civil society observers were 'locked out' of the conference venue, generated a high degree of criticism. As a result, Climate Action Network International (CAN-I)[11] called on the COP President to ensure better engagement of civil society in future negotiations. The President of Bolivia, one of the six dissenting nations to the Copenhagen Accord, established the World People's Conference on Climate Change and the Rights of Mother Earth (held in Cochabamba in April 2010). The aim of the World People's Conference was to challenge the dominant ecological modernization discourse under the UNFCCC and to propose an alternative, grassroots and indigenous-focused 'green radicalism' (Stevenson & Dryzek 2012).

For some months following Copenhagen there was considerable soul searching among attending ENGOs regarding the outcomes of the international negotiations and demobilization evident in the nascent climate action movement. Australian CAGs, in contrast, appeared less directly impacted. Consistent with their community-based concerns they focused their attention on matters of local significance. This was consistent with the prevailing mood that I found among those who attended Klimaforum,[12] the vibrant grassroots forum in Copenhagen. At Klimaforum there was little faith in a positive global outcome being reached through the formal negotiations. Instead, people's optimism lay with the capacity of the many local and community-based initiatives from around the world being showcased there.

The unprecedented scale of interest and involvement from civil society in the 2009 Copenhagen Climate Change talks called into question the capacity of the current mainstream negotiations to adequately address the concerns of global citizens on the most pressing social issue of our time. In this sense, Copenhagen represented a turning point in the relations between civil society and the current regime. Since the Copenhagen talks, civil society organizations have maintained a significant presence at the annual UNFCCC COPs but not in the numbers nor with the degree of protestation evident in Copenhagen. The public's concerns also shifted after 2009 to more immediate economic threats to their wellbeing. Many of the grassroots organizations that emerged and grew rapidly from 2006–2009 started to dissipate and their memberships declined.

Grassroots 'upsurge'

The years 2006–2009 were therefore a period of heightened public concern around climate change matched with political upheaval and international civil society mobilization. It was during this time that significant grassroots climate activism emerged. Rosewarne *et al.* (2014), in their book *Climate Action Upsurge*, detail this phenomenon through an ethnographic study of climate activists within Australia. However, it is interesting to note that this period of rapid escalation and then demobilization can be tracked in a similar way in other Western nations. The UK provides a particularly informative example because it was a significant site of both grassroots mobilization and its decline.

Climate Camps

A Climate Camp, according to Pearse *et al.* (2010), is a 'spatial intervention' located as closely as possible to a source of significant carbon emissions, such as a power plant, airport or coalmine. Climate Camps create a temporary community that is directed at learning about and taking direct action on fossil fuel expansion activities. 'As such, they create ideological power as counter-sites, designed to unmask and contest plans to expand carbon-intensive infrastructures and industries' (Pearse *et al.* 2010, p. 82).

The first Camp for Climate Action was held in the UK in 2006 (Doyle 2009). In the following years Climate Camps spread to sites across the UK, Europe and Australia (Rosewarne *et al.* 2014) where they exhibited 'an anarchist ethos and act[ed] as cultural laboratories where demonstrations of technologies and techniques for sustainable, low carbon living are on show' (North 2011, p. 1582). As such, Camps tended to attract the more committed and radicalized activists rather than those just commencing their collective climate action journey. As Doyle expresses, Climate Camps sought to address the isolation of individual protestors through collective action and bring people together into a 'community of resistance'. The experience of the Camp was then intended to be 'a platform to inspire individuals to adopt these ways of living in their local communities' (Doyle 2009, p. 110). Camps were therefore considered temporary model communities of alternative and sustainable lifestyle practices (Doyle 2009; Pearse *et al.* 2010). Deliberative, participative and non-violent direct action processes were central to their operation and they aimed to be wholly inclusive and non-hierarchical (Doyle 2009). Camps incorporated a particular model of modified consensus decision-making, group deliberative processes and support that derives from anarchist practice and can be observed in other contemporary social change movements, in particular the World Social Forum and the Occupy movement. In 2011, Camp for Climate Action in the UK decided to no longer hold annual Climate Camps and embarked on a process of reflection on the future strategy for organizing and action. There have been no further Camps within Australia since that time.

Transition Towns

Transition Towns[13] also mark their beginnings in 2006 in the UK and have since 'rhizomically' spread internationally (Bailey *et al.* 2010). Transition Towns aim to insulate their communities from the duel impacts of peak oil and climate change by relocalizing production in order to reduce dependence on the currently unsustainable modes of production within the carbon-based economy and build community resilience to future shocks (Dryzek *et al.* 2013). The two main issues of concern to the Transition Movement are peak oil and climate change. Transition Initiatives share three principal characteristics: they engage members in personal action; provide community-based activities, such as the development of Energy Descent Plans and skills for relocalization; and have international appeal. Feola and Nunes (2014) observe that relocalization is a key theme of the Transition Movement that requires reduced dependency on global markets and oil dependent transport. Relocalization also creates a rationale for 'transitioners' to focus their energies on a discrete set of interests, such as 'food, transport, energy and local currencies' (Feola & Nunes 2014, p. 234).

The Transition Movement has attracted a significant degree of research interest, possibly because of its rapid development and spread. More recently, researchers have considered Transition Initiatives as exemplars of community-scale climate governance 'experiments' (Bulkeley *et al.* 2015; Hoffmann 2011) from which can be drawn significant learning on how bottom-up social change occurs. Seyfang and Haxeltine (2012) found that Transition Town memberships share particular characteristics and tend to be over-represented by a particular type of person: female, aged 45–64; 'extremely well educated'; professionally employed but not highly paid. Members display characteristics of ' "post-materialists" who eschew high-status jobs and consumption in favour of personal fulfilment and (in particular environmental) activism' (Seyfang & Haxeltine 2012, p. 388)[14] and engage with less radical agendas and confrontational tactics than, for example, participants in Climate Camps. As Bailey *et al.* (2010, p. 598) put it, their emphasis is on local action that 'allows relocalisers and other survivalists to avoid having to persuade politicians to redesign economic systems while simultaneously appealing to grassroots supporters in order to create momentum for broader political and economic reforms'.

Feola and Nunes' (2014) recent case study of the Transition Movement identifies several factors that contribute to its success. First, they note that successful Transition Towns create social links with other members of their local community, such as local authorities and businesses, thus 'building capacity and empowering social actors' (p. 247) as well as having an external impact through improved environmental performance or by the development of social innovations, such as local currency schemes. However, the root of their success can be tracked to their centrally organized resources and training and expanding knowledge networks globally. Transition Initiatives are least successful when they fail to engage with other actors (p. 247).

Carbon reduction action groups (CRAGs)

CRAGs consist of members from a local community who come together to measure, reduce and potentially trade their personal and/or household carbon emissions. The first CRAG was formed in the UK in 2006, with further groups developing in the USA, Canada, China and Australia (Krakoff 2011). At their height in 2008 there were 25 groups operating throughout the UK until their eventual decline in 2010 (Hielscher 2013). About half a dozen CRAGs were active at one time within Australia. Each CRAG set up an agreed range of emission sources that would be measured, accounted for and then 'claimed'. Carbon emissions from air travel, home heating, car travel, electricity consumption and public transportation could be included within a CRAG's scheme, with each group member being allocated a personal carbon 'ration' for each year (Krakoff 2011, p. 29). If a group member exceeded their annual ration there would be an opportunity to purchase or trade additional allowances. CRAGs therefore set up a group accountability scheme to assist their members in understanding the bases of their individual or household carbon footprint and tangible measures to reduce it.

Hielscher's detailed innovation history of the rise and fall of CRAGs in the UK from 2006–2010 provides some useful measures for the success and failure of community-based collectives such as CRAGs. She notes, for example, that their demise could be traced to several key factors. CRAGs relied on an organic process for spreading to other communities as there was no core, centralized establishment or organization. A more systemic spread may have been expected if CRAGs had a central organizing platform or philosophy such as exists in the Transition Movement. CRAGs were self-selecting, relying principally on members' existing social networks of friends and family. While this bred a high degree of trust and support among the group it likely limited group membership as they failed to engage broader sectors within their local communities. The groups lacked wider structural support and networks, which could have assisted when they came up against the systemic issues that constrain the individual and/or household from reducing their GHG emissions. Finally, the longevity of the CRAGs was limited by their lack of a more encompassing vision that could create a broader audience. This may have provided the ability for groups to evolve and change in response to varying social, political and economic conditions.

There is further evidence to suggest that community-based collectives engaged in climate action rose at the same time across many Western nations (Burgmann & Baer 2012; Krakoff 2011; Wolf & Moser 2011).[15] It is only recently that the burgeoning groundswell from the grassroots has claimed some attention from scholars; however, they are primarily seen either as a means for states to link up their citizens' individual and household carbon reduction actions or sites for devolving state responsibility for climate action. Transition Towns are the most commonly cited example of a grassroots movement rising from local communities to create an alternative, 'new and sustainable materialism' (Dryzek *et al.* 2013). Much less is known about community-based collectives outside of the major ENGOs that act primarily in an advocacy role for greater political action on climate change. For the most part these types of grassroots organizations fly under the radar and remain largely invisible to mainstream organizations and the state. Some exceptions follow: low carbon communities in the UK, according to the Low Carbon Communities Network,[16] numbered more than 400 groups with an additional 400 supporting members in 2012; hundreds of community-led renewable energy generation initiatives have developed within the UK with community renewable energy projects thriving across the UK, Europe, Australia and the USA (Gross & Mautz 2015). Perhaps, though, the most significant show of citizen strength derived from the grassroots is exemplified by the mobilization of over 1,000 groups that supported the 400,000 strong People's Climate March[17] held in New York

City in September 2014. The march was held in the lead-up to the international meeting called by the UN President, Ban Ki-moon, in an effort to create a sense of urgency and commitment by nations in the lead-up to the Paris Climate Change talks to be held in December 2015.

In the following section I outline a case study that tracks one type of grassroots social innovation, namely, Australian CAGs. CAGs emerged in 2006 from their local communities in order to take both practical and political action towards climate change mitigation. Their passage of rise and subsequent decline and continuing evolution provides a detailed case of community-based climate agency.

Australian climate action groups (CAGs)

CAGs can be considered to be as varied as the communities that they draw their members from and their activities tend to align with the motivations of their core active membership. Their membership ranges from a few people to several thousand[18] and they engage in different forms of action, including: holding local talks and information stalls; coordinating bulk buys of solar panels and hot water systems; developing local wind farms; political advocacy; direct action; and civil disobedience.

Since their emergence around 2006, CAGs have taken measures to better organize and build their movement on a regional, state and national level in an effort to increase their influence, effectiveness and political power. National climate summits[19] have been held annually since 2009, and in 2010 the Community Climate Action Network was established. The aim of the Network is to 'build a diverse, participatory grassroots climate action movement' through better coordination of groups' activities on a national basis, promotion of communication among groups, support for existing state and regional networks, and coordination of national activities.

Some CAGs have also joined the peak national non-government organization responsible for climate change action within Australia, the Climate Action Network Australia (CANA). CAGs represent a significant component of the CANA membership and their influence on CANA policy development and direction has become more evident in recent years. CANA is a member of CAN-I,[20] which is the peak global climate change NGO that contributes to international climate change policy, primarily through the UNFCCC negotiations and related fora. In more recent times CAGs have joined other national alliances responding to emerging issues, in particular Lock the Gate,[21] which campaigns against coal seam gas production and Solar Citizens,[22] which advocates for solar energy at the household, community and national levels.

My research with CAGs was undertaken following the United Nations Copenhagen Climate Conference held in December 2009. As described above, this was a period characterized by civil society disappointment in the failure of the Copenhagen talks to reach a global binding agreement; it was also a period where the moral failings of successive Australian governments to act decisively on climate change fuelled public distrust, and when public concern around climate change had started to decline. Research was undertaken with eight Australian CAGs. Focus group discussions were conducted with each CAG and form the primary data source for the case study. These are augmented by the results of scoping interviews with the major Australian civil society and non-government climate action organizations, personal observations and reflections as a participant in the climate action movement within Australia that included attending two Climate Camps and two national Community Climate Action Network summits and attendance at both COP15 and Klimaforum in Copenhagen. Documentary evidence, such as CAG websites, have also informed the case study.

The selection of CAGs for involvement was purposive, based on their different types of geographical location – inner or outer suburban areas of major cities and rural/regional towns – and sought to include groups that employed different types of voluntary climate action, ranging from overt political action (such as direct action, civil disobedience) to more consumer-based activities (such as bulk-buying of solar panels) to community education and awareness raising. One CRAG was included. The eight focus groups were held between November 2009 and May 2010 and included 40 adults in total (20 women and 20 men). Several themes became apparent through the analysis of the transcribed recordings of the focus groups, which help to understand the types of people involved in CAGs, their motivations for taking climate action and the impact that they aspire to on a personal, group and societal level.

Motivation for voluntary action on climate change

Participants reported varying reasons for taking voluntary action on climate change. These ranged from concerns for their children or grandchildren, nature and the environment, resource conservation and social justice. For the most part participants demonstrated a high degree of knowledge of the science of climate change which fed their motivation for action. In most groups participants mentioned Al Gore's film, *An Inconvenient Truth*, as important in generating their awareness of climate change as an issue. Underpinning their concerns was a strong desire to 'do the right thing', indicating that their actions were based on a sense of moral obligation.

Types of individual and collective (group) action undertaken

The types of action taken by participants varied considerably across the groups. In terms of individual actions, participants were engaging in activities, such as: retrofitting their homes for lower carbon emissions; using public transport or cycling rather than driving a car; becoming vegetarian;

and turning off their hot water systems. The types of actions undertaken by CAG participants both individually and collectively were distinct from those of the general public in that CAG members' actions required significant investments in time and money. Some of the lifestyle practices adopted by CAG members go well beyond what would be considered normed social behaviours as they involve a considerable degree of discomfort, or in Maniates and Meyer's (2010) terms, an 'environmental politics of sacrifice'. Group activities included: overt political campaigns, lobbying and direct action; community education and awareness-raising; and bulk buying of solar panels.

Individual and collective agency around climate change

Participants stressed the importance of their individual responsibility for action on climate change but understood that this responsibility needs to be shared with other social actors, and in particular with governments. According to the CAG participants, governments hold the power to create the changes required to transition to a low carbon emissions pathway. Most groups were highly politically engaged and saw their role in collective action in influencing government policy and practice. The groups worked to support and enhance their individual agency by increasing confidence, providing skills in their political practices and fostering reflexivity.

Constraints and enablements for action

Participants identified many different reasons why others in the community failed to get involved in action on climate change. These included: apathy, denial, fear, ignorance, feeling disempowered, lack of immediate danger and an increase in individualism within society. On the other hand, constraints for the participants were almost universally expressed as a lack of time, money and energy. Enabling aspects of the groups were mostly associated with their providing support, skills and confidence.

Scale of influence and action

For the most part, participants sought to influence their families, members of their local communities and their local politicians. They sought to expand their influence by recruiting more members to their groups and by linking with other local community organizations, including other CAGs in their region, state or Australia-wide. Participants were often involved in other community initiatives related to the environment or social justice issues. Several participants noted the importance of building greater community resilience as a type of insurance against the prospect of future climatic catastrophe.

Communicating climate change

For some groups, their focus was on encouraging community members to undertake small and simple steps towards a more sustainable and less carbon-intensive lifestyle. Others took on a more overt political role through, for example, being involved in actions to publicly shame their local political member. Influencing public opinion was another strong element of their communication strategies and involved letter writing to the local newspaper and use of the internet and social networking.

These themes are introduced briefly here and are drawn out in detail in the remaining chapters. Before turning to that more detailed analysis, I discuss some additional theoretical conceptions that are paramount to understanding how grassroots action on climate change can hold the key to broader scale social transformation.

Conceptualizing community action on climate change

Sustainability transitions theory

While Beck's risk theory helps to broadly frame the issue of climate change within the context of risk, globalization and postmodernity, I now turn to Sustainability Transitions Theory (STT), which has been instrumental in developing ideas around sustainability, grassroots innovations and social change and provides a more nuanced understanding of how change can occur from the grassroots.

STT is a middle range theory (MRT) (Geels 2011) that draws from diverse theoretical sources, including innovation studies, sociology, institutional theory, science and technology studies, political science and governance to analyse the co-evolution of society and technology (Geels 2011; Grin *et al.* 2010). It has been widely employed in the study of technology (such as electricity use, transport etc.) and policy systems (de Haan & Rotmans 2011; Loorbach & Rotmans 2010). More recently its application has been directed towards processes of grassroots innovation and social change from the 'bottom up' (Hargreaves *et al.* 2011; Middlemiss & Parrish 2010; Seyfang & Smith 2007). The pluralist nature of STT also makes it relevant to a transdisciplinary exploration of climate change from the perspective of societal change.

Socio-technical transitions occur, according to the theory, when innovative and radical solutions to issues of sustainability (described as 'niches') are able to challenge and ultimately overthrow the dominant system or 'regime' (Seyfang *et al.* 2010, p. 3). An STT approach acknowledges that shifting to a low or zero carbon future requires changes in both actors and structures as individual lifestyles and household-level behaviours are embedded in wider social, cultural, technological and institutional systems. Traditionally, STT has been used to understand how new technologies (or new practices) emerge and then transition into wider adoption throughout society. More recently STT has been applied to social innovations that emerge from the grassroots of civil society and that have the potential to translate into the mainstream. I will argue that STT theory offers a useful heuristic for developing an appreciation of why community collectives, such as CAGs, have arisen as a particular and distinct grassroots community-based phenomenon in response to climate change and how they could and do engage in broader scale processes of social change.

According to Grin *et al.* (2010), there are four conceptual notions that underpin the transitions of social and technological systems aimed at achieving sustainable development. First, systems (economic, cultural, technological, ecological, institutional) do not develop in isolation but *co-evolve* in a process of cyclical, iterative change (Grin *et al.* 2010, p. 4). Second, a transition can be conceived as occurring across three levels: niche, regime and landscape. This is known as the multi-level perspective (MLP) (Geels 2005; Geels 2011) and is commonly used to frame transition processes. (The MLP is explained in more detail below.) Third, the pathway of the transition is *multiphase* (Grin *et al.* 2010, pp. 126–31) and together these phases of change form an S-curve (illustrated at Figure 4.1) or rather an ideal representation for a societal change process.

In reality, Grin *et al.* (2010) note that these phases may lead to alternative and 'non-ideal' outcomes (illustrated in Figure 4.2). In this S-curve diagram they identify alternative system progressions of system breakdown, backlash and lock-in. They also note that the S-curve does not replicate the timeframes required for societal transitions, which they argue usually occur over at least one generation or 25 years (Grin *et al.* 2010, p. 128). Nor does the S-curve acknowledge the relative mutability of the change phases, which may incorporate varying degrees of acceleration or slow down dependent on what

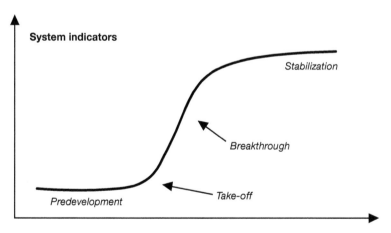

Figure 4.1 The different phases of a transition (Rotmans *et al.* 2001)
Source: Reproduced from Grin *et al.* 2010, p. 130

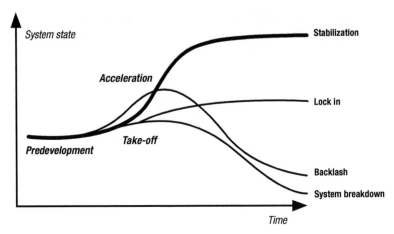

Figure 4.2 Alternatives for S-shaped curve
Source: Reproduced from Grin *et al.* 2010, p. 131

other impacts are operating outside of the particular transition (for example, unimagined events such as wars or large natural or man-made disasters). Grin *et al.* (2010, pp. 129–30) observe that the multi-phase framework is:

> Primarily employed as a descriptive ordering framework for the direction, pace and magnitude of a transition, describing the changes in phases, and as an explanatory framework for explaining the driving forces and mechanisms behind the phases and their changes (from relative order and stability to chaos and instability and vice versa).

Lastly, sustainability transitions involve *co-design and learning*. Sustainability transitions engage processes of social learning involving a 'synthesis of theoretical knowledge, practical knowledge and practical experience' (Grin *et al.* 2010, p. 5). In other words, successful sustainability transitions require *knowing* and *doing* that is both reflexive and shared. Social learning, according to Reed *et al.* (2010, p. 5), includes the following three aspects. First, social learning must demonstrate that a change has occurred in understanding in the individuals involved. Second, it must go beyond the individual to be situated within wider social units or 'communities of practice' (Wenger 1999) within society. Thirdly, social learning occurs through social interactions and processes between actors within a social network.

Implied by these four conceptual precursors is that sustainability transitions are 'very complex and comprehensive phenomena' and it cannot be assumed that a particular 'normative orientation' towards sustainable development will result in the shaping of transitions (Grin *et al.* 2010, p. 3). Denoting that direct and instrumental interventions around sustainable development (for example, to support a governmental policy position) may lack the impetus for creating change or may not deliver the intended outcomes.

The multi-level perspective (MLP)

Geels (2014, p. 23) describes the MLP in relation to sustainability transitions as an 'interplay' between three analytical levels: 'niches (the locus of radical innovations), socio-technical regimes (the locus of established practices and associated rules that enable and constrain incumbent actors in relation to existing systems) and an exogenous socio-technical landscape.'

Niches, or in other words, the 'micro level', are sites of innovation and transformative change. Action at the micro level is structured by the incumbent regime, or 'meso' level. The broader structural context for interaction between niches and regimes is provided at the 'macro' level by landscapes (Scrase & Smith 2009). Transitions emerge when the dynamic interactions between these multiple levels of niche, regime and landscape set up a mutual reinforcement effect (Grin *et al.* 2010, p. 4). As Scrase and Smith (2009, pp. 709–10) argue, climate change is a topic well suited to analysis using this multi-level perspective:

> This 'landscape' consists of material, demographic, ideological and cultural processes that operate beyond the direct influence of actors in any given regime and provide 'gradients for action' (Geels, 2004). Landscape processes, political or otherwise, bear down upon regimes, generating stress and creating opportunities. Broad societal concerns over climate change are one such stress. The hope is that these processes of niche development and regime destabilization will, over time, generate a transition to a low carbon socio-technical regime. This could involve a gradual evolution or a more disruptive transformation: the STT perspective provides a conceptual framework for considering both.

Processes of change therefore need to overcome the inherent inertia created by path dependence and 'lock-in' of existing institutions, practices and social conditions. Raven *et al.* (2010) argue that there are three dimensions of regime lock-in: institutional, social and technological. First, institutional structures such as laws, regulations or cultural values, 'are often very rigid, preventing the breakthrough of social innovations' (p. 59). Second, the social dimensions of lock-in are created by actors and social networks being 'blind' to alternatives, lending support to existing systems that represent 'incumbent organizational capital and institutionalized power' (p. 59). Third, the technological 'hardware' that is employed in supporting existing technologies and infrastructures often involves large investments (both material and non-material) that embed them within the existing regime. Given the inertia and embeddedness of regimes, it follows that key to achieving a sustainability transition is the ability to influence and/or disrupt the incumbent regime.

Structuration in sustainability transitions

The MLP lends a scalar sensitivity to the sustainability transitions thesis. However, importantly, rather than being geographical or spatial, the scale levels of the MLP represent 'degrees of structuration' (Grin *et al.* 2010, p. 4), so that 'the higher the scale level the more aggregated the components and the relationships and the slower the dynamics are between these actors, structures and working practices' (Grin *et al.* 2010, p. 4).

The structuration or 'stickiness' that pertains to each of the multiple levels varies. In the niche level, actors are most free from structure and the 'options for agency' (Raven *et al.* 2010, p. 62) provide 'the variation environment for radical innovations' (Raven *et al.* 2010, p. 61). In the regime, actors are more tightly bound through the dominant sway of existing institutions, processes and regulations. At the landscape level, processes of change are the slowest as actors are most bound to structures such as cultural norms, for example. Raven *et al.* (2010, p. 62) state that actors cannot influence the landscape level at all, but the landscape level 'can have a major influence on their behaviours and choices'.

Earlier I noted that Gidden's structuration theory expresses a duality of structure. Actors are not only embedded in structure, which is defined as consisting of rules and resources, but they also act to reproduce structures (Grin *et al.* 2010, p. 42). Structures are required for action and can be both enabling and constraining (Grin *et al.* 2010, p. 43). As structuration theory has been a particularly important informant to STT, I extend here some of the ideas essential to structuration theory that have been taken up within the sustainability transitions literature.

While the idea of actors and structures could be conceived along a singular plane of interaction, Grin *et al.* further emphasize the multi-dimensionality of structures. Drawing from Giddens (1979) they define three types of structures: of signification (meaning); of legitimization (norms); and of domination (power) and state that all three dimensions are involved in social action. Giddens (1979, pp. 81–2) explains these three dimensions as being combined in different ways in social practices. He states:

> The communication in meaning in interaction does not take place separately from the operation of relations of power, or outside the context of normative sanctions. All social practices involve these three elements. It is important to bear in mind what has been said previously in respect of rules: no social practice expresses, or can be explicated in terms of, a single rule or type of resource. Rather, practices are situated within intersecting sets of rules and resources that ultimately express features of the totality.

There are two types of context for the interaction between actors and structure: social systems and social structure (Giddens 1979). Social systems

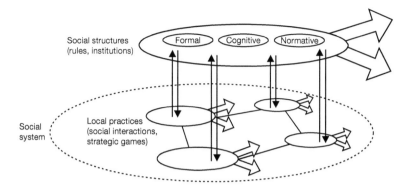

Figure 4.3 Social system and social structure (adapted from Deuten, 2003, p. 37)
Source: Reproduced from Grin *et al.* 2010, p. 451

are concerned with the interactions between actors in local practices. These can be conceived as horizontally oriented interactions that involve mutually dependent actors in processes of say, negotiation, conflict or exchange (Grin *et al.* 2010). The social structure represents the vertically aligned rules and resources that are formal, cognitive and normative (Grin *et al.* 2010, p. 45). The directionality and dimensionality implied in the distinction between social systems and social structures (illustrated in Figure 4.3) have been instrumental to the formulation of STT.

Reflexivity in action is the final element of structuration theory that provides a crucial understanding of the basis for sustainability transitions that I will note here. Previously I have stated the importance of reflexivity within risk theory as a counter to globalization, as society is forced to look back upon itself and question the fundamental risk conditions that characterize modernity as well as the role of traditional institutions of authority, such as the state. In Chapter 3, I argued that a lack of reflexivity poses one potential constraint to the realization of individual agency and the uptake of pro-environmental behaviours and that reflexivity is an essential element in the activation of agency for climate change mitigation practices. According to Grin *et al.* (2010, p. 233), reflexivity is a type of reflection where actors 'scrutinize their conduct' and 'which is quintessential for *Re*-structuration'. Grin *et al.* (2010, pp. 233–4) describe this process:

> Reflexivity never just concerns a particular action, but considers the flow of conduct, extending well into the past as well as anticipating the future. Giddens thus speaks of reflexive monitoring. In reflexive monitoring, agents consciously reflect on the intended and unintended consequences of their own actions. They do so in relation to the structural conditions in which they find themselves, taking into account the potential of change in structural context, both through their conduct and through

exogenous trends. . . . Reflexive monitoring adds to the capacity of actors to re-evaluate past experience and the present status quo, or, in the words of Beck *et al.* (2003: 12; cf. 1.2) to break through the dominance of the past over the future.

The process of reflexive monitoring in sustainability transition action therefore requires actors who possess agency and can result in changed futures when 'hegemonic ties' (Seyfang *et al.* 2010, pp. 5–6) to unsustainable trajectories are broken.

Sustainability transitions are conceived as the result of relatively rare conjunctions of factors that rely on the dual processes of radicalism at the grassroots and the more gradual and larger shifts required in landscape norms and practices (Raven *et al.* 2010). Due to the complexity inherent in this conjunction, a further implication is that the time scale for change cannot be predicted. Transitions may occur gradually as over time niche-innovations become adopted into mainstream practice and institutional arrangements. Otherwise, rapid step change may occur where fractures in societal norms arise suddenly at the landscape level. For example, the Fukushima nuclear reactor disaster in Japan caused by a tsunami rapidly led the German government to commit to shutting down all its nuclear power plants by 2022.[23] The sudden change in landscape conditions arguably forced regime change faster than existing niche, grassroots pressure.

STT has been critical to the development of my understanding of how social change processes targeted towards achieving sustainability develop from the local and community scale, of how these processes are expressed in voluntary group action, and of how they can transition to the global scale. There are several elements of the theory (explained above), which highlight the potential for applying a sustainability transitions theoretical approach to research into grassroots community action on climate change. First, the MLP provides a multi-scalar framework useful for determining the relationship between local community-scale action and the global scale. Second, by incorporating structuration in the MLP the potential for agents to enact radical innovation that can alter the extant regime is exposed.

In summary, STT offers an analytic construct for positioning local grassroots community-based action within a wider social change framework. It explains behaviour change from a collective or social perspective rather than an individual perspective; it explains how innovations emerge and translate across the multiple levels of niche, regime and landscape; and it argues that for change to be successful it needs to be consistently adopted at the local (micro), national (meso) and international (macro) scales (Moloney *et al.* 2010, p. 7621).

The limitations of STT lie in its level of abstraction and lack of empirical application to more complex and pluralistic problems such as climate change (Hargreaves *et al.* 2011). Sustainability transition researchers have tended to focus on supply-side aspects of technological innovation, such as systems of energy supply, rather than address demand-side issues such as sustainable consumption, for example, thus failing to fully acknowledge civil society's central role in social transitions (Hargreaves *et al.* 2011, p. 5). The political role of niches is not explicated and nor is the question of how power relations play out between the multiple levels of niche, regime and landscape (Meadowcroft 2011). There is a need therefore for complementary theoretical framings to be employed in developing a fuller understanding of how grassroots action can translate into society-wide changes. To this extent Smith, Seyfang and others suggest that social movement theories may provide a complementary addition to transitions theory by revealing the collective identities and interests that form the basis of collective action targeting climate change.

Sustainability transitions, civil society and social movements

Grin *et al.* (2010) acknowledge that STT, as a nascent research field, contains significant gaps and potential areas for future exploration. They concede the bias towards the technological in socio-technical transitions and suggest that greater emphasis on the social aspects of change is required, in particular with regard to how social processes may facilitate or co-emerge with niche development. Innovations are often found to originate from the civil society sector, grassroots community organizations, social movements, new businesses and other 'outsiders' (Raven *et al.* 2010, p. 59). Recent attention has turned to the role of civil society in social innovation and the role of collective and community-scale agency in multi-level change processes, areas often neglected in transitions research in favour of the more traditional focus on the market and state-based actors (Hargreaves *et al.* 2011, p. 4).

Seyfang and Smith (2007), in determining how 'grassroots innovations' may shift existing regimes, extend contemporary thinking on how sustainability transitions may occur within civil society. They define 'grassroots innovations' as: 'Networks of activists and organizations generating novel bottom-up solutions for sustainable development; solutions that respond to the local situation and the interests and values of the communities involved' (Seyfang & Smith 2007, p. 585).

They comment on the many, varied and growing types of local community-based projects emanating from the grassroots such as organic gardens, food cooperatives, low impact housing developments, community composting and farmers' markets. Each constitutes a 'local sustainability' grassroots innovation or 'niche'.

Seyfang and Smith employ a framework that identifies three ways that niche influences successfully *diffuse* into mainstream (regime) practice. First, through replication – that is, niches can bring about aggregate changes. As a case in point, Seyfang and Smith employ the example of Transition Towns, which have replicated rapidly from their origin in 2006 through many communities throughout the UK and other countries. As noted above, there are now hundreds of such initiatives active worldwide. Second, diffusion occurs through growth in scale and influence of niches by attracting more participants. As an example, the largest community-based CAG in Australia started from a group of 40 people and has now grown to over 2,000 members.[24] Third, diffusion occurs through translation of niche ideas to broader mainstream audiences.

The second component of the framework deals with the *processes* that extend successful niche growth and emergence. The three processes consist of:

- managing expectations so that grassroots niches can attract greater involvement by establishing 'widely shared, specific, realistic and achievable' expectations;
- building networks of wider support throughout their local communities and by broader stakeholder engagement;
- processes of 'social learning' (Seyfang & Smith 2007, p. 589) whereby knowledge is built and shared and groups are involved in reflecting on the 'assumptions and constraints of mainstream systems' (Seyfang & Haxeltine 2010, p. 5).

There are important implications of this work, in my view, for how local, collective and grassroots action can influence and potentially instigate broader social change. Hielscher *et al.* (2011, p. 6), for example, argue:

> This framing of community action for sustainability as 'innovative' allows us to make novel contributions to the sustainability transitions literature around 'grassroots innovations', which are distinct from the existing literature in terms of: context (civil society rather than the market economy); their driving force (social and/or environmental need, rather than rent seeking); the nature of the niche (alternative values as opposed to incubation from market forces); organisational forms (diverse forms including voluntary organisations, cooperatives and community groups, rather than firms); and the resource base (grant funding, voluntary input, mutual exchange, rather than returns on investment). Little is known about the conditions under which community-led innovations do or do not diffuse into wider society.

STT therefore offers a way to imagine 'the ways that civil society groups generate radical innovations in niches, how they challenge existing regimes and how they influence landscape values' (Hargreaves *et al.* 2011, pp. 4–5).

Application of social movement theory

The application of STT to radical innovations emanating from civil society and its relation to social movements has recently become a focus of research conducted by Smith (Smith 2007; Smith 2011) and Seyfang with others (Hargreaves *et al.* 2011; Hielscher *et al.* 2011; Seyfang *et al.* 2010). In brief, they take two different social movement theoretical models as their point of comparison with STT. Seyfang *et al.* (2010) apply New Social Movement (NSM) theory to an analysis of Transition Initiatives in the UK.[25] According to the authors (Seyfang *et al.* 2010, pp. 14–5), NSM theory can explain who joins movements, and why and how this might impact on the potential growth of a niche, thereby emphasizing group deliberation and how collectives develop a common identity and purpose:

> The application of NSM theories with a transitions perspective thus provides a way to link analysis of macro-social trends with the micro-level interactive social processes within which participants in the movement talk, argue, debate, build relationships and engage in ongoing or renewed social practices.

Smith (2012) brings a different perspective to the relationship of social movement theory to sustainability transitions by utilizing a resource mobilization (RM) approach (see endnote 25). Grassroots innovations can be understood through niche theory, that is, it can explain how radical and novel change can emerge and replicate from the grassroots. Social movement theory, on the other hand, can assist in understanding how path-dependent regimes can be 'unsettled' (Smith 2012, p. 183). One of the key roles of social movements is to challenge and destabilize the status quo and Smith (2012, p. 183) argues that: 'in combination, these processes will determine how environmentalist forces in civil society will influence the mainstream of sustainability energy transitions'. In effect, in working together, these two processes of challenging and destabilizing facilitate sustainability transitions through the dual actions of unsettling regimes and nurturing niches (Smith 2012). Social movement research examines movement identities, contexts, actions and outcomes within the context of 'socio-economic and cultural change and for their relations to states, markets and cultures' (Smith 2012, p. 191). Smith proposes that an understanding of the processes of regime destabilization can be enhanced through the adoption of the broad spectrum of political analysis that 'conventional social movement research' provides (Smith 2012, p. 191). Social movement analysis, in adopting a multi-level transitions perspective, can also be broadened through: taking into account how regimes can shape civil society movements; identifying opportunities for regime destabilization; and exploiting changing landscape conditions (Smith 2012).

The work of Smith, Seyfang and others on complementary theoretical frames around grassroots innovations, regime destabilization and social change therefore extends the analytic potential of STT when applied to research on community-based climate change action. The incorporation of social movement theory into STT allows more meaningful analysis of the social and political change promise of local-scale, collective and community-based action on climate change.

Complementary theories

In the absence of a growing social movement around climate change it is of interest here to examine briefly other potential forms of grassroots organization and mobilization theory that touch on processes of change from the local and grassroots level through community-based action and their potential for wider societal adoption. There are two that I mention briefly here that offer complementary framing to STT – polycentrism (Ostrom 2010); and the green public sphere (Torgerson 1999, 2008a, 2008b, 2010).

The green public sphere

Torgerson proposes an alternative conception to environmental politics and green social movements, which he terms the 'green public sphere'. What I find appealing about this notion is that, rather than conceptualizing the grassroots as a building block of some great, unified climate movement, Torgerson's 'green public sphere' provides a more pluralist account of political and social activism. For the most part, Torgerson is critical of the notion of environmental social movements (and social movements more generally), and is wary of the 'instrumentalist overtones accompanying the trope of "movement"' (Torgerson 2008b, p. 29). This distancing is conspicuous in the defining features of the green public sphere which he describes as:

> Not a movement or even a movement of movements, the green public sphere is animated by exchanges of differing opinions. Central to the green public sphere, moreover, is ambivalence between common identity and radical difference. This ambivalence may necessarily be constitutive of a green politics for a divided planet.
>
> (Torgerson 2008b, p. 31)

Torgerson distinguishes the green public sphere from instrumental notions of green politics and convergent views of environmentalism based on an obsession with bringing unity to the green movement (Torgerson 1999). The idea of building a green movement as a unified '*we*' is disparaged as 'despite all talk of diversity and inclusiveness – . . . elements that cannot merge with the movement's essential identity must be pruned away and, in effect excommunicated'. Instead, Torgerson argues for a green public sphere that would 'make meaningful disagreement possible' (Torgerson 1999, p. 19). But neither should a view of green politics based on 'possessive individualism' be adopted that relies on a collectivity of individual 'good deeds' (Torgerson 1999, p. 131). Reminiscent of my discussion in Chapter 3 on the individualization of responsibility, Torgerson believes that emphasizing such individual acts of personal responsibility 'deflects attention from systemic patterns of incentives ... that serve to shape and direct the behaviour of the possessive individual', thereby reinforcing existing regime-influenced behaviours. Rather, it is the context of individual action that is important and, in particular, the opportunities 'to engage in debates of the green public sphere' (Torgerson 1999, p. 131).

Following Hannah Arendt and occupying similar territory to John S. Dryzek, Torgerson sees politics as a space for debate and 'meaningful disagreement' and suggests that operationalizing green politics requires the joining of an environmental ethics with a discursive ethos (Torgerson 1999, p. 120). Torgerson positions discourse (which naturally involves human communication) at the heart of the green public sphere. The importance of dialogue and debate is core to Torgerson's (1999, p. 129) thesis, as

> an interchange of considered opinions, debate can foster an imaginative interplay of identities, interests and perspectives that encourages evaluations and judgements from an enlarged viewpoint. More than political outcomes are important, for the very process takes on value for those who participate in it.

The intrinsic importance of politics lies in its performance, rather than purely in its functional and constitutive enactment and how narrow self-interest and uniformity of ideas are moderated through sweeping discursive engagement. In this way, Torgerson's key emphasis on diversity of opinion, discourse and debate in the public sphere *as* politics (after Arendt) prefigures the importance of social learning both to the individual and the collective. The green public sphere can be conceptualized therefore as a 'network of spaces' in which public communication occurs and where 'the local and global intersect' (Torgerson 2008b, p. 28). In this way, Torgerson provides a different political analysis of social movements than Smith and Seyfang but shares their evaluation of how grassroots collectives engaging in environmental action at the local and community scale can nevertheless, through discursive engagement, form alternative networks that serve to counter the extant regime of advanced industrial society.

Polycentrism

In a similar vein to Torgerson, Elinor Ostrom argues against coordinated global response and global governance structures as the sole means of successful climate change action. Drawing from decades of research into community governance of common pool resources (an example of a common pool resource could be a local irrigation system), Ostrom recently extended her thesis to incorporate climate change (Ostrom 2009). Climate change, according to Ostrom, presents a potent example of a 'global "public bad"' where maintaining the common pool resource of clean air (or, in other words an unpolluted global atmosphere) represents a 'global public good' (Ostrom 2009, p. 5). She argues that while current global efforts have largely failed, 'chaotic' and 'messy' polycentric action is viable. Polycentrism is offered as a counter to what Ostrom perceives as the dominant reply to a problem that is global, coordinated and central. Polycentrism implies that many centres of action operating at multiple scales can be equally, if not more, effective than global-scale responses (Ostrom 2012). Ostrom's poly-centrism concept hence displays significant similarities with the multi-level perspective of STT:

> Polycentric systems tend to enhance innovation, learning, adaptation, trustworthiness, levels of cooperation of participants, and the achieve-ment of more effective, equitable, and sustainable outcomes at multiple scales, even though no institutional arrangement can totally eliminate opportunism with respect to the provision and production of collec-tive goods (Toonen 2010). Enabling citizens to form smaller-scale collective consumption units encourages face-to-face discussion and the achievement of common understanding. Creating larger collective con-sumption units reduces the strategic behaviour of the wealthy trying to escape into tax havens where they could free ride on the contributions of others. Further, creating polycentric institutions related to climate change helps to fulfil the 'matching principal' in international law that problems involving multiple levels (e.g. global, national, regional and small scales) should involve contributions at each of these levels (Adler, 2005).
>
> (Ostrom 2010, p. 552)

Rational individuals can participate in collective action around a common pool resource where the conditions for cooperation exist. Ostrom (2009) identifies a range of important variables that enhance such cooperative arrangements and that can feasibly occur at the grassroots. Some to note in particular are: the prime role of trust and reciprocity among actors in cementing cooperative collective arrangements; the provision of an even playing field; and the reinforcing formulation of co-learning that occurs within collective action and which helps to generate higher levels of social capital over time (Ostrom 2009). Further, repeated opportunities for associ-ational behaviour can create patterns of group trust and reciprocity, assisting civic engagement, reversing the erosion of social capital and potentially facilitating the creation of a deliberative public sphere (Hoffman & High-Pippert 2010) – similar to Torgerson's notion of the green public sphere.

Both Ostrom's polycentrism and Torgerson's green public sphere extend the notion of how grassroots social innovations concerned with climate change can instigate change processes from their local community settings. Both acknowledge that diverse actors need to be engaged in the process and both stress the importance of networked connections between collectivities. Furthermore, both acknowledge the central role of collective action for nurturing trust and cooperation among actors and social learning achieved through group deliberation and reflection. They emphasize group dynamics and the centrality of discourse and deliberation within collectivities as key contributors to grassroots inspired social change.

Torgerson re-conceptualizes the role of social movements in an alternative model of green politics, the green public sphere. Stressing the importance of ideological pluralism, discourse and a human-centred ecological rationality, the green public sphere represents a re-imagining of a post-industrial regime based on a core of green and moral values. Torgerson's thesis illuminates how CAGs, situated as they are outside of the state, might contribute to this alternative post-industrial and low carbon regime through their expressed collective values and the role of discourse, debate and differing opinion within CAGs and their networked spaces. Finally, Ostrom's polycentrism, expressive of a collective agency, identifies the important interpersonal relations of trust, reciprocity and cooperation as central to group action and the multi-scale governance of the global atmospheric commons.

Notes

1 Walk Against Warming was an annual event held throughout Australian cities and towns and aligned with the Global Day of Climate Change Action.
2 Krakoff 2011 notes a similar rise in the USA in grassroots climate action groups.
3 The Australian Senate is one of two Houses of Parliament. The Senate consists of 76 senators elected from each Australian state and territory under a system of proportional representation. Together with the House of Representatives, the two houses share the power to make laws. Under Australia's Constitution both houses are required to pass any new legislation.
4 The Constitution provides a method for resolving deadlocks which might arise in the event of a disagreement between the houses. If the Senate twice fails to pass a bill from the House of Representatives, under certain specified conditions, the Governor-General may simultaneously dissolve both houses, in which case elections are held for all seats in both houses, www.aph.gov.au/About_Parliament/Senate, accessed 8 June 2015. This is known as a double dissolution.
5 Quotations from research participants are noted by their name (pseudonyms are used throughout); age at time of research; and group code. CAGs were recruited from the two most populous Australian states, New South Wales (NSW) and Victoria (VIC).
6 'A hung Parliament results when no party has more than half the MPs in the House of Representatives, which means no party can pass laws without gaining support from other parties or independent members of the House', Liddy, M. (2011), 'Australia's hung Parliament explained' ABC News, 17 November 2011, www.abc.net.au/news/2010–08–23/australias-hung-parliament-explained/954880, accessed 13 January 2012.
7 See www.climatechange.gov.au/media/whats-new/clean-energy-legislation.aspx, accessed 18 December 2011.
8 See www.climatechange.gov.au/en/government/clean-energy-future/legislation.aspx, accessed 13 January 2012.

9   Fisher implies that this will result from a form of punitive action from the UNFCCC, a claim which cannot be supported with current UNFCCC statements.
10 'Massive turnout for Walk against Warming', www.abc.net.au/news/stories/2009/12/12/2769874.htm, accessed 24 June 2011.
11 CAN International represents over 900 environment and development NGOs from more than 100 countries. See www.climatenetwork.org/, accessed 3 June 2015.
12 Klimaforum was a free grassroots 'People's Summit' held at the same time as the United Nations Copenhagen Climate Conference. Klimaforum attracted in the order of 50,000 people in Copenhagen in 2009 and has been held at subsequent climate change conferences. http://klimaforum.org/, accessed 5 March 2012.
13 According to the Transition Network website in November 2014 there were 1,196 initiatives registered with 472 official initiatives and 702 'muller' initiatives (that is, not yet officially part of the network) globally, www.transitionnetwork.org/, accessed 3 June 2015.
14 Bailey *et al.* (2010) also support this view.
15 By 2009 up to 200 Climate Action Groups had formed throughout Australia (Burgmann & Baer 2012) and could be found throughout major cities, regional cities and small towns.
16 See www.lowcarboncommunities.org/, accessed 4 June 2015.
17 See http://peoplesclimate.org/, accessed 26 April 2015.
18 BREAZE for example has over 2,000 members. www.breaze.org.au/, accessed 29 April 2011.
19 See http://climatesummit.org.au/, accessed 29 April 2011.
20 See www.climatenetwork.org/, accessed 1 February 2012.
21 www.lockthegate.org.au/, accessed 3 June 2015.
22 www.solarcitizens.org.au/, accessed 3 June 2015.
23 'Germany: Nuclear power plants to close by 2022' BBC News Europe, 30 May 2011, www.bbc.co.uk/news/world-europe-13592208, accessed 12 July 2011.
24 See www.breaze.org.au/, accessed 1 March 2012.
25 Bates *et al.* (2005) offer three distinct schools of social movement theory: collective behaviour and social movements research, resource mobilization theory, and new social movement thinking (p. 16). In brief the distinction between resource mobilization (RM) and new social movement (NSM) theories is that RM is concerned largely with the organizational capacities and processes that build and contribute to social movements (pp. 16–17). NSM is more interested in cultural issues and framing and the processes of deliberation that occur among social movement members (Bates *et al.* 2005, p. 17).

References

Bailey, I., Hopkins, R. & Wilson, G. 2010, 'Some things old, some things new: the spatial representations and politics of change of the peak oil relocalisation movement', *Geoforum*, vol. 41, no. 4, pp. 595–605.
Bates, P., Bevan, H. and Robert, G. (2005) *Towards a million change agents – a review of the social movements literature: implications for large scale change in the NHS*. Literature review. National Health Service NHS, UK, accessed 3 May 2011, www.institute.nhs.uk/images//documents/BuildingCapability/NewModels/social%20movement/nhs_social_movement.pdf.

Boykoff, M.T. 2007, 'From convergence to contention: United States mass media representations of anthropogenic climate change science', *Transactions of the Institute of British Geographers*, vol. 32, no. 4, pp. 477–89.

Bulkeley, H., Castan Broto, V. & Edwards, G.A.S. 2015, *An urban politics of climate change. experimentation and the governing of socio-technical transitions*, Routledge, London.

Burgmann, V. & Baer, H. 2012, *Climate Politics and the Climate Movement in Australia*, Melbourne University Press, Melbourne, Australia.

Christoff, P. 2010, 'Cold climate in Copenhagen: China and the United States at COP15', *Environmental Politics*, vol. 19, no. 4, pp. 637–56.

de Haan, J. & Rotmans, J. 2011, 'Patterns in transitions: understanding complex chains of change', *Technological Forecasting and Social Change*, vol. 78, no. 1, pp. 90–102.

den Elzen, M.G.J. 2010, *The Emissions Gap Report: Are the Copenhagen Accord Pledges Sufficient to Limit Global Warming to 2 degrees or 1.5 degrees?*, United Nations Environment Program (UNEP), accessed 20 August 2011, www.unep.org/publications/ebooks/emissionsgapreport/index.asp.

Dimitrov, R.S. 2010, 'Inside Copenhagen: the state of climate governance', *Global Environmental Politics*, vol. 10, no. 2, pp. 18–24.

Doelle, M. 2010, 'The legacy of climate talks in Copenhagen: hopenhagen or brokenhagen?', *Carbon and Climate Law Review*, vol. 1, pp. 86–100.

Doherty, B. & Doyle, T. (eds) 2008, *Beyond borders: environmental movements and transnational politics*, Routledge, Taylor & Francis, London.

Doyle, J. 2009, 'Climate action and environmental activism: the role of environmental NGOs and grassroots movements in the global politics of climate change', in T. Boyce & J. Lewis (eds), *Climate change and the media*, Peter Lang Publishing, New York, pp. 103–16.

Dryzek, J.S., Norgaard, R.B. & Schlosberg, D. 2013, *Climate-challenged society*, Oxford University Press, Oxford.

Feola, G. & Nunes, R. 2014, 'Success and failure of grassroots innovations for addressing climate change: the case of the transition movement', *Global Environmental Change*, vol. 24, no. 0, pp. 232–50.

Fisher, D. 2010, 'COP-15 in Copenhagen: how the merging of movements left civil society out in the cold', *Global Environmental Politics*, vol. 10, no. 2, pp. 11–7.

Garnaut, R. 2008, *The Garnaut climate change review. Final report*, Cambridge University Press, Port Melbourne, Australia.

Geels, F.W. 2004, 'From sectoral systems of innovation to socio-technical systems: insights about dynamics and change from sociology and institutional theory.' *Research Policy*, vol.33, no. 6–7, pp. 897–920.

Geels, F.W. 2005, 'Processes and patterns in transitions and system innovations: refining the co-evolutionary multi-level perspective', *Technological Forecasting and Social Change*, vol. 72, no. 6, pp. 681–96.

Geels, F.W. 2011, 'The multi-level perspective on sustainability transitions: responses to seven criticisms', *Environmental Innovation and Societal Transitions*, vol. 1, no. 1, pp. 24–40.

Geels, F.W. 2014, 'Regime resistance against low-carbon transitions: introducing politics and power into the multi-level perspective', *Theory, Culture & Society*, pp. 21–40.

Giddens, A. 1979, *Central problems in social theory: action, structure, and contradiction in social analysis*, University of California Press, Berkeley, CA.

Grin, J., Rotmans, J. & Schot, J. 2010, *Transitions in sustainable development: new directions in the study of long term transformative change*, Routledge, New York.

Gross, M. & Mautz, R. 2015, *Renewable energies*, Routledge, UK.

Hall, N.L., Taplin, R. & Goldstein, W. 2010, 'Empowerment of individuals and realization of community agency', *Action Research*, vol. 8, no. 1, pp. 71–91.

Hanson, F. 2010, 'The Lowy Institute Poll 2010', *Lowy Institute for International Policy, Sydney*.

Hargreaves, T., Hazeltine, A., Longhurst, N. & Seyfang, G. 2011, *Sustainability transitions from the bottom up: civil society, the multi-level perspective and practice theory*, Working Paper 2011–01, University of East Anglia, Norwich.

Hielscher, S. 2013, *Carbon rationing action groups: an innovation history*, Community Innovation for Sustainable Energy Project. Project report. University of Sussex; University of East Anglia, accessed 4 June 2015, http://sro.sussex.ac.uk/53354/.

Hielscher, S., Seyfang, G. & Smith, A. 2011, *Community innovation for sustainable energy*, Centre for Social and Economic Research on the Global Environment (CSERGE), Working Paper 2011–03, CSERGE, Norwich, UK.

Hoffman, S.M. & High-Pippert, A. 2010, 'From private lives to collective action: recruitment and participation incentives for a community energy program', *Energy Policy*, vol. 38, no. 12, pp. 7567–74.

Hoffmann, M. 2011, *Climate governance at the crossroads*, Oxford University Press, Oxford.

IPCC 2007, 'IPCC fourth assessment report: climate change 2007', contribution of Working Group I to the *Fourth Assessment Report of the Intergovernmental Panel on Climate Change*, 2007, Cambridge, UK.

Jamison, A. 2010, 'Climate change knowledge and social movement theory', *Wiley Interdisciplinary Reviews: Climate Change*, vol. 1, no. 6, pp. 811–23.

Jones, B. 2010, *Democratic challenges in tackling climate change*, Whitlam Institute, University of Western Sydney, Australia.

Krakoff, S. 2011, *Planetary identity formation and the relocalization of environmental law*, Working Paper, 03-11, University of Colorado, Boulder, CO.

Loorbach, D. & Rotmans, J. 2010, 'The practice of transition management: examples and lessons from four distinct cases', *Futures*, vol. 42, no. 3, pp. 237–46.

McGaurr, L. & Lester, L. 2009, 'Complementary problems, competing risks: climate change, nuclear energy and the *Australian*', in T. Boyce & J. Lewis (eds), *Climate change and the media*, Peter Lang, New York, pp. 174–85.

McGregor, I.M. 2011, 'Disenfranchisement of countries and civil society at COP-15 in Copenhagen', *Global Environmental Politics*, vol. 11, no. 1, pp. 1–7.

Maniates, M. & Meyer, J.M. 2010, *The Environmental Politics of Sacrifice*, The MIT Press, Cambridge, MA.

Meadowcroft, J. 2011, 'Engaging with the *politics* of sustainability transitions', *Environmental Innovation and Societal Transitions*, vol. 1, no. 1, pp. 70–5.

Middlemiss, L. & Parrish, B.D. 2010, 'Building capacity for low-carbon communities: the role of grassroots initiatives', *Energy Policy*, vol. 38, no. 12, pp. 7559–66.

Moloney, S., Horne, R.E. & Fien, J. 2010, 'Transitioning to low carbon communities–from behaviour change to systemic change: lessons from Australia', *Energy Policy*, vol. 38, no. 12, pp. 7614–23.

Neilsen and Environmental Change Institute 2007, *Climate change and influential spokespeople: a global Nielsen online survey* accessed 7 April 2011, www.eci.ox. ac.uk/publications/downloads/070709nielsen-celeb-report.pdf.

North, P. 2011, 'The politics of climate activism in the UK: a social movement analysis', *Environment and Planning A*, vol. 43, pp. 1581–98.

Ostrom, E. 2009, *A polycentric approach for coping with climate change*, Report no. 5095, The World Bank Development Economics, Office of the Senior Vice President and Chief Economist, Washington.

Ostrom, E. 2010, 'Polycentric systems for coping with collective action and global environmental change', *Global Environmental Change*, vol. 20, no. 4, pp. 550–7.

Ostrom, E. 2012, 'Nested externalities and polycentric institutions: must we wait for global solutions to climate change before taking actions at other scales?', *Economic Theory*, vol. 49, no. 2, pp. 353–69.

Pearse, R., Goodman, J. & Rosewarne, S. 2010, 'Researching direct action against carbon emissions: a digital ethnography of climate agency', *Cosmopolitan Civil Societies Journal*, vol. 2, no. 3, pp. 76–103.

Raven, R., Bosch, S.v.d. & Weterings, R. 2010, 'Transitions and strategic niche management: towards a competence kit for practitioners', *International Journal of Technology Management*, vol. 51, no. 1, pp. 57–74.

Reed, M.S., Evely, A.C., Cundill, G., Fazey, I., Glass, J., Laing, A., Newig, J., Parrish, B., Prell, C., Raymond, C. & Stringer, L.C. 2010, 'What is social learning?', *Ecology and Society*, vol. 15, no. 4.

Rogelj, J., Nabel, J., Chen, C., Hare, W., Markmann, K., Meinshausen, M., Schaeffer, M., Macey, K. & Hohne, N. 2010, 'Copenhagen Accord pledges are paltry', *Nature*, vol. 464, no. 7292, pp. 1126–8.

Rootes, C. 2008, 'The first climate change election? The Australian general election of 24 November 2007', *Environmental Politics*, vol. 17, no. 3, pp. 473–80.

Rootes, C. 2011, 'Denied, deferred, triumphant? Climate change, carbon trading and the Greens in the Australian federal election of 21 August 2010', *Environmental Politics*, vol. 20, no. 3, pp. 410–7.

Rosewarne, S., Goodman, J. & Pearse, R. 2014, *Climate action upsurge. The ethnography of climate movement politics*, Routledge, London and New York.

Scrase, I. & Smith, A. 2009, 'The (non-)politics of managing low carbon socio-technical transitions', *Environmental Politics*, vol. 18, no. 5, pp. 707–26.

Seyfang, G. & Haxeltine, A. 2010, Growing grassroots innovations: exploring the role of community-based social movements for sustainable energy transitions, CSERGE Working Paper EDM 10–08, CSERGE, Norwich, UK.

Seyfang, G. & Haxeltine, A. 2012, *Growing grassroots innovations: exploring the role of community-based initiatives in governing sustainable energy transitions*, Environment and Planning C: Government and Policy, vol. 30, pp. 381–400.

Seyfang, G., Haxeltine, A., Hargreaves, T. & Longhurst, N. 2010, *Energy and communities in transition – towards a new research agenda on agency and civil society in sustainability transitions*, CSERGE Working Paper EDM 10–13, CSERGE, Norwich, UK.

Seyfang, G. & Smith, A. 2007, 'Grassroots innovations for sustainable development: towards a new research and policy agenda', *Environmental Politics*, vol. 16, pp. 584–603.

Smith, A. 2007, 'Translating Sustainabilities between green niches and socio-technical regimes', *Technology Analysis & Strategic Management*, vol. 19, no. 4, pp. 427–50.

Smith, A. 2012, 'Civil society in sustainable energy transitions', in G. Verbong & D. Loorbach (eds), *Governing the energy transition: reality, illusion or necessity.* London, Routledge, pp. 180–202.

Stevenson, H. & Dryzek, J.S. 2012, 'The discursive democratisation of global climate governance', *Environmental Politics*, vol. 21, no. 2, pp. 189–210.

Stewart, R.G. 2013, *Climate change in a new democratic age: why we need more, not less, democratic participation*, vol. 9, Whitlam Institute, University of Western Sydney, Parramatta, Australia.

Torgerson, D. 1999, *The promise of green politics: environmentalism and the public sphere*, Duke University Press, Durham, NC.

Torgerson, D. 2008a, 'Constituting green democracy: a political project', *The Good Society*, vol. 17, no. 2, pp. 18–24.

Torgerson, D. 2008b, 'Expanding the green public sphere: post-colonial connections', in B. Doherty & T. Doyle (eds), *Beyond borders: environmental movements and transnational politics*, Routledge, Taylor & Francis, London, pp. 17–34.

Torgerson, D. 2010, 'Nature and political theory', *Contemporary Political Theory*, vol. 8, no. 3, pp. 340–50.

Wenger, E. 1999, *Communities of practice: learning, meaning, and identity*, Cambridge University Press, Cambridge.

Wolf, J. & Moser, S.C. 2011, 'Individual understandings, perceptions, and engagement with climate change: insights from in-depth studies across the world', *Wiley Interdisciplinary Reviews: Climate Change*, vol. 2, no. 4, pp. 547–69.

5 People like me

The role of agency in voluntary climate change action

Introduction

In Chapter 3, I argued that there is an inherent emphasis in developed societies on locating responsibility for climate change, both in terms of its causes and effects, with individual actors. The expectation is that through their personal- and private-sphere behaviours, actors possess the ability to effectively reduce their greenhouse gas emissions. This 'individualization of responsibility' for climate change mitigation takes place in the context of a neoliberal discourse that is dominant throughout the developed world so that the political ideology of individualism now extends into each person's lifestyle choices and behaviours.

This raises several questions around the promotion of individualized responsibility for climate change mitigation in the context of broader social change. In particular, whether the adoption of individual 'carbon conducts'[1] will lead to the collective uptake of social practices of carbon reduction or indeed whether individual action will challenge structurally embedded high GHG emitting behaviours, that is, shift our currently fossil fuel dependent economy. I argued therefore in Chapter 3 that due to a range of constraints on personal actions, individual agency is being significantly thwarted and that broad social change demands concomitant changes to social (collective) and cultural practices. In this chapter, I address more directly the question of whether the individualization of responsibility for voluntary climate change action will lead to broader processes of societal change. I do so by drawing on the results of my empirical research with community-based, grassroots CAGs.

In Chapter 3 I argued that individual responsibility for climate change action needs to be understood within the context of what Giddens (1984) describes as the 'duality of structure'. As structures are both enabling and constraining, they provide 'both the medium and the outcome of action' (Grin *et al.* 2010, p. 42). In accordance with this position, the predominant approach to climate change action promoted at the individual and household scale is flawed as it encourages atomistic and inconsequential action and does not address the structural limitations that reinforce continuing cycles of unsustainability. Further, I argue here that people like those that form the

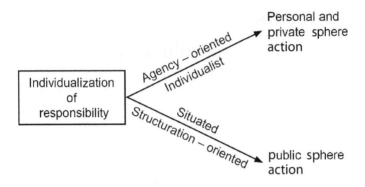

Figure 5.1 Individualization of responsibility
Source: Developed from Middlemiss 2010 (Kent 2012)

basis of my research (i.e. members of community-based collectives such as CAGs) are able to take voluntary action to mitigate the effects of climate change because CAGs possess particular characteristics and are able to surmount the constraints that reinforce the status quo. In this way, CAGs represent one potential model for community-scale climate action success.

Middlemiss (2010) has taken up this point. She sets up a theoretical framework that focuses on the tension between an *agency-oriented* (which she calls 'individualist') perspective of individual responsibility with an approach borne out of *structuration* (which she calls 'situated') where individual agency is conditioned by structural enablements and constraints. This lends an important perspective to understanding the tension in the two positions described above.

The important point here is the differences between an agency-oriented (individualist) approach and a structuration perspective on the individual-ization of responsibility. An agency-oriented approach leads to the indivi-dualization of responsibility played out in personal- and private-sphere behaviour or otherwise leads to disempowerment and denial (Norgaard 2011). In contrast, a structuration perspective on the individualization of responsibility suggests that individual actors undertake action within their personal and private spheres but remain reflective of the systemic conditions that both structure and restructure their respective interplay. Based on this understanding, actors come together in collective, public sphere action.

In what ways then are members of CAGs expressive of agency on climate change? First, CAG memberships consist of a particular type of person – a person who not only enacts their responsibility for climate change in their personal and private spheres of behaviour but is also aware of the limitations of this action. Their action is 'situated' (Middlemiss 2010) within its social context where it is understood that to be effective, action needs to be politically focused, collective and conducted in the public domain. Second, the constraints to agency of individuals who join CAGs are overcome through their involvement with their group. They are personally empowered and reflexive around their action on climate change. CAGs are therefore expressive of a collective agency where the whole is greater than the sum of its parts. In other words, individual agents active on climate change within their local communities realize the advantages of group actions that cannot be explained on the basis of their individual agency alone. As Lorenzoni *et al.* (2007, pp. 452–3) find:

> The majority of individuals consulted in our studies accepted that individuals play a role in causing climate change and that they should be involved in action to mitigate it. On the whole however they felt that individual action would have little effect in comparison to other, large scale emitters. Participants generally argued that it was not worthwhile

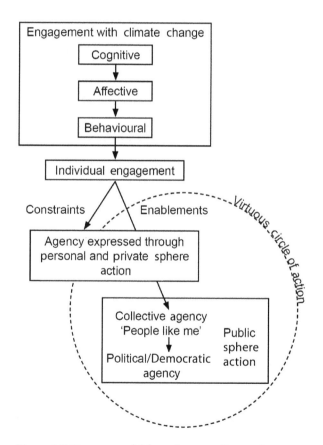

Figure 5.2 Process model for voluntary climate change
Source: Kent 2012

taking action at this individual level given its limited efficacy. They certainly saw climate change as a collective problem to be tackled at a collective level.

This understanding of the key role of collectives and collective action in societal change around climate change remains largely hidden to policy makers who continue to promote the ideal of 'super-majorities' consisting of 'the individual behaviours of the many' (Maniates 2012).

Beyond this I propose that my research generates an understanding of a developmental process at play that determines why certain people join with others in collective climate change action, and others do not. This process is mapped in Figure 5.2 and explained throughout the following sections.

How do members of CAGs express their responsibility for taking action on climate change?

The individualization of responsibility for action on climate change can be considered to follow one of two distinct pathways (Figure 5.1). The individualization of responsibility can be acted out through personal- and private-sphere behaviour where the focus is on individual practices, such as the 'low hanging fruit' of changing household light bulbs or reducing car idling times (Maniates 2012). This represents 'agency-oriented' behaviour (Middlemiss 2010), while an individualization of responsibility acted out through political and public sphere action represents 'situated' (Middlemiss 2010) behaviour, where actors link their behaviour to the 'social deter-minants of practice' (Middlemiss 2010, p. 152). In other words, they acknowledge the structural enablements and constraints to their individual and collective agency.

Middlemiss found that her research participants (members of a church-based ecology group focused on sustainable consumption) tended to express their responsibility for sustainable consumption in individualistic rather than collective terms. In particular, they separated their individual responsibility from politics and 'rarely linked the responsibility for sustainable consump-tion to structural players (e.g. business and government)' (Middlemiss 2010, p. 151). In contrast, CAG members expressed their responsibility for taking climate change mitigation action in terms of a shared responsibility where government has a significant role, expressed in the words of CAG members Bill and Bernadette below:

> *We're all responsible, in the sense that we've all contributed to climate change, and we all do what little we can ourselves, but solutions in the sense we're looking at whose responsible for changing it, its gotta be broader large scale political change.*

> (Bill, 60, NSW1)

It's gotta come from the government, its gotta come from above … this is an emergency and we really need to…. Try and open the government's eyes and ears and minds to what the people are saying: 'this is an emergency, get on with it'.

(Bernadette, 72, VIC3)

While CAG members describe their responsibility for taking action on climate change in both individual and collective terms, for most (like Bill above), responsibility for climate change extended well beyond the individual's private-sphere actions into the public and political realms.

CAG members possess individual agency, complemented by the benefits the group provides, as expressed by David (63, VIC4): *'Being part of a group is certainly part of it, though I would act anyway, ineffective as it might be and unconfident as I may be, I would still be giving it a go.'*

The group facilitates individual agency through: enhancing member confidence and commitment to take action (particularly political forms of action); building trust between group members; development of a group profile that provides legitimacy, authenticity and authority for their actions; and contributing to a public good. In several cases, participants noted that they would not have been confident in taking political action alone and that the group provided a supportive and safe environment for testing their convictions through riskier forms of activism.

Well that's what we're in it for, that's what we join a group for so we can take community action. A person on your own you wouldn't be motivated or you wouldn't be feeling up to it or you'd feel shy, but when you're with some other people it makes all the difference.

(Bernadette, 72, VIC3)

According to Louis (2009), collective action 'can be psychologically motivating when it expresses group emotions such as anger, moral outrage or guilt' (p. 729) and can work in 'a virtuous circle of action and reinforcement even in the absence of movement "success"' (p. 730), expressive of the reinforcing effect described above. The group as a 'real-life social group' (Simon & Klandermans 2001) provides an avenue for convergence around a shared opinion or common cause. The issue of climate change forms the basis of moral concern and responsibility to take action. Areas of conflict are reduced and the group comes to share similar ideas, which also 'make things possible'.

Group members also learn from each other and from their actions (both individual and collective) so that the group becomes a place for social learning. Members gain a greater understanding of climate change but also the opportunity to discuss and reflect within the group setting. In this way, CAGs demonstrate 'social learning in practice' (Moloney *et al.* 2010, p. 7622). According to Reed *et al.* (2010, p. 5) social learning consists of the following three elements: it demonstrates that a change in understanding has taken place in the individuals involved; it goes beyond the individual to be situated within wider social units or communities of practice within society; and it occurs through social interactions and processes between actors within a social network. This type of citizen engagement 'schools' (Hendriks 2006) CAG members in a view of democracy that is allied with a generative notion of power ('power-with') that comes from association with others and sharing something together (Hendriks 2009, p. 178).

Members of CAGs express their responsibility for taking action on climate change both individually and collectively. They perceive responsibility as something that is shared between a government and its citizens. Moreover, in the face of government inaction on climate change, CAG members express legitimacy, authority and authenticity. The group enhances each individual's agency, providing confidence, skills and a place for shared learning and reflection.

What motivates CAG members to take action on climate change?

Individual participants were motivated to take action around climate change for varying reasons. These included: a primary concern for nature and the environment; perceived government inaction; concern for future generations (older participants in particular noted concern for their grandchildren); a response to overconsumption and wastefulness; a concern for social justice; and as an expression of community service, caring and resilience. For some participants, climate change is representative of a broader more holistic problem characterized by human unsustainability.

For the most part, participants were well informed regarding the science of climate change, believed that it is anthropogenically produced and agreed on the need for urgent and concerted action to mitigate its effects. How they 'know' climate change was a key motivation for group involvement. Further, their knowledge increased over time about the risks that climate change poses and this worked to create even greater motivation to act.

> *I feel like I didn't really understand the problem until two years after the climate group had already been running and my personal motivation went to a whole new level after that. It was just like . . . I have to devote my life to this now.*
>
> (Lenore, 28, NSW2)

Not all participants however were convinced of global warming: two positioned themselves as sceptical of the science but otherwise were concerned more generally with issues of local and global environmental sustainability, exemplified in Jerry's words: '*I suppose I look at it more as sustainability not climate change*' (Jerry, 63, VIC2).

Underpinning the cognitive awareness of climate change evident in the focus group participants' responses was a deeper moral attachment to the issue, which created a strong sense of individual responsibility and willingness to take action. For some participants, understanding the science of climate change had become obsolete in the face of government intransigence and the level of inaction around the issue. The more salient issue was the moral basis to act. '*I feel [it] is a moral thing, it's tied up in so many different philosophies and religions and lessons in life*' (Jackie, 39, NSW4).

CAG members were motivated to take action on climate change for varying reasons, such as a concern for: family, nature and the environment; overconsumption and wastefulness; political inaction; or social justice. For the most part their motivations around climate change stemmed initially from an understanding of the science on climate change but it is a sense of moral obligation that drives them in their personal actions and their decisions to seek out and join with 'like-minded' others.

How do CAG members engage with climate change as an issue?

Lorenzoni *et al.* (2007) offer three preconditions for effective individual engagement, which they define as: 'a personal state of connection with the issue of climate change, in contrast to engagement solely as a process of public participation in policy making' (p. 446). Engagement with climate change, according to the authors, requires the concurrent aspects of the *cognitive*, *affective* and *behavioural*. In other words it is not enough for people to know about climate change in order to be engaged; they also need to care about it, be motivated and able to take action (Lorenzoni *et al.* 2007, p. 446).

These three aspects of engagement are reflected in the CAG focus group responses.

Cognitive

> *The thing is if you look at the Goddard Institute of NASA, look at the data coming through and there's no argument the data's there. So people need to look at the data.*
>
> (Jeffrey, 64, VIC3)

> *I just feel that I've got too much knowledge to ignore it. I couldn't live with myself if I didn't do anything about climate change.*
>
> (Mandy, 32, VIC1)

Irrespective of the constructed nature of climate change knowledge (as discussed in Chapter 2), members of CAGs in general displayed great confidence in the scientific underpinnings of climate change. The science of climate change initially alerted participants to the scale, magnitude and consequences of the issue and formed a strong motivator for their action. This understanding was evident within each of the CAGs included in the research and arguably extends to those concerned about climate action more generally, as much of the climate movement expresses its concerns around climate change in line with the dominant scientific discourse (Burgmann & Baer 2012). Many of the CAG participants indicated they had formal education in disciplines that gave them either a detailed knowledge of climate science (through science, geography, engineering, agriculture for example) or otherwise, as highly educated people, an ability to grasp the complex nature of the subject. In this way, CAG participants distinguish themselves from the general public based on their ability to understand the implications of scientifically constructed climate change knowledge.

Of particular interest to policymakers is what the public knows about climate change and the motivations underlying their actions. Social research surveys have been used to track these trends over time (I discuss this social research in Chapter 3). They reveal that, while in general, community understanding of the commonly held scientific explanations of the causes of global warming and the role of humans in contributing to it has risen, a significant percentage of the adult population remains confused, misinformed or otherwise ignorant. Contributing to public confusion and uncertainty around the climate issue, there is a concerted campaign being waged to discredit both climate science and the credentials of climate scientists more generally (Hamilton 2007; Oreskes & Conway 2010).

Most CAGs were established following the Australian release of Al Gore's film, *An Inconvenient Truth*, coinciding with the time of greatest levels of public concern regarding climate change (Neilsen and Environmental Change Institute 2007), and many participants cited the film as a key motivator for the formation of their group. *An Inconvenient Truth* aimed to translate the complex science of climate change, both in terms of its causes and effects, into a readily understood and actionable global problem. Apart from Al Gore, other academic and popular writers have been influential: the writings of James Hansen (Hansen 2007, 2008) in particular were cited by CAGs. James Hansen, formerly of NASA in the USA and a distinguished climatologist, is a long-term advocate for strong climate change action. He argues for an atmospheric CO_2-equivalent target of 300 ppm (parts per million) which would require capping global temperature rise well below the UNFCCC's accepted two degree limit to prevent dangerous climate change. Several focus group participants mentioned his discourse on climate tipping points (Hansen 2008; Hansen et al. 2008). For some, 'tipping points' generated a new or renewed sense of urgency around climate change action:

I went to the climate summit at the beginning of last year and heard [DS] who was talking about tipping points and I'd never really got my head around tipping points before and what that actually meant. If we hit those points there was no way we could return from that, and that's when ... My personal motivation went to a whole new level.

(Lenore, 28, NSW2)

This 'climate change-as-catastrophe' discourse (Beck 1992, 2006b; Hamilton 2010; Hansen 2007; Hulme 2008; Spratt & Sutton 2008) resonated deeply within the CAGs generating a 'social scare' (Ungar 1995) or 'moral shock' (Pearse *et al.* 2010), precipitating their action. According to Rosa and Dietz (1998), issues such as global warming, which are communicated through scientific discourse, and through scientific elites, require associated 'dramatic real-world events' in order to reach lay publics. Ungar (1995), argues that these real-world events 'unleash authentic social scares' related to scientific claims. Ungar provides as an example the droughts of the summer of 1988, which first aroused public concern on climate change despite decades of scientific understanding. The year 2006 provides the same conditions that Ungar describes for creating a 'social scare'. Pearse *et al.* (2010, p. 90) describe 'moral shocks' as moments of 'awakening' or 'disjuncture' where individuals reflect on particular events, creating new forms of understanding and mobilizing them towards activism. In other words, CAG members' ability to understand the science communicated on climate change, their *cognitive* ability, led to their *affective* engagement with the issue.

Affective

While a cognitive awareness of climate change may have been the initial inspiration for people's action on climate change, the emotional engagement of CAG participants was a particularly important underlying motivation. There was an affective stimulus at the root of most participants' involvement in climate change action. For some, this related closely to their 'circle of care'.[2] Children and grandchildren were an important raison d'être for taking action on climate change:

I've got four kids and I'm worried about their future and what it will be like for them so ... That's one of the main reasons why I do it but also ... because I care about what happens to our planet.

(Raelene, 42, VIC1)

I have seven grandchildren ... [and] ... my wife and I wish to set some sort of example in the hope that they will become more aware than their parents of the need to act. So it's terribly altruistic.

(Ken, 74, VIC2)

For many participants the emotional toll of engaging in climate change action related to a deep sense of despair regarding this 'diabolical' problem and the unfolding uncertain future:

> *It's incredibly hard what we are doing and it's incredibly emotional and ... every single person in the movement struggles with that all the time and struggles with, is it worth putting our energy into it and we do just want to give up ... not keep going, and so, as we've said, the group's really important in dealing with that ... We don't actually talk about how we deal with that great uncertainty of the future and the deep sadness that we feel about the future of the planet and its people and the worry and the despair and it's important ... to acknowledge that.*
> (Michele, 28, NSW2)

This sense of desolation could lead to disempowerment, denial and 'choosing not to choose' (Macnaghten 2003) to take action around climate change. Instead, this emotive force contributed to the 'moral shock' (Pearse *et al.* 2010) experienced by CAG members and became a 'call to action' – in other words, a strong disincentive to apathy and inaction. An important distinction is revealed here on how CAG members differ from the majority within their communities:

> *The difference between us, who try to do something and people who think it's important but don't, you know, that's complex but ... people I know say that they're not frightened enough yet and I think there's something in that. It suggests to me that even though intellectually they know this is a serious issue, they don't actually know this is a serious issue yet. But people will, the penny will drop.*
> (David, 63, VIC4)

An important point is revealed here. CAG participants, based on their knowledge of climate change and their emotional responses to it, choose to engage in action and to accelerate their capacity to act by working within a group. Others within the community, though potentially equally knowledgeable, display a different affective response. Much has been written about this, particularly within the psychological literature. However, I suggest that the lack of motivation for individual and collective advocacy around climate change expressed in apathy or denial, for example, represents a point of critical bifurcation (see Figure 5.3) around community action on climate change.

Even during periods of high levels of stated public concern around climate change, people have failed to take concerted action (Hulme 2009; The Climate Institute 2010). Norgaard (Norgaard 2006; Norgaard 2009) observes that denial of climate change and inaction by the public can be attributed to 'the social organization of denial', and that there is both a psychological and sociological basis to inaction, conceived as ' "the mental processes of attending and ignoring" ' (Norgaard 2006, p. 374) (citing Zerubavel 1997, p. 11). The social organization of denial occurs in the contexts of the individual, of social norms of behaviour and of the broader political and economic situation. She further argues that rather than a deficit in knowledge about climate change leading to '... the failure to integrate this knowledge into everyday life or transform it into social action' (Norgaard 2009, pp. 28–9), *people not only don't want to know but don't know how to know.*

Inaction therefore needs to be understood in the context of people's belief that they are unable to effectively act on an issue as complex, all-encompassing yet intangible as climate change. This belief is based not only on their factual knowledge but also on their inability to overcome their feelings of deep despair (Macy 1995). Norgaard considers peoples' feelings of helplessness to be symptomatic of inadequate political and economic structures and the realization that 'one's government and/or the world community at large could not be relied upon to solve this problem' (Norgaard 2009, p. 30). In this sense, despondency is matched with a lack of trust in those who should be most capable of resolving 'wicked' global problems such as climate change. So, in response, people turn to those matters most readily within their control. As one of Norgaard's (2009, p. 32) respondents states: 'I suppose that's why my family has become more important to me, my everyday life, that which is near' (Nilsen, 184, 1999).

This also supports my argument that a bifurcation occurs in response to the 'moral shock' of climate change. Members of CAGs, for example, express their agency as *moral agents* able to enact their collective agency

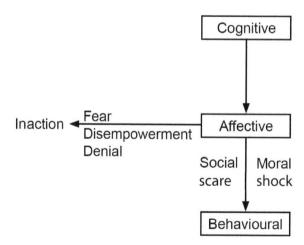

Figure 5.3 Bifurcation in action
Source: Kent 2012

through their political actions. Others turn to their closest circle, their family, and devote their efforts to lowering their carbon emissions within their personal and private spheres.

Behavioural

The third co-existent prerequisite for engagement on climate change (Lorenzoni *et al.* 2007) is people's motivation and ability to act. CAG participants described an extensive range of actions that they were taking within their homes and lifestyles but in addition to this, participants undertook various forms of collective and political action.

All participants were engaged in individual and/or household-level actions to mitigate climate change as well as forms of collective (group) action. Individual actions ranged from household-level behaviour such as switching off standby power, purchasing energy saving equipment and retrofitting homes with renewable energy items. Lifestyle level changes included changing their diets, growing their own food, adopting alternative transport practices such as downsizing from a car to a motorbike, using public transport or riding a bicycle. For some CAG participants, individual action involved a high degree of personal sacrifice – moving from paid to volunteer work, giving up flying (the 'Achilles heel' of carbon footprint reduction (Krakoff 2011, p. 38)), constructing a home aquifer for water supply, turning off the home's hot water, and showering only every second day. These types of activities demonstrate a high level of individual responsibility matched with the personal capacity to undertake such action:

> *I think there is a place for every type of action or protest, there's a scale* [murmurs of agreement in the background] *and it's about what purpose they serve . . . For example doing a hunger strike is not going to change the climate, but that's not the point of the hunger strike, maybe it's to get publicity and it's not about changing the climate as such, so I think everything has a place on the spectrum and things appeal to different people.*
>
> (Bethany, 20, VIC4)

Collective actions focused on: developing broader community networks and alliances to support climate change action at the community and wider scales (state and/or national); enhancing the capacity of other community members through awareness-raising activities and by making available specific tools or equipment for generating lower carbon households (bulk purchase PV or solar hot water, home energy audit kits etc.); forms of political/ citizen-based action including petitions, letters and phone calls to politicians and more direct action focused at sites of political power such as protests, sit-ins and rallies; and more radical forms of civil disobedience, such as blocking coal infrastructure.

Both individual and collective forms of voluntary action provided a sense of empowerment to participants, which increased their involvement in both individual and collective actions. The group provided a secure and emotionally supportive space for individuals to experiment with expressions of agency around climate change mitigation and provided a place where shared knowledge, values and beliefs around climate change could be expressed. Furthermore, volunteering with groups allowed participants to develop and enhance skills in areas such as media, event organization, political lobbying and advocacy, and non-violent direct action and civil disobedience.

Evidence from the focus groups suggests that for some groups the normed behaviour and shared values resulted in quite significant changes in lifestyle practices. These included some of the more committed personal behaviours such as reducing personal showering routines or, for one participant, taking up cycling in her seventies. These actions go beyond incremental changes in lifestyle and indicate a directly political counter to dominant cultural norms.[3] However, tensions were revealed for some group participants who felt that their personal actions were secondary to more political forms of action geared towards agitating for more broad scale societal level change:

> *Around the time the group formed the Howard government was running that campaign 'Be Climate Clever', you know, change your light bulbs or whatever it was. And I think over the ten years of his government we had a message that was put out to the public constantly which was taking action on climate change looks like individual lifestyle behavioural change ... and there was no sense that actually our governments have a responsibility in taking action on these issues and making the structural changes required to really deal with them. So ... when the group ... formed, I think being aware of that and looking to change ... the bigger political landscape was really important and it still is, to me.*

(Lenore, 28, NSW2)

CAGs may be non-partisan but they are, for the most part, engaged in political processes (although not powerfully) and are better described as geographically based 'communities of interest' (Seyfang & Smith 2007, p. 597) or ideological niches, which set themselves apart as 'other' or 'alternative' to the mainstream. In this sense, CAGs demonstrate their position in public space where they can act in ways that are informal, un-structured, communicative and strategic, but which may also be outside and against the state (Hendriks 2006).

In summary, CAG members undertake significant actions ranging from changes in social practices quite removed from accepted degrees of comfort (Shove 2003) and extant social norms – some participants for example reduced their energy use by bathing only in cold water – to enacting novel forms of collective political action through direct action and civil disobedience. The adoption of these more radical lifestyle practices by some CAG members are examples of the desire 'to make the personal political', a type of lifestyle politics (Spaargaren & Mol 2008) or 'an environmental politics of sacrifice' (Maniates & Meyer 2010). Engagement in effective mitigation of climate change requires more than citizen *participation* in democratic processes, it must be *enacted* by them. Dobson (2006) describes this as a 'thick cosmopolitanism', which he defines as a recognition of each person within 'a common humanity' (p. 169). Thick cosmopolitanism requires not only an acknowledgement of the principles of cosmopolitanism, but also that people carry out political action. In other words, they need 'to "be" cosmopolitan' (p. 169). In this sense, CAG members *are* cosmopolitan as they act out their deep concerns regarding climate change and human survival through their political expression. As Bethany (VIC4, 20) states: '*As in compelled, as in I have this information how can I not do something? . . . I have an obligation, how can I not? It would be selfish of me not to.*'

CAG members are engaged in a progression of voluntary collective climate change action. CAG members engage with climate change cognitively, affectively and behaviourally. They have come to know climate change as a catastrophic problem through an understanding of scientifically constructed climate change knowledge. CAG members were influenced by Al Gore's film, *An Inconvenient Truth*, with many groups forming around the time of the film's release. This coincided with significant landscape-level real-world events, generating a 'social scare' (Ungar 1995) and prompting CAG members to reflect on these socially situated conditions. However, rather than leading to despair and inaction, this 'moral shock' (Pearse *et al.* 2010) precipitated CAG member action both within their personal and private spheres and through collective public-sphere action.

Alternative pathways to public sphere and collective agency

At this point, I turn to consider some presumptions I've made regarding engagement with climate change as an issue as a precursor to both individual and collective action.

If CO_2 turns out not to be true, then what we're doing could be damaged. If CO_2, global warming turns out not to be true, then what we're doing and what we necessarily must do to make this Earth better for everybody could be damaged by that not being true . . . Because you talk about the denialists and the believers, well, we shouldn't have the denialists and believers, we should be focused on what we need to do to make this a better Earth and whether CO_2's the culprit or whether the sun's the culprit or what's going to happen next, I don't know, but *that doesn't alter all the actions taken by people around this table have been toward a sustainable future, and so, if everybody did that then the big political argument wouldn't really matter.*

(Jerry, 63, VIC2)

The above statement by Jerry, a climate change sceptic, prompts the question: do people have to be engaged with climate change as an issue to effectively address the causes and effects of unsustainability? In other words, is climate change the subject that needs to be addressed or are there other contexts beyond this specific problem set to be considered? To place Jerry's quote in context, VIC2, a CRAG, possessed certain characteristics that delineated it from the other CAGs.

In selecting a CRAG for study, I hoped to extend the range of types of participants and climate action groups in my research. VIC2 demonstrated a number of features which diverged widely from those of the other groups. First, it was evident from the focus group that the members of the CRAG were not operating according to the general understanding of a carbon rationing group. CRAGs aim to support and facilitate both individual and *collective* reduction in personal and household carbon emissions. In VIC2 however this was not the case, with members considering themselves as individual advocates for carbon reduction behaviour, not collective agents.[4] Second, there was considerable tension within this group, specifically around understandings of the scientific basis for climate change. In particular, Jerry (63) held sceptical views on whether global warming was occurring and whether humans were contributing to it. This generated significant debate among the participants and raised particular questions for me: do people have to be concerned specifically about climate change in order to act on it? What are the specific elements of climate change that cause individual's greatest concern? Finally, if your approach to taking climate change action is based on an 'agency-oriented' individualization of responsibility, why get involved in a group at all? I consider these questions in light of my research in the following section.

Climate change as a heuristic

Several CAG participants commented on how climate change brings together a range of long-term issues and concerns for them. Climate change then becomes a problem set, a way to synthesize and filter concerns that might extend beyond the environment to capture more broadly their concerns about the economic system, politics, social justice, food and water security – matters that have increasingly become captured under the expression 'sustainable development' or 'sustainability'. In this way, climate change works to 'connect the dots' on other issues and provides a *reflexive heuristic* for group members. As Hulme (2010, p. 267) describes, climate change is 'both a resourceful idea and a versatile explanation which can be moulded and mobilized to fulfil a bewildering array of political, social and sociological functions'.

While for many of the research participants their initial focus on climate change was mediated through their knowledge of climate change science, the phenomenon of climate change itself (for example, as a result of increasing GHG emissions) was over time becoming less central to their actions. Climate change came to represent, as stated by Michele (28, NSW2): *'everything that's wrong with society coming to a head'* or otherwise for Randall (70, NSW1): *'It's quite extraordinary really that all the things that have interested me and concerned me for the last 20 years have come together and relate in some way to climate change.'*

Thus climate change becomes a coda for the root causes of societal unsustainability and a motivation that surpasses the disempowerment brought on by the fear of catastrophic climate change. There was diminished interest here in personal and household carbon mitigation behaviours or in calculating carbon footprints and a much greater emphasis on community engagement, direct action, social movement building and political change. Climate change in this way becomes a tool for focusing energy and honing skills around a broader social and political project. As Hulme (2009, p. 322) observes:

> Climate change is everywhere. Not only are the physical climates of the world everywhere changing, but just as importantly the idea of climate change is now found to be active across the full parade of human endeavours, institutions, practices and stories. The idea that humans are altering the physical climate of the planet through their collective actions, an idea captured in the simple linguistic compound 'climate change', is an idea as ubiquitous and as powerful in today's social discourses as are the ideas of democracy, terrorism or nationalism. Furthermore climate change is an idea that carries as many different meanings and interpretations in contemporary political and cultural life as do these other mobilising and volatile ideas.

For others, another pathway is suggested. There is also the potential for the mundane, routine and natural to render the intangibility of climate change into a more accessible and understandable phenomenon, one which could be extended to a broader audience. Hulme portrays this as the 'banal cosmopolitanism' of climate change suggesting that human experiences of climate and weather are 'losing their place-based character', assuming a new, powerful and global storyline of climate change (Hulme 2010, p. 272).

As Jasanoff (2010, p. 235) puts it:

> Science is not the only, nor the primary, medium through which people experience climate. We need no warrant other than our senses and

memories, supplemented by familiar recording devices such as the calendar or the gardeners' almanac, to register the vagaries of the weather, the changing of the seasons, the fertility of the soil, the migration of birds, or the predation of insects.

Here Jasanoff conveys the constant reminder of the natural world to our state of being. In this way, the weather becomes the universal language of climate and climate change (as discussed in Chapter 2) separate to our cognition. Weather binds the unbounded nature of climate change to a specific place and thereby grounds individual and collective imaginations to tangible, observable and felt local phenomena (Jasanoff 2010). This is also reflected in Kirsten's (62, VIC4) statement below:

> *Perhaps it's to do with the sort of people who have . . . the more active imagination? . . . whether it is just somehow to do with the sort of personality people have that leads them then to think yes, I really feel this.*

It could be argued, therefore, that there are both localizing and globalizing tendencies in human responses to the real potential of catastrophic global warming. In the local lies the capacity for people to make real something that seems ephemeral and boundless; in the global lies the certainty of climate change as a universal phenomenon grounded in the everyday humdrum nature of our experience of the weather:

> *Yeah it's in the everyday but you know everyone talks about the weather but you . . . think how boring! But it's central to how we live and it's that whole 'God the weather today! O, Melbourne weather!' But it's not normal, it's not normal to have a massively long summer and no rain but it's not concrete at the same time.*
>
> (Bethany 20, VIC4)

According to Räthzel and Uzzell (2009), people experience a spatial biasing between the local and global in relation to issues of global environmental concern that creates a disjuncture for individual action and may explain why people fail to act around issues such as climate change. Through a closer engagement with how we know, feel and experience the weather, the issue of climate change changes from being an abstract global issue to a tangible local concern. Revealed through this conundrum is the potential for linking up community-based collectives and accelerating wider scale citizen action on climate change.

Summary

To summarize my argument to this point (illustrated in Figure 5.4): first, individual agency for climate change action requires a 'moral shock' or 'social scare' to precipitate a high degree of individual concern and responsibility. Second, in order to engage with the issue effectively (i.e. cognitively, affectively and behaviourally), individuals must be able to overcome feelings of denial and despondency and this is achieved through coming together in groups to produce collective agency. Third, while climate change has been presented here as the prime focus of community response, I make the case that it represents a potent heuristic or 'focal point' (Parks & Roberts 2010) for collective political action on a broader range of issues relating to sustainability and justice. (I draw this point out further in the next chapter.) Lastly, I suggest that the construction of climate and its confluence with our understanding of weather or other natural phenomena can provide an alternative to the positivist scientific and technological framing of climate change. Translating a global intangible into a local, concrete and observable phenomenon may address individual inaction based on feelings of disempowerment and where appeals based on the plight of distant others fail. Certainly there is growing support for this position based on social research findings that indicate that local weather events impact on people's perception of climate change.

There remain some gaps in the logic of this progression. First, the question remains: is there is a particular type of person who engages in collective voluntary climate change action? This is an important consideration as, if wider scale change is to be achieved, it is essential to recognize how the influence of this sub-group can be extended throughout the broader community. The second concern is: can the broader activation of these particular traits be harnessed and, if so, how? Also, is it only certain communities that have the capacity to support these collectives (Middlemiss & Parrish 2010)?

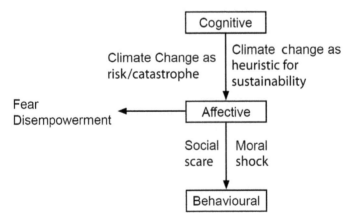

Figure 5.4 Engagement with climate change
Source: Kent 2012

People like me

Members of CAGs represent a particular subset within their local communities and society generally. Many of the characteristics that distinguish CAG members – they tend to be well educated, middle class and financially comfortable, for example – are indicative of their capacity to undertake climate change action. These characteristics also form the basis of their group identity.

CAG individual and group characteristics

Tranter (2010) describes membership of environmental organizations in Australia in terms of active and passive membership and notes that older people are not only more likely to be involved in environmental organizations but are also more active members. He states that: 'one's stage of the lifecycle might be important here, as many older people with relatively greater autonomy from family and work responsibilities are able to devote more time to participation' (p. 421). This was reflected in the comments of older participants across the focus groups exemplified in the quotation from David (63, VIC4): '*I decided when I retired that I would involve myself again with what seemed to be and still seems to be the big issue of our time.*'

Apart from time and autonomy, older participants offered other benefits to groups. In NSW1, for example, participants noted that their members were not only actively engaged with their local community, but they were also respected members of the community that held (or have held) positions of relative power and authority. Older participants were for the most part, tertiary educated professional people, though mostly retired or semi-retired from their professional work. These participants fall within what Inglehart calls the 'cognitively mobilized' – that is they are 'highly educated, articulate, politically skilled and informed' (Tranter 2010, p. 417). Tranter (2011) more recently characterizes this group as a particular 'elite' who are not only highly educated but who also possess post-materialist values:

> In general terms, consistent predictors of environmental concern in Australia include holding post-materialist values, engaging in eastern spiritual practices (perhaps reflecting alternative lifestyles and consumption practices), professional occupation and, to an extent, tertiary education. Gender differences are also apparent, with men less likely than women to favour environmental protection over economic growth, to claim they would pay extra tax to protect the environment, or to believe global warming poses a serious threat to their way of life
>
> (Tranter 2011, p. 92)

According to Inglehart (1997, p. 4), *post-materialist* values, that is, those that prioritize self-expression and quality of life, are demonstrative of post-war generations who have emerged from the industrialization era with unprecedented levels of economic security. Ingelhart and others have tracked this phenomenon throughout nations for 30 years through the World Values Survey.[5] Among the catalogue of findings from the survey, cultures of modernity/postmodernity are characterized by a shift from survival to self-expression values, which create higher levels of personal empowerment among citizens. CAG members therefore are representative of a particular subset within Australian society who tend to eschew a mainstream consumerist lifestyle to adopt alternative and more sustainable ways of living. CAG members, according with Inglehart (1997), display post-materialist values.

These characteristics however were shared by the younger cohort of participants, as stated by Michele (28, NSW2) below:

> *We're middle class people that have spare time and have professional jobs and we have intellectual histories and we have supportive families. So there's a whole lot of social factors that allow us the time to think about these problems and divert energy to them. I mean if I'm from a working class family and I have three kids my biggest problem is the mortgage. I don't have any of that so I have the luxury of being able to think about and acting on broader issues.*

The CAG participants presented as 'a very particular group, not representative of the general public' (Howell 2011, p. 185) in that they are middle class, highly educated people often freed up from immediate family responsibilities who have higher levels of risk perception regarding climate change and high levels of motivation to take action. In this respect, they share characteristics with the members of Transition Towns, who were found by Seyfang and Haxeltine (2012) to be over-represented by a particular type of person (as discussed in Chapter 4).

In summary, CAG participants in Australia are representative of a particular 'elite': mostly white, middle class, highly educated and financially secure. They are drawn to others with similar backgrounds and values – they are 'like-minded people' who can forge a collective identity around the issue of their greatest concern, climate change. 'People like me' was a consistent refrain among the CAG participants, nuanced in several different ways as illustrated below.

• Grouping together with similar others created group cohesion, conflicts were minimised and decision-making simplified. Within the collective, trust can flourish, confidence can build and learning is facilitated. In other words, there are many social advantages to collectives that contain like-minded people.

I guess ... it's nice to all think the same way about things and in other ways that's a limitation because you're coming from the one place so you end up having the same kinda ideas about things.

(Michele, 28, NSW2)

Collective action can work in 'a virtuous circle of action and reinforcement even in the absence of movement "success"' (Louis 2009, p. 730). The reinforcing action described above appears to be an example of this. The issue of climate change forms the basis of moral concern and responsibility to take action. Areas of conflict are reduced and the group comes to share similar ideas, which also make collective action possible.

• There are, on the other hand, potential disadvantages to group uniformity. CAGs found it difficult to increase their membership and to expand their influence and commitment to voluntary political action into the broader community. In almost all cases, stagnation in group membership was cause for significant frustration among CAG participants:

Most of the meetings and rallies and things we go to consist of the converted and that is, that is very frustrating and it hasn't changed over the last coupla years.

(Bernadette, 72, VIC3)

Yeah, absolutely, we had a huge, we had a huge non-renewal rate last year.

(Raelene, 42, VIC1)

[Jack interrupts]: So once they'd got their PVs [photovoltaics] on the roof ... they didn't renew their membership. It was purely to get that and then that was it.

(Raelene, 42, VIC1)

Seyfang and Haxeltine (2012) similarly note Transition Towns have difficulty in attracting a newer and broader membership. Their outreach activities attract 'principally "insider" activists, rather than "newcomer" members of the public' (Seyfang & Haxeltine 2012). They suggest that to broaden the appeal of Transition Towns beyond 'a small group of like-minded [environmental] activists' (p. 15) will require diversifying membership through effective communication with wider audiences (Seyfang & Haxeltine 2012). Hielscher (2013) also states this point in relation to self-selecting groups (such as CRAGs) that may have a limited and less inclusive vision.

• The age of CAG participants was also raised by several groups. CAG participants fell within two main age groupings that align with different life stages. Younger participants were largely single, without children or otherwise significant financial or family responsibilities; older participants (making up the majority in my research cohort) in the main were retired or close to retirement with time to spend on voluntary community activities. Groups consisting of older members (several groups consisted entirely of active members aged 55 years and older) lamented the lack of younger members. There is another discriminating factor potentially at play. The older participants in NSW1 were proud of the respect that they generated within their local community. The group's position within their regional town lent both credence to their work and by inference, a sense of authority, power and influence to the participants themselves:

> We know people too and linked to this age group there's a lot of people in [CAG] who are very well connected in this community. We can draw on people, we can be accepted by the council, we're not regarded as ratbags,[6] if we raise an issue it's dealt with with respect. If we call a meeting, an impressive group of people come. So there's a distinct advantage in this group of people.
>
> (George, 62, NSW1)

The lack of diversity in CAG membership therefore provokes questions regarding the role of CAGs in social movement development around climate change. For example, can social movements build from particular community 'elites' which can generate cohesion and expertise but may also alienate other sectors of the community? Archibugi and Held (2011, p. 18) note that: 'the English, American, French and Russian revolutions, all fought in the hope of empowering the bourgeois, the citizen and the proletariat, were led by elites.' However this would appear to be the antithesis of theoretical proposals for wide-scale social change progression that relies on diversity, inclusion and egalitarianism such as rendered in Torgerson's green public sphere, Dryzek's deliberative democracy (Dryzek 2001, 2008, 2009) and Beck's (2006a) cosmopolitan vision. The potential tension between the collective identity of CAG members and broader social engagement in climate action is explored further in Chapter 6.

Constraints and enablements

Earlier in Chapter 3, I outlined three constraints to individual agency that I put forward as contributing to inaction around climate change: lack of personal empowerment, lack of trust and lack of reflexivity. A key question that my empirical work sought to answer was: in what ways do CAG members overcome constraints to individual agency? At this point I should make it clear that I don't suggest that these three factors alone delimit climate action. Rather, I have applied them as an empirical 'test' to determine how actors who come together in collectives in order to undertake voluntary activities around climate change demonstrate the ability to surmount barriers to action.

Following from my argument above, I suggest that there are two elements that may determine why those who become CAG members differ from citizens of the wider community in terms of their individual agency. In the section above: 'People like me', I propose that those who join community-based climate action groups are from a particular 'elite'. In the following section I argue that members of this 'elite' are enabled to act on climate change as they are both individually and collectively empowered. They develop interpersonal trust through the membership of the group and their collective processes, but apart from this maintain trust in the political processes that allow structural change to occur. Finally, they are reflexive agents, able to utilize their engagement (cognitive, affective and behavioural) on climate change as *cosmopolitan* agents[7] who can link aspects of their individual agency to creating global climate change solutions.

Power

Personal empowerment plays an important role in determining how individual agency around climate change can enact broader scale change, yet it remains under researched in relation to collectives (Drury & Reicher 2009). Much of the literature concerning community climate change action has tended to focus on people's feelings of disempowerment as a core reason for their inaction (Moser 2009; Norgaard 2009). Paterson and Stripple (2010) go further and propose that power is deliberately set by capital and the state as a structural impediment to collective agency. They state that: '[there] is no pre-existing collective political community which can be invoked, and which needs to "act"; rather, it is a collectivity which has to be constantly made and remade' (p. 344).

Individual carbon reduction practices within the *'private sphere'* are exploited as a collective *'public good'* (Paterson & Stripple 2010, p. 347), creating not only the individualization but also the privatization of action aimed at lowering global carbon emissions. Under the 'conduct of carbon conduct' (Paterson & Stripple 2010), such action precludes any political challenge to the structural propensities towards unsustainability but instead acts to channel the desires of individuals through, for example, the carbon market (Paterson & Stripple 2010, p. 344).

Paterson and Stripple argue that individualized forms of climate change action expressed through a range of 'carbon conducts' (here however they include collective forms such as CRAGs) are both 'inadequate environ-mentally . . . and regressive socially' (Paterson & Stripple 2010, p. 342). They describe the 'conduct of carbon conduct' to mean

> a government of people's carbon dioxide emissions that does not work through the authority of the state or the state system, but through

people's governing of their own emissions. Different regimes of 'carbon calculation' operate so individuals either work on their emission-producing activities or to 'offset' their emissions elsewhere. The conduct of carbon conduct is therefore government enabled through certain forms of knowledge (measurements and calculations of one's own carbon footprint), certain technologies (the turning of carbon emissions into tradeable commodities), and a certain ethic (low carbon lifestyle as desirable).

(Paterson & Stripple 2010, p. 347)

Paterson and Stripple characterize five 'carbon governmentality' practices that individuals adopt in governing their own emissions: they act as 'counters, displacers, dieters, communitarians, or citizens' (p. 359). These practices operate to mould individuals 'as particular types of subjects' and because they emphasize personal responsibility for carbon management they are reflective of the power dynamics that operate under neoliberalism (p. 359). Individual freedoms read as these types of 'carbon conducts' act to depoliticize citizens (they are in effect disempowering) and channel individuals' energies into 'increasingly elaborate practices of self-monitoring and management' (p. 359). The power of the state in its unsustainability is thereby reproduced and reinforced through the conduct of these actors. Further, the role of the group in developing collective agency is questioned in this interpretation as the group simply enables individuals to enact their personal carbon lowering behaviours without challenging the regime state. So how then are CAGs empowered around climate change? The question of power was not so much spoken but implied within the CAG focus groups. However, it became clear that CAG participants could be distinguished from their broader communities by the fact that they were empowered to take action and specifically sought out a collective of like-minded people to do so:

> *I think you've got an action side and you have a socializing side and giving you that confidence that you can do something bigger than the individual.*
>
> (Rod, 60, NSW3)

> *The more germane issues for the general community is what power do we have or can we fix it? How do we wield some power to bring change?*
> (Solomon, 52, NSW3)

Hendriks (2009) describes such generative notions of power as 'power-with' or 'power-to' and as 'a community conception of power' (p. 178). Drawing on Arendt, Hendriks states that such power comes from collectives that engage in communal action. Power of this type is not directed towards domination but rather seeks to overturn or resist it (Kahane 2010):

This power is generative, it involves sharing something or becoming something, not just giving or demanding or consuming. It expands in its exercise. It finds a way to call on people to connect with something larger than themselves.

(Guinier and Torres 2002, p. 141 cited in
Hendriks 2009, p. 178)

Certainly, CAGs acknowledged that their group played a core facilitatory function, with individual group members extending themselves beyond their individual agency. As Linda and Lenore stated:

> *When I first got involved in the group I started to be more politically active. I started to go to protests and meetings, and sit-ins which I've never done before ... I think now when people say, 'hey let's go chain ourselves to something', I'm much more likely to go 'Yeah, OK, why not?'*

(Linda, 27, NSW2)

> *I think for me personally one of the really critical things that allows me to act is knowing that I have the support of other people around me and that I'm not doing it alone, and that makes me far more brave and gutsy than I ever would.*

(Lenore, 28, NSW2)

Implied in this notion of 'power-with' is participation in democratic processes. Hendriks (2009, p. 179) suggests a central role for deliberation and discourse in this expression of 'people power': 'The deliberative process provides the powerless (for example, marginalized groups, everyday citizens and so on) with a degree of autonomy to collectively reconsider policy issues, and in some cases, the possibility to redefine the "problem" itself.'

Further, the deliberative processes played out in the informal and unstructured spaces of social life (Hendriks 2006, p. 497), such as CAGs, have been shown to reinforce the ability of actors to engage in political procedures by building self-confidence, knowledge and awareness (Hendriks 2009, p. 180). The empowerment of CAGs and their members thereby becomes a counterpoint to state power. It assists community co-determination around important concerns such as climate change, fosters virtues of trust and reciprocity, and cultivates social learning in democracy (Hendriks 2006; Moloney *et al.* 2010). In other words, CAG members become individually and collectively empowered through their action and develop skills in the practice of democracy. They act as *democratic agents*.[8]

Trust

> *The impression I get is that most people are mistrustful, they don't know what to believe. You find some kindred spirits every now and then.*
>
> (Terry, 55, VIC2)

The discourse of trust–distrust is pervasive within contemporary politics, particularly where a distinct political partisanship is being displayed around important issues such as climate change (Tranter 2011). Since the 1960s there has been a continual decline in citizen engagement and participation in democratic politics in its traditional forms, fuelled by a reduction in citizen knowledge and interest in politics and increasing distrust of government (Hetherington 1998; Saward 2008; Schyns & Koop 2010). Decline in civic engagement remains a fundamental problem for contemporary democracy (Hoppner & Whitmarsh 2010). Supporting evidence for this position is found in both politico-economic (Hetherington 1998; Nye *et al.* 2010; Saward 2008) and psycho-social (Blake 1999; Hoppner & Whitmarsh 2010; Lorenzoni *et al.* 2007) research. Political distrust is so pervasive within present-day society that it extends beyond an individual attribute to be adopted as a social and cultural norm. Distrust of politics presents as systemic and endemic to the modern social condition, leading to a lessening of social capital, which is widely considered as essential to the effective and efficient functioning of modern societies (Schyns & Koop 2010, p. 151).

The phenomenon of rising levels of citizen distrust in both political institutions and political actors within contemporary western democracies, according to Mansbridge (1997, pp. 148–9) leads to: increased cynicism, decreased interpersonal trust, reduced optimism, increasingly negative media coverage of the government and more publicity on corruption. Mansbridge's list of consequences is surprisingly reflective of contemporary politics in neoliberal societies and of the regard that citizens currently hold for politicians and governments of all persuasions. Most importantly, it describes a set of societal conditions that are distinctly unhealthy for a modern democracy.

Declining political trust has significant implications for democracy as it can lead into a cycle of further political and democratic dysfunction as 'without public support for solutions, problems will linger, will become more acute, and if not resolved will provide the foundations for renewed discontent' (Hetherington 1998, p. 804). Schyns and Koop argue that this will lead to a lack of support for and legitimacy of democratic governments. Underlying this disengagement is a perceived lack of agency, as Dahlgren (2009, p. 70) expresses:

> People increasingly do not feel inspired by what the politicians propose that society collectively could and should be. Likewise, citizens do not embody a sense of popular efficacy that they can, via democracy's institutions and mechanisms, impact on societal development.

Against the prevailing social norm, members of CAGs spoke repeatedly of taking political action around climate change with the specific aim of generating action by politicians and governments. For example, Polly (25, VIC4) said:

> *I've become more political. I'd written letters to politicians before but I'm not naturally a particularly political person. Being involved in [CAG] has one, convinced me that more of that is necessary and, more people have to get involved even if initially it's not something that they are particularly comfortable with and so more prepared to act in an overtly political way.*

It is appropriate here to consider in what ways the actions of CAG members demonstrate trust in political institutions. CAG responses to political structures demonstrate that while they may sit *outside* of the state, they do not necessarily position themselves *against* it (Dryzek *et al.* 2003). In other words, their belief in the legitimacy of government remains. If anything, CAGs set themselves as *legitimizing agents*, their role being to ensure that governments remain accountable, transparent and authentic to their citizens (Dryzek 2009). I suggest this is not an agenda of radicalism that seeks to create wholesale social change. Rather, CAGs are operating here as cosmopolitan agents in order to legitimize state power, with the hope that in turn the state will bring about a social 'good' (Archibugi & Held 2011), such as a concerted effort to mitigate against dangerous climate change. Bethany (20, VIC4) expresses this well:

> *We have legitimacy. This is a science based issue so we are trying to use the science that we have . . . We're not just raving lunatics with our own agenda, trying to force other people to change because we believe that is the way it should be.*

It is wrong to suggest here that CAGs are purely focused on political action. They also strongly believe that their collective action needs to be directed towards influencing public opinion and attracting the main-stream community to their 'cause', namely climate action. This was evident in the emphasis of CAGs on community outreach, awareness-raising and education.

In summary, I have argued that CAG members surmount the constraint of lack of trust by demonstrating that, through their actions they are cosmopolitan, democratic and legitimizing agents. They are 'actors with authority' (Biermann *et al.* 2009) undertaking political action despite heightened community distrust in existing government and political arrangements for mitigating the effects of dangerous climate change.

Reflexivity

The third enablement for agency is reflexivity. Archer defines reflexivity as: 'the regular exercise of the mental ability, shared by all normal people, to consider themselves in relation to their (social) contexts and vice versa' (p. 4). According to Archer (2007, p. 5) the modernizing conditions of our fast changing, globalizing world requires increasing levels of reflexivity. In asking 'what exactly do people do?' Archer (2007) suggests that there is a need to examine the *'variability* in the actions of those similarly socially situated and the differences in their processes of reflexivity' (p. 6, emphasis in text). In other words, what is the relationship between people deliberating on an issue of concern and the action people take in their social lives? (Archer 2007, p. 37).

So in what ways do CAG members display reflexivity in relation to their actions and how is this different from the attitudes of those who choose not to take public sphere action on climate change? CAG participants were quite literal in demonstrating their role as reflexive agents in climate change action: '*I just want to be able to look myself in the eye in the mirror and say well at least I tried, at least I spent my energy and time . . . in a good, constructive way*' (Linda, 27, NSW2).

Those inactive on climate change within the community were otherwise characterized as people who 'don't want to look'. CAG members in fact suggested that a lack of personal responsibility for climate change action is linked to the failure to employ reflexive thinking on the part of those that choose not to act:

> *They are so focused on their lives and living day to day . . . it's just about survival, they're not looking at other aspects of their lives.*
>
> (Jerry, 63, VIC2)

> *But you know this divides. They're saying, well, they oughta do something about it and it's shocking what's happening, but don't want to look.*
>
> (Kirsten, 62, VIC4)

I have already shown that CAG members are highly educated people who are often less burdened with the concerns of managing their day-to-day lives and hold post-materialist values. As a particular 'elite' within their communities, it could be expected that they possess the capability and the time to critically think and reflect on the problem of climate change. Bethany's statement below supports this contention:

> *Well it's my upbringing. The privileges I've had, perhaps my education, where I've gone to school, where I fit into society . . . financial things are not so much of a worry for my family so therefore I've been able to think about other things beyond those immediate to do's, have to*

cover those first. It's just that extra knowledge and then I've got the time to be able to do something about it as well. So you've got to be able to cover all those personal bases first and then you think about the wider world and how you can affect it.

(Bethany, 20, VIC4)

CAG members perceived others within their community who were not overtly active or otherwise concerned about climate change as lacking reflexivity. According to CAG participants, others are disempowered, overly individualistic, hedonistic, ignorant, failing to connect issues, not affectively engaged or morally outraged enough. I expected the CRAG members (VIC2) who were initially drawn to their group by the free gifts and subsidized solar panels provided by their council to demonstrate not only more individualistic but also less reflexive tendencies. However, this was not the case:

But it could cause wars. If one part of the Earth became unsustainable and they say we're going to live here now, it's on.

(Jerry, 63, VIC2)

So much of what we have we waste and we overconsume and people in other developing countries would probably like the same basic essentials that we take for granted.

(Terry, 55, VIC2)

Other CAG members equally demonstrated the ability to link their local and community-based concerns with broader notions of unsustainability:

Back in the sixties and seventies we thought that it was going to be so much leisure by year 2000 because technology would improve productivity, but we all chose not to ... take leisure but to take more consumption, we all worked far more. Why did we do that? I've never understood that. Why didn't we just say, let's work half as much with the technology productivity improvements. Let's just have half the wages but we never said that. We said no, no, we'd have more trips, more furniture, more new cars, more everything that's where we went wrong.

(Wayne, 68, NSW4)

They made links, for example, between climate change and consumption, climate change and population, and even climate change and (resource) wars, demonstrating the distinct ability of CAG members to apply 'critically reflexive systemic thinking' as the basis for their 'ethically and morally grounded' actions (Gregory 2000, p. 493). The collective again both supported and enhanced individual reflexivity, providing a safe space for dialogue and debate, and aiding mutual learning.

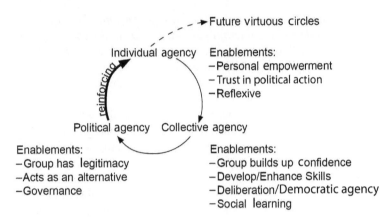

Figure 5.5 Virtuous circle of agency
Source: Kent 2012

Earlier, I argued that disempowerment, distrust and lack of reflexivity constrain individual agency for environmental problem solving. All are potentially potent inhibitors of political engagement that must be overcome to extend the potential of citizen participation in climate change governance. CAG participants, on the other hand, display enabling characteristics as cosmopolitan, democratic and legitimizing agents. I illustrate this process in Figure 5.5.

I represent this process as a virtuous circle.[9] As the participants in my research cohort have expressed above, members possess individual agency. They have overcome the constraints to agency of disempowerment, lack of trust in political institutions and political actors, and a lack of reflexivity required to address the global risk issues of modernity, and specifically, climate change. Their individual agency is enhanced by their involvement in the group. Their CAG enables the development of collective agency. Involvement in the group bolsters individual members' confidence around their voluntary actions. CAG members have the opportunity to develop and practise skills that contribute to both their individual and collective agency in climate change action. They act as political agents and in the process of group dialogue and deliberation, they practice democracy. This political agency acts to further enhance their individual agency and emboldens CAG members in fulfilling both their individual and collective responsibility for climate change through their voluntary actions. Linda (27, NSW2) expresses this process well:

> so you start off being nervous about coming along to a meeting and
> you do it and it doesn't kill you and it actually was quite fun and ...
> you realize you can survive through that and then the next step is OK,
> well, come along to ... an event of some sort and then a couple of

months later you're being interviewed on national radio or standing in front of some building waiting for a policeman to take you away [general laughter]. *It's not a very gradual process.*

The groups consider their collective political and democratic agency as providing a form of legitimacy that under the conditions of Beck's organized irresponsibility positions them as a type of alternative governance for legitimate grassroots climate change advocacy and action. It remains to consider how these traits and capabilities might be harnessed to activate agency in the wider community. This is the focus of the next chapter.

Notes

1 Paterson & Stripple (2010) describe five 'carbon conducts' commonly promoted for individual and/or household uptake: carbon footprinting, carbon offsetting, carbon dieting, CRAGs and PCAs.
2 Peter Singer 2011 refers to the 'expanding circle' in arguing that an ethical approach should expand our circle of concern from those near such as family and close friends to distant others.
3 Maniates and Meyer (2010) describe this as the 'environmental politics of sacrifice'.
4 Personal communication, convenor of VIC2 CRAG who states: '*In setting up a CRAG I did not set out to form a group as such but to empower individuals to act and become advocates*', email dated 12 October 2011.
5 See http://worldvaluessurvey.org/, accessed 28 June 2011.
6 The Macquarie Dictionary defines ratbag as: 'a person of eccentric or non-conforming ideas or behaviour'; 'a person whose preoccupation with a particular theory or belief is seen as obsessive or discreditable', www.macquariedictionary.com.au, accessed 26 October 2011.
7 Archibugi and Held (2011) distinguish between collective groups 'having a personal cosmopolitan lifestyle and holding cosmopolitan values' (p. 13). They argue that a cosmopolitan democracy relies on support from those that hold cosmopolitan values. I use the term cosmopolitan agents to represent actors who hold cosmopolitan values.
8 List and Koenig-Archibugi (2010) define democratic agency as: 'The collection of individuals in question has the *capacity* (not necessarily actualised) to be organized, in a democratic manner, in such a way as to function as a state-like group agent' (p. 91).
9 The Oxford Dictionary defines a virtuous circle as 'a recurring cycle of events, the result of each one being to increase the beneficial effect of the next', Oxford Dictionary Online, accessed 31 January 2012, www.oxforddictionaries.com.

References

Archer, M.S. 2007, *Making our way through the world: human reflexivity and social mobility*, Cambridge University Press, Cambridge.
Archibugi, D. & Held, D. 2011, 'Cosmopolitan democracy: paths and agents', paper presented to the *Global Governance: Political Authority in Transition. ISA Annual Convention 2011*, Montreal PQ, 16–19 March 2011.

Beck, U. 1992, *Risk society: towards a new modernity*, trans. M. Ritter, Sage, London.

Beck, U. 2006a, *Cosmopolitan vision*, Polity, Cambridge, UK.

Beck, U. 2006b, 'Living in the world risk society', *Economy and Society*, vol. 35, no. 3, pp. 329–45.

Biermann, F., Betsill, M.M., Gupta, J., Kanie, N., Lebel, L., Liverman, D., Schroeder, H. & Siebenhuner, B. 2009, *Earth system governance: people, places and the planet. Science and implementation plan of the Earth System Governance Project*, ESG Report 1, IHDP: The Earth System Governance Project, Bonn.

Blake, J. 1999, 'Overcoming the "value-action gap" in environmental policy: tensions between national policy and local experience', *Local Environment*, vol. 4, no. 3, pp. 257–78.

Burgmann, V. & Baer, H. 2012, *Climate politics and the climate movement in Australia*, Melbourne University Press, Melbourne, Australia.

Dahlgren, P. 2009, *Media and political engagement*, Cambridge University Press, Cambridge.

Dobson, A. 2006, 'Thick cosmopolitanism', *Political Studies*, vol. 54, pp. 165–84.

Drury, J. & Reicher, S. 2009, 'Collective psychological empowerment as a model of social change: researching crowds and power', *Journal of Social Issues*, vol. 65, no. 4, pp. 707–25.

Dryzek, J.S. 2001, 'Legitimacy and economy in deliberative democracy', *Political Theory*, vol. 29, no. 5, pp. 651–69.

Dryzek, J.S. 2008, 'Two paths to global democracy', *Ethical Perspectives*, vol. 15, no. 4, pp. 469–86.

Dryzek, J.S. 2009, 'Democratization as deliberative capacity building', *Comparative Political Studies*, vol. 42, no. 11, pp. 1379–1402.

Dryzek, J.S., Downes, D., Hunold, C., Schlosberg, D. & Hernes, with H.-K. 2003, *Green states and social movements: environmentalism in the United States, United Kingdom, Germany and Norway*, Oxford University Press, Oxford.

Giddens, A. 1984, *The constitution of society: outline of the theory of structuration*, University of California Press, Berkeley, CA.

Gregory, W.J. 2000, 'Transforming self and society: a "critical appreciation" model', *Systemic Practice and Action Research*, vol. 13, no. 4, pp. 475–501.

Grin, J., Rotmans, J. & Schot, J. 2010, *Transitions in sustainable development: new directions in the study of long term transformative change*, Routledge, New York.

Hamilton, C. with research assistance from Downie, C. 2007, *Scorcher: the dirty politics of climate change*, Black Ink Agenda, Melbourne, Australia.

Hamilton, C. 2010, *Requiem for a species: why we resist the truth about climate change*, Earthscan, London, Washington, D.C.

Hansen, J. 2007, 'Climate catastrophe', *New Scientist*, vol. 195, no. 2614, pp. 30–4.

Hansen, J. (ed.) 2008, Tipping point: perspectives of a climatologist in E. Fearn, ed., *State of the wild 2008-2009: A global portrait of wildlife, wildlands, and oceans*. Wildlife Conservation Society/Island Press, pp. 6–15.

Hansen, J., Sato, M., Kharecha, P., Beerling, D., Berner, R., Masson-Delmotte, V., Pagani, M., Raymo, M., Royer, D.L. & Zachros, J.C. 2008, 'target atmospheric CO_2: where should humanity aim?' *Open Atmosphere Science Journal*, vol. 2, pp. 217–31.

Hendriks, C.M. 2006, 'Integrated deliberation: reconciling civil society's dual role in deliberative democracy', *Political Studies*, vol. 54, pp. 486–508.

Hendriks, C.M. 2009, 'Deliberative governance in the context of power', *Policy and Society*, vol. 28, pp. 173–84.

Hetherington, M.J. 1998, 'The political relevance of political trust', *American Political Science Review*, vol. 92, no. 4, pp. 791–808.

Hielscher, S. 2013, *Carbon rationing action groups: an innovation history*, Community Innovation for Sustainable Energy Project, Project report. University of Sussex; University of East Anglia, accessed 4 June 2015, http://sro.sussex. ac.uk/53354/.

Hoppner, C. & Whitmarsh, L. 2010, 'Public engagement in climate action: policy and public expectations', in L. O'Neill, S. Whitmarsh & I. Lorenzoni (eds), *Engaging the public with climate change: behaviour change and communication*, Earthscan, London, pp. 47–65.

Howell, R.A. 2011, 'Lights, camera . . . action? Altered attitudes and behaviour in response to the climate change film The Age of Stupid', *Global Environmental Change*, vol. 21, no. 1, pp. 177–87.

Hulme, M. 2008, 'The conquering of climate: discourses of fear and their dissolution', *Geographical Journal*, vol. 174, no. 1, pp. 5–16.

Hulme, M. 2009, *Why we disagree about climate change: understanding controversy, inaction and opportunity*, Cambridge University Press, Cambridge.

Hulme, M. 2010, 'Cosmopolitan climates: hybridity, foresight and meaning', *Theory, Culture and Society*, vol. 27, no. 2–3, pp. 267–76.

Inglehart, R. 1997, *Modernization and postmodernization: cultural, economic and political change in 43 societies*, Princeton University Press, New Jersey.

Jasanoff, S. 2010, 'A new climate for society', *Theory, Culture and Society*, vol. 27, no. 2–3, pp. 233–53.

Kahane, A. 2010, *Power and love: a theory and practice of social change*, Berrett-Koehler, San Francisco, CA.

Kent, J. 2012, 'Third sector organisations and climate change: a case study of Australian Climate Action Groups', *Third Sector Review*, vol. 18, no. 1, pp. 53–76.

Krakoff, S. 2011, *Planetary identity formation and the relocalization of environmental law*, Working Paper 03-11, University of Colorado, Boulder, CO.

List, C. & Archibugi, K. 2010, 'Can there be a global demos? An agency-based approach', *Philosophy & Public Affairs*, vol. 38, no. 1, pp. 76–110.

Lorenzoni, I., Nicholson-Cole, S. & Whitmarsh, L. 2007, 'Barriers perceived to engaging with climate change among the UK public and their policy implications', *Global Environmental Change*, vol. 17, no. 3-4, pp. 445–59.

Louis, W.R. 2009, 'Collective action – and then what?', *Journal of Social Issues*, vol. 65, no. 4, pp. 727–48.

Macnaghten, P. 2003, 'Embodying the environment in everyday life practices', *The Sociological Review*, vol. 51, no. 1, pp. 63–84.

Macy, J. 1995, 'Working through environmental despair', *Ecopsychology: restoring the earth, healing the mind*, vol. 2, pp. 240–59.

Maniates, M. & Meyer, J.M. 2010, *The environmental politics of sacrifice*, The MIT Press, Cambridge, MA.

Maniates, M.F. 2012, 'Everyday possibilities', *Global Environmental Politics*, vol. 12, no. 1, pp. 121–5.

Mansbridge, J. 1997, 'Social and cultural causes of dissatisfaction with U.S. government', in J. Joseph, S. Nye, P.D. Zelikow & D.C. King (eds), *Why people don't trust government*, Harvard University Press, Cambridge, MA, pp. 133–53.

Middlemiss, L. 2010, 'Reframing individual responsibility for sustainable consumption: lessons from environmental justice and ecological citizenship', *Environmental Values*, vol. 19, no. 2, pp. 147–67.

Middlemiss, L. & Parrish, B.D. 2010, 'Building capacity for low-carbon communities: the role of grassroots initiatives', *Energy Policy*, vol. 38, no. 12, pp. 7559–66.

Moloney, S., Horne, R.E. & Fien, J. 2010, 'Transitioning to low carbon communities – from behaviour change to systemic change: lessons from Australia', *Energy Policy*, vol. 38, no. 12, pp. 7614–23.

Moser, S.C. 2009, 'Costly knowledge – unaffordable denial: the politics of public understanding and engagement on climate change', in M.T. Boykoff (ed.), *The politics of climate change: a survey*, Routledge, London, pp. 155–81.

Neilsen and Environmental Change Institute 2007, *Climate change and influential spokespeople: a global Nielsen online survey*, accessed 7 April 2011, www.eci.ox.ac.uk/publications/downloads/070709nielsen-celeb-report.pdf.

Norgaard, K.M. 2006, 'People want to protect themselves a little bit: Emotions, denial, and social movement nonparticipation', *Sociological Inquiry*, vol. 76, no. 3, pp. 372–96.

Norgaard, K.M. 2009, *Cognitive and behavioural challenges in responding to climate change: background paper to the 2010 World Development Report*, The World Bank, Policy Research Working Paper 4940, http://econ.worldbank.org.

Norgaard, K.M. 2011, *Living in denial: climate change, emotions, and everyday life*, The MIT Press, Cambridge, MA.

Nye, M., Whitmarsh, L. & Foxon, T. 2010, 'Sociopsychological perspectives on the active roles of domestic actors in transition to a lower carbon electricity economy', *Environment and Planning A*, vol. 42, pp. 697–714.

Oreskes, N. & Conway, E.M. 2010, *Merchants of doubt: how a handful of scientists obscured the truth on issues from tobacco smoke to global warming*, Bloomsbury Press, New York.

Parks, B.C. & Roberts, J.T. 2010, 'Climate change, social theory and justice', *Theory, Culture and Society*, vol. 27, no. 2–3, pp. 134–66.

Paterson, M. & Stripple, J. 2010, 'My Space: governing individuals' carbon emissions', *Environment and Planning D: Society and Space*, vol. 28, pp. 341–62.

Pearse, R., Goodman, J. & Rosewarne, S. 2010, 'Researching direct action against carbon emissions: a digital ethnography of climate agency', *Cosmopolitan Civil Societies Journal*, vol. 2, no. 3, pp. 76–103.

Räthzel, N. & Uzzell, D. 2009, 'Changing relations in global environmental change', *Global Environmental Change*, vol. 19, no. 3, pp. 326–35.

Reed, M.S., Evely, A.C., Cundill, G., Fazey, I., Glass, J., Laing, A., Newig, J., Parrish, B., Prell, C., Raymond, C. & Stringer, L.C. 2010, 'What is social learning?', *Ecology and Society*, vol. 15, no. 4.

Rosa, E.A. & Dietz, T. 1998, 'Climate change and society', *International Sociology*, vol. 13, no. 4, pp. 421–55.

Saward, M. 2008, 'Representation and democracy: revisions and possibilities', *Sociology Compass*, vol. 2, no. 3, pp. 1000–1013.

Schyns, P. & Koop, C. 2010, 'Political distrust and social capital in Europe and the USA', *Social Indicators Research*, vol. 96, no. 1, pp. 145–67.

Seyfang, G. & Haxeltine, A. 2012, 'Growing grassroots innovations: exploring the role of community-based initiatives in governing sustainable energy transitions', *Environment and Planning C: Government and Policy*, vol. 30, pp. 381–400.

Seyfang, G. & Smith, A. 2007, 'Grassroots innovations for sustainable development: towards a new research and policy agenda', *Environmental Politics*, vol. 16, pp. 584–603.

Shove, E. 2003, 'Converging conventions of comfort, cleanliness and convenience', *Journal of Consumer Policy*, vol. 26, no. 4, pp. 395–418.

Simon, B. & Klandermans, B. 2001, 'Politicized collective identity: a social psychological analysis', *American Psychologist*, vol. 56, no. 4, p. 319.

Singer, P. 2011, *The expanding circle: ethics, evolution and moral progress*, Princeton University Press, Princeton, NJ.

Spaargaren, G. & Mol, A.P.J. 2008, 'Greening global consumption: redefining politics and authority', *Global Environmental Change*, vol. 18, pp. 350–9.

Spratt, D. & Sutton, P. 2008, *Climate code red: the case for emergency action*, Scribe, Carlton North, Victoria, Australia.

The Climate Institute 2010, *Climate of the nation. Australians' attitudes towards climate change and its solutions*, The Climate Institute, Sydney, Australia.

Tranter, B. 2010, 'Environmental activists and non-active environmentalists in Australia', *Environmental Politics*, vol. 19, no. 3, pp. 413–29.

Tranter, B. 2011, 'Political divisions over climate change and environmental issues in Australia', *Environmental Politics*, vol. 20, no. 1, pp. 78–96.

Ungar, S. 1995, 'Social scares and global warming: beyond the Rio Convention', *Society and Natural Resources*, vol. 8, pp. 443–56.

6 Social transitions from the local to the global

Introduction

CAG members undertake voluntary activities on climate change both as individual and collective agents. They are both personally and collectively empowered, have overcome feelings of political distrust and have built trusting relationships with their CAG peers. They approach their climate action reflexively, reflecting on their individual and collective motivations and they position climate change within its broader social context. CAGs have legitimacy and they represent an alternative governance derived from the grassroots. In coming together in collectives in mutual learning and deliberation, they develop skills in democracy and they practise democracy. In Chapter 5, I laid out a model (Figure 5.5) that sets out the determinants for this process. The aim of this chapter is to discuss how CAGs realize their potential to influence public opinion and political action, both within and beyond their local community context in order to infiltrate wider society. In particular I address the following questions: can CAGs be considered niches? And, if so, do CAGs represent a niche that could affect the regime?

These questions are considered from the perspective of the recent but growing scholarship that seeks to understand the role of grassroots community-based action on climate change and sustainability, supported by a burgeoning of local and community-based sustainability initiatives (Feola & Nunes 2014; Seyfang & Smith 2007). For the most part this scholarship seeks to extend STT from its historic interest in demand-side socio-technical innovations into areas of civil society concern (Geels 2011; Grin *et al.* 2010; Hielscher *et al.* 2011), such as citizen engagement and participation in sustainability initiatives, social learning, governance and community collectives' contributions to social capital (Hoffman & High-Pippert 2010; Rauschmayer *et al.* 2015). Furthermore, the multiplicity of sustainability initiatives that are central to these grassroots movements is occurring counter intuitively, according to Middlemiss and Parrish (2010, p. 7559). Grassroots initiatives are supported by volunteers with little power or influence, and few resources for creating change. The concept of change arising from the 'bottom up' is not universally supported and in many cases, particularly when considering hegemonic power interests, is treated with hostility

(p. 7560). This chapter in particular addresses the emergence of community-based groups from the grassroots seeking to entrench low carbon pathways and to establish alternative energy systems and practices counter to the structural power of extant regimes.

Can CAGs be considered niches?

First, I take up the question of whether community-based grassroots collectives can contribute to broader scale social change and if so, how. I am interested here in how transitions frameworks are being applied in order to understand pathways for social change that emerge from the grassroots, and how groups such as CAGs operate as niches, that is, pockets of radical social innovation with regime change potential.

The role of collective agency within groups such as CAGs and the nature of collectives in terms of their member characteristics, individual and group agency, and social change potential remain largely under researched. However, there has been a more recent turn in the sustainability transitions literature to consider the role of community-based collectives in social innovation and change. As Shove (2010, p. 278) observes, this literature creates and exploits the 'intellectual space' in order to: 'think . . . seriously and systemically about how environmentally problematic ways of life are reproduced and how they change.'

In particular, the notion of 'grassroots innovations' (Seyfang & Smith 2007) has been instrumental in expanding ideas around how radical changes at the grassroots may translate into regime spaces. This notion has been taken up more recently by researchers in their theoretical and empirical work (Feola & Nunes 2014; Howaldt *et al.* 2010; Kirwan *et al.* 2013; Ornetzeder & Rohracher 2013; Reeves, Lemon & Cook 2014) and applied to collectives active on climate change and low carbon transitions.

In Chapter 4, I set out one of the leading principles of STT, the MLP (Geels 2005), which has been influential in characterizing grassroots innovations. According to Geels, regimes support incremental change, possess stabilizing patterns and are path dependent. Niches, in contrast, sit outside of the regime, often as 'protected spaces' (Geels 2011, p. 27), which 'work on radical innovations that deviate from the existing regime' (Geels 2011, p. 27). Just like research and development laboratories (Geels uses these as an example), CAGs consist of particular social 'elites' or 'enclaves' (Dryzek 2009) ripe with the potential to explore new forms of action within their local communities in order to influence both public opinion and political actors. As CAGs sit outside of the state, often distinct from more mainstream ENGOs active on climate change campaigning and advocacy, they are not beholden to mainstream practice. They have the capability of working outside the hegemony. Or perhaps, as others suggest (Feola & Nunes 2014; Middlemiss & Parrish 2010), grassroots initiatives may simply go unnoticed, given that they generally consist of small groups of volunteers active within their local communities.

Geels (2011) makes another important observation on the application of the MLP to sustainability transitions in acknowledging that the MLP itself is useful as a 'heuristic device' that assists in guiding researchers through questions and problems (p. 34) rather than a distinct object of truth. As Geels (2011, p. 29) states:

> An important implication is that the MLP does away with simple causality in transitions. There is no single 'cause' or driver. Instead, there are processes in multiple dimensions and at different levels which link up with, and reinforce, each other ('circular causality').

In other words, the MLP assists in conceptualizing messy change progressions (Ostrom 2009).

Structuration and niches

To further explore whether CAGs are grassroots niches it is important to draw on the critical role that structuration theory plays in the transitions literature. Geels illuminates this by exposing a more nuanced explication of the relationship between the different levels of niche, regime and landscape. A noted criticism of the MLP has been the perception that these three levels operate as a nested hierarchy (Geels 2011). Geels clarifies that, instead, they are differentiated by their different degrees of *structuration*. At the niche level there is least structuration, or 'stickiness', of actors to the prevailing structural conditions which explains why grassroots sustainability initiatives have proliferated across local communities. Or as Lash and Wynne put it: 'In effect structural change forces social actors to become progressively more free from structure. And for modernization successfully to advance, these agents must release themselves from structural constraint and actively shape the modernization process' (in Beck 1992, p. 2).

If the vision here of social change premised on *individualization* is to be realized, then the question of if and how actors are freed from structural constraints becomes the chief consideration. So in what ways are CAG members freed from structural constraints? In the previous chapter I argued that CAGs are enabled through overcoming the constraints of disempowerment, distrust and lack of reflexivity. Accordingly, as agents are most free from structure in niches and as niches are the least structured elements in the MLP, new ways of local-level community-based practice (actions/behaviours), governance (political processes) and deliberation (democratic processes) can be developed and trialled. CAG members, as I have shown in Chapter 5, adopt social practices that go against accepted social norms to directly address unsustainable behaviours. They actively engage in political processes even though they take a non-partisan approach to their climate action and may not be schooled in politics. Through their conversations and group deliberations they develop their skills in localized democracy and make localized democracy a reality. CAG niches act as the loci of social learning and experimentation, which can be replicated across other communities with the potential to translate into wider scale regime change. This positions grassroots social innovations, such as CAGs, central to community-based social change on climate change.

Niche formation

As discussed earlier, Al Gore's film, *An Inconvenient Truth*, was a significant marker for CAG formation (five of the eight groups specifically referenced their formation around the time of the film's release) and indeed that time represents the pinnacle for grassroots climate group formation in other Western liberal democracies. The film was released in Australia on 14 September 2006 to coincide with a visit from Al Gore and corresponded with high levels of public concern about climate change. All except two of the groups formed around this time (late 2006 to early 2007) with one group forming later in 2007 and another re-formed in 2009. '*We asked for people who were concerned about climate change and that was just ... when Al Gore's film was coming out and we had 50 or 60 people come along*' (Walter, 40+[1], NSW3).

> *I think I must have seen Al Gore's film, called ... An Inconvenient Truth, yes that's what first drew my attention to climate change so when I saw the advert about this group I went along 'cause I realize this is a very new but important topic.*
>
> (Daphne, 65, VIC3)

While a town or community meeting or other gathering (such as Walk against Warming) precipitated CAG formation for some groups, preceding this was often a more informal series of conversations or discussions held in someone's home or the local pub where people could exchange their views and ideas around the issue:

> *When J[acob] and I were talking about climate change and we thought that the conversation was really, kind of an important aspect of social change, we felt, OK, part of what we'll do is, we'll just set up a regular conversation with some other people we knew well ... and we just met once a month or so and it was the discussing of things you sorted out a bit of knowledge ... The natural progression was then to take action on that knowledge and ... that's how [CAG] was begun.*
>
> (Walter, 40+, NSW3)

These conversations contributed to a shared understanding of group members' beliefs, values, concerns and motivations around climate change.

What prefigures a niche, and is this important to consider when differentiating community climate action? I have argued that CAG formation is precipitated by a 'moral shock' or 'social scare'. Part of my reasoning relates to the surge of CAG formation following the Australian release of Al Gore's film, *An Inconvenient Truth*. According to Neilsen and the Environmental Change Institute (2007), the international impact of the film coincided with the period of greatest concern regarding the threat of dangerous climate change. Does this equate with a niche creation 'moment'? A poll of 32 community groups active on climate change in the UK undertaken by the Grassroots Innovations[2] project showed a wave of group formation between 2005 and 2010, which peaked in 2007, and has since waned. Middlemiss and Parrish (2010) note that one of their two study groups, the Bollington Carbon Revolution, commenced in September 2006. The Transition Towns movement also began in September 2006 (Scott-Cato & Hillier 2010). The first Camp for Climate Action occurred in the UK in 2006 and it was at this time that CRAGs commenced (Hielscher 2013). These examples exhibit strong parallels with the formation of Australian CAGs, which occurred during a period of high public concern and political attention, and it appears to be no coincidence that grassroots niches active on climate change formed around this time, coalescing around the concurrent landscape-level trends.

Since their peak time of formation in late 2006, there has been a decline in the numbers of CAGs commencing and this is matched with the Grassroots Innovations project findings, associated with a steady reduction in mainstream community concern on climate change (Hanson 2011). The multi-phase perspective describes different phases of socio-technical transition: emergence, take-off, acceleration and stabilization (Geels 2011; Grin *et al.* 2010) (see Figure 4.1). This idea is useful when considering the role of niches in transitions as not all innovations will succeed and result in new forms of stable regimes. Rather, as Geels (2011) explains, a process of change can be conceptualized whereby:

> (a) niche-innovations build up internal momentum, (b) changes at the landscape level create pressure on the regime, and (c) destabilisation of the regime creates windows of opportunity for niche-innovations. These can be related to the multi-phases: emergence, take-off, acceleration and stabilization (Rotmans *et al.* 2001).
>
> (Geels 2011, p. 29)

While niche success can lead to stabilization in new regime conditions, in Chapter 4, I noted the alternative pathways to stabilization laid out by Grin *et al.* (2010) (illustrated in Figure 4.2). Extant regime situations can lead to system lock-in, which makes them resistant to the forces of change, to backlash where the forces resisting change are reinforced or otherwise to system breakdown. This brings me to consider whether new waves of grassroots action around climate change are evident that can contribute to the building of civil society action and regime destabilization or, otherwise, potentially lead to stagnation.

A current example is the significant grassroots action that is coalescing around the issue of coal seam gas (CSG) development. This is an issue that extends beyond Australia with an aggressive industry push evident in the UK, the USA, South Africa and Europe to rapidly develop and exploit accessible gas resources with the justification that they replace coal, which has higher GHG emissions.[3] Groups such as the Lock the Gate Alliance[4] have established and multiplied rapidly in recent times in response to the socio-technical advance of the CSG threat, which is quickly taking advantage of a short-term market demand for gas. The collectives forming around the CSG issue in Australia are responding to different landscape conditions than those that precipitated the development of CAGs. For a start, this issue has more recently attracted attention but is gaining rapid momentum. Rather than a *moral shock* or *social scare* of a global nature, group formations are motivated around more localized threats, for example, to agricultural land and the pollution of local water sources. I suggest that these grassroots collectives arising around CSG are therefore forming under different conditions than those that were relevant and activating for CAGs. In particular, the discourses of concern in the CSG debate relate more to locally relevant conditions such as farm heritage and local water resources than the 'climate change-as-catastrophe' discourse common in my CAG group discussions. There is a considerable display of self-interest here too. CSG is a distinctly local issue with the Lock the Gate campaign successfully exploiting the ability for farm owners to close their gates to gas company exploration on their land.

There are similarities between the CSG and community climate change action campaigns and the issues are being linked to strengthen the movement generally; however, differing motivations are evident in the more 'cosmopolitan' (Hulme 2010) concerns of CAGs. This opens another area for future fruitful investigation, that is: what are the differing routes of niche formation? How are different niche actors characterized? What motivates their collective action within their local communities?

To this point I have considered CAGs as niches with sustainability transition potential. I have discussed their formation in relation to a particular historical and political 'moment'. The concatenation of decades of scientific evidence (for example, through the IPCC) and numerous serious events and natural catastrophes focused climate change as the 'celebrity' issue of the time (Ungar 1995). I have also raised questions regarding what might precede the formation of a niche, whether the formation of niches relies on certain actors and whether niche formation is dependent on local community conditions and contexts. In the next section I consider the latter question.

Community capacity and niche formation

Earlier I made the statement that CAGs are as diverse as the communities that they emerge from. Indeed CAGs can be found in communities across Australia and through my research I sought to draw from CAGs in different geographic locations and community settings. My purpose was to develop a more generalizable sample. However, recent scholarship raises the question of whether the formation of CAG niches is dependent on their local community contexts.

Middlemiss and Parrish (2010) make an important distinction regarding the characteristics of the communities that grassroots innovations emerge from. They use community capacity as a descriptor, arguing that communities require both social capital and resources in order to effectively host 'low carbon' niches. Incorporated within their notion of successful community capacity building are the requirements of increased social capital, resource availability, which they note is 'lower in places experiencing poverty and [social] exclusion' (p. 7560), and democratic decision-making or deliberative capacity: 'As such taking responsibility for one's ecological impact means agents acting according to the capacity that is afforded to them by their contexts' (Middlemiss & Parrish 2010, p. 7561).

It is possible that only certain types of communities possess the conditions which support the development of grassroots innovations. This needs to be acknowledged in a similar way to the 'elite' status of CAG members, when considering the potential for niche formation and transition into regimes spaces. Earlier I alluded to the benefits that collectives provide to their members, and it may be expected that some of these are likely to penetrate CAGs' local communities, thereby 'changing the capacity of the communities in which they are active' (Middlemiss & Parrish 2010, p. 7561).

CAGs adopt social practices that counter unsustainable behaviour, involve social learning in developing the skills to affect their campaign objectives and enact democracy through their group deliberations. I therefore consider CAGs as grassroots innovations; that is, they are sites of radical social innovation involved in collective political action on climate change that emerge spontaneously from the 'bottom up'. However CAGs, in a similar way to other 'grassroots innovations', have failed to replicate and grow further in recent years. Rather, their influence has spread through linking with other grassroots networks. In the following section I expand upon some recent scholarship that contributes to an understanding of CAGs as niches with regime change potential.

CAGs as niche projects

One of the more salient features of CAGs is that their membership consists of a particular group of people, largely middle class, highly educated and comfortable financially, who possess post-materialist values (Tranter 2010,

2011). I use the term *people like me* to describe this group. While collectively CAGs across Australia have been acknowledged to possess diverse characteristics, the question arises whether a larger climate action movement could grow from groups that individually represent a select few within their local communities. CAG members were also cognisant of this, commenting on the difficulty they had in attracting new members to expand their groups. They also believed much more extensive engagement with climate change throughout the broader community would be required in order to achieve the level of change necessary to mitigate against dangerous climate change, especially within the timeframe required:

> *But how do we increase the people who are receptive to this? We are always banging on to those people who are converted, converting the converts. Can we bring more people into the fold?*
>
> (Alfred, 65, VIC2)

> *it's got to be a pretty amazing grassroots action that can do that but if it happens it's gonna be along the scale of the Vietnam Moratorium ... before it is succeeding.*
>
> (Solomon, 52, NSW3)

> *I think influencing individuals within the ... local community, like getting the community galvanized around the issue so it's not just a few individuals scattered around.*
>
> (Marcia, 36, NSW4)

CAG members are reflecting here on the difficulties involved in expanding their group membership and diversity, which they recognize is essential for successfully translating climate change concern into the public and political arenas. I described the three mechanisms of niche diffusion set out by Seyfang and Smith. To recap briefly here, these are: replication, for example by CAGs forming in more communities; growth, for example by individual groups attracting more members; and translating CAG influence into the mainstream. As illustrated above, CAGs are experiencing difficulty in diffusing from their grassroots niche into the regime in order to effect broader social change. CAGs are failing to grow the scale and influence of their grassroots niche by attracting more participants and effectively broadening their appeal through engaging with mainstream audiences.

Based on this evidence, I came to wonder whether CAGs were capable of, or indeed required to, expanding beyond their membership in order to effect change. Was there some other means whereby niches could grow and translate in order to bring about change? For example, are there similar groupings of 'like-minded people' involved in other issues rather than specifically engaged in political action on climate change? People involved, for example, in the development of eco-villages and co-housing or community gardens and community-supported agriculture, Transition Towns and community renewable energy developments (Dryzek *et al.* 2013; Gross & Mautz 2015; Scoones *et al.* 2015). Arguably these different grassroots groups consist of 'like-minded people' that coalesce around post-materialist values that are similar to those of my CAG research cohort. Recent scholarship has come to light that supports this contention.

Raven *et al.* (2010) develop the idea that niches consist of a number of *local projects* (p. 65), where each project represents a particular type of radical innovation or sustainability experiment. They describe these projects as occurring simultaneously and developing 'through a social learning process', which builds a 'new trajectory':

> Transition experiments, carried by local networks, provide space for local activities. The outcomes give rise to learning processes that may be aggregated into generic lessons and rules. Outcomes are also used to adjust previous expectations and enroll more actors to expand the social network.
>
> (Raven *et al.* 2010, p. 65)

Further to the notion of Raven *et al.* concerning sustainability niches as multiple and varied local projects, Hielscher *et al.* suggest that this extension to niche theory captures a local-to-global mechanism:

> niches from individual projects and initiatives which are seen as 'carried by local networks and characterised by local variety' towards the 'global level'. . . . Instead of regarding individual community initiatives as numerous niches, it is a number of them or even the totality of groups that create the 'global level' niche.
>
> (Hielscher *et al.* 2011, p. 12)

Utilizing this theoretical frame, CAGs can be conceived, then, as a local *niche project* or subset of a much broader sustainability niche. This foregrounds the potential for CAGs to aggregate with other groups of like-minded people, thereby developing broader networks and expanding into much wider social coalitions. Among CAGs nationally such 'aggregation activities' have certainly occurred through the development of state and national organizing bodies and a national summit held since 2009. Expanded social networks can also be seen with the more recent incorporation of issues related to health and climate change and the interest of some trade unions. As noted earlier in Chapter 4, CAGs have also become more active in national campaigns and advocacy work through membership in CANA, joining the Solar Citizens campaign,[5] and the Lock the Gate Alliance, thus providing evidence for these aggregating tendencies.

So it can be seen how this newer theoretical perspective on niche projects can be related to 'community innovations' emerging from civil society. Specifically Hielscher *et al.* explore the concept of niche projects through community-led sustainability energy projects in the UK. They note that

> groups aim to develop holistic approaches to climate change that could potentially drive a more systemic change. It might therefore make more sense to conceive of all the diverse community-led energy initiatives together as one niche, as they share a common focus on 'sustainable energy'.
>
> (Hielscher *et al.* 2011, p. 13)

These recent evolutionary perspectives on niche formation, niche projects and sustainability transitions are reminiscent of Torgerson's notion of the green public sphere (Chapter 4). Local grassroots niche projects develop and expand as 'issue-linkages' (Pattberg & Stripple 2008) are recognized and adopted. For example, at the Climate Camps I attended in 2009 and 2010, issue-linkages were evident that sought to expand climate change action beyond a narrow band of grassroots interests. Grassroots organizations concerned with forest issues Australia-wide were well represented at the 2010 Climate Camp (which was situated close to the Bayswater B power station in the Hunter Valley, NSW), and so was the nascent national Lock the Gate Alliance campaigning against the development of CSG. It should be noted the Lock the Gate Alliance could be considered as a niche project on CSG, which has more recently coalesced into a niche, as in response to the rapid escalation of the issue the alliance now consists of 252 groups[6] across Australia including many grassroots organizations, such as CAGs. The green public sphere is captured in another recent example, the People's Climate March held in New York City in September 2014. The march involved over 1,500 groups that came together under a common platform calling for strong international action on climate change. In looking over the participating groups, rather than a unified movement, the march consisted of a coalition of diverse groups with representation from environmental, faith, gender rights, union and social justice organizations and interests, many of them drawn from the grassroots of their local communities.[7] As Foderaro (2014) observed:

> The diversity of the demonstrators made for some odd juxtapositions. On West 58th Street, the minaret of an inflatable mosque bobbed next to a wooden replica of Noah's Ark the size of a school bus. Nearby Capuchin Franciscan monks in flowing brown robes, who were in town from Rome for the march, mingled with nuns, while a group flying a pagan flag beat a drum.

These types of coalitions are consistent with the 'aggregation activities' described by Raven *et al.* (2010) and incorporate a diversity of grassroots initiatives engaged in discursive deliberation and collective action. These aggregations and social learning activities are also described by Seyfang and Smith (2007) as essential processes for translating niche issues into the mainstream regime. The conceptualization of multiple and aggregated niche projects formulating into a 'global' niche thereby extends the normative power of STT in ascribing local grassroots collectives (such as CAGs) with regime change potential. In the same way I propose that given the nature of climate change as representative of 'everything that's wrong with society coming to a head' (Michelle, 28, NSW2) and the nature of CAGs as representative of community members with strong moral and political concerns, these types of common political 'projects' can be harnessed from the grassroots in order to develop a 'global' sustainability niche.

However, Hielscher *et al.* (2011) suggest that the concept of niche projects still fails to account for notions of politics and power, a specific critique of STT (Geels 2014; Grin *et al.* 2011; Meadowcroft 2011). Hielscher *et al.* (2011, pp. 16–17) suggest that social movement theory may fill this gap by 'inform[ing] transitions theory and reveal[ing] the political roles niches must adopt in sustainability transitions'. They go on to ask: 'How do community energy niches develop collective *identities* and *interests*; what repertoires of activism press for reforms?' Their questions raise several issues and points of departure from my proposition, which I consider below.

First, it appears that the political roles of community innovations may be played down in the account of Hielscher *et al.* or that Hielscher *et al.*, similar to their critique of Transition Towns, believe these community energy niches possess a certain political naivety or a lack of interest in politics (Scott-Cato & Hillier 2010; Seyfang *et al.* 2010). This contrasts to my research findings on CAGs as in almost all cases there was an acknowledgement by participants of their roles as political agents in grassroots climate change action. As I've argued in Chapter 5, CAG members are further enabled and empowered through their individual, collective and political engagement, creating a virtuous circle of increasing capabilities. To the extent that CAG members are empowered and claim legitimacy in political engagement, I consider CAGs do fill a political role in reform of climate change policy within Australia.

Second, while I don't discount the importance of including social movement theory in the notional understandings of grassroots climate action, I have suggested that the development of 'collective identities and interests' may be counterproductive to the creation of an alternative governance built on grassroots innovations. I have drawn on the scholarship of Dryzek, Torgerson and Ostrom to argue for a more open and diffuse notion of grassroots-initiated social change based on a diversity of discourses, on widespread discussion and debate, and on positions of group trust and cooperation.

Third, regarding the fundamental question Hielscher *et al.* (2011) expressed above regarding how reform succeeds from the grassroots: I have no argument with it – this remains an essential question for investigation that I take up below.

Developments in the sustainability transitions literature have recently addressed questions regarding how a 'political orientation' (Meadowcroft 2011, p. 70) can be applied to sustainability transitions and the role of power in this process (Avelino 2009; Geels 2014; Grin *et al.* 2010; Grin *et al.* 2011). Meadowcroft (2011) asserts that politics is manifest on each level of the MLP. At the niche level he identifies the role of governments in either protecting or exposing niches. In doing so, governments encourage or discourage innovation (p. 71). (Notably, this bears some similarity to the processes of state inclusion and exclusion proposed by Dryzek *et al.* (2003).) I take this to be a rather narrow view of the political potential of sustainability niches as it assumes that the state will be the primary if not the sole arbiter of grassroots innovation and does not consider the role of sustainability niches outside of the state, where in fact they may have greater political change potential (Dryzek *et al.* 2003). Meadowcroft in fact concludes with a similar tranche of questions to Hielscher *et al.*, but focuses on 'institutional reform' rather than 'repertoires for activism' (Hielscher *et al.* 2011, p. 17) asking

> what institutional contexts are favourable to orienting and accelerating sustainability transitions; which reforms to democratic institutions can improve their capacity to negotiate sustainability transitions; and what sorts of institutional innovations focused on the environment and sustainability can make a difference.
>
> (Meadowcroft 2011, p. 73)

Again a distinct tension is revealed here between the role of the state and the grassroots in regime change. To what extent does the state play a mediating role in regime change and how does it reinforce structural constraints to change? Can grassroots niches only encourage regime change by putting pressure on the state through, for example, galvanizing favourable public opinion? Or is there a role for grassroots niches outside the state that complements the role of other actors that work within the state? Grin *et al.* in addressing some of these thorny questions concerning state power and grassroots collective agency state:

> At the basis of the understanding of the politics involved in strategic agency is the realisation that the regime embodies power: the rules, resources and actor configurations which are part of the regime will privilege practices over others. . . . Similarly, the dominant discourses that are part of the regime have significant structuring effects on struggles for legitimacy. Thus, transitions both presuppose and bring about a shift in standards of legitimacy. Seen this way, the challenge for strategic agents thus becomes to make transition dynamics and the

political dynamics associated with it reinforce each other sufficiently so as to gradually tilt the balance of power and legitimacy between incumbent and sustainability practices. This is essentially a diffuse, distributed process that may lead to convergence through common visions or through the graduate, self-reinforcing structuring of practices.

(Grin *et al.* 2011, p. 80)

In effect what Grin *et al.* describe illustrates a type of minimal or inconsequential regime shift (Smith 2007) to achieve niche success, where niches are required to compromise on their original visions and consequently there is a 'wider diffusion of a more shallow sustainability' (Smith 2007, p. 446). This is unlikely to provide the conditions for rapid, wide-scale change in energy and societal transition required to prevent catastrophic climate change. This is a point that Geels (2014) takes up in proposing that too much focus has been applied to the potential of transition from niches, when the 'destruction' of the embedded fossil fuel regime would be a more worthy focus.

The notion of niche projects therefore nuances understanding of CAGs as niches with regime change potential. CAGs represent a particular type of grassroots political collective taking action on climate change. They possess similarities with other types of community-based collectives active around issues pertaining to sustainability. The linkages that CAGs create contribute to the development of a sustainability niche. Here the potential of Torgerson's green public sphere may be realized as coalitions develop between diverse groups of actors emerging from the grassroots. However, questions remain in relation to how niches gain and assert power. I take this up below in discussing how CAGs seek to influence political actors in order to achieve their sustainability aims and their perceptions on how change occurs.

CAGs as niche grassroots innovations that influence the regime

If CAGs are to successfully negotiate beyond their innovative social niche to influence other state and non-state actors and disrupt (or indeed, 'destroy') the dominant market-driven economic rationalism of contemporary politics, their influence and power will need to grow. Previously I discussed the key change processes for successful niche growth and regime influence proposed by Seyfang and Smith (2007) and taken up more recently in the sustainability transition scholarship interested in local community-based grassroots innovations. The success factors for niche growth and translation are noted below.

Niches are 'cosmopolitan spaces' which can influence regimes through:

- Replication – that is, niche 'cells' can develop in different locations and aggregate to create change (Seyfang & Haxeltine 2012).

- Grow in scale – that is, niches can increase their influence by networking beyond their niche to attract a greater range and diversity of actors (Seyfang & Haxeltine 2012).
- Ideas and practices can be translated into mainstream settings (Seyfang *et al.* 2010; Smith 2007).

Successful niche emergence and growth require the following three key processes:

- Grassroots niches need to have widely shared, specific, realistic and achievable goals. In other words, niches need to live up to their promises on performance and effectiveness (Seyfang & Haxeltine 2012).
- Niches network with many different stakeholders who can support niche emergence.
- Learning processes go beyond 'everyday knowledge' to 'second-order learning' (or reflexive learning) wherein 'people question the assumptions and constraints of mainstream systems altogether' (Seyfang & Haxeltine 2012).

I've found this a very useful reflective tool for engaging in thinking around my CAG case study and have applied five elements of this framework to my analysis in order to define their emergence and growth within the wider climate action movement within Australia and their regime change potential. The five elements are: replication, networks, growth, translation, and social/reflexive learning.[8] The elements are discussed below.

Replication through fragmentation

CAGs emerged and replicated rapidly following the surge of public concern around climate change promulgated by Al Gore's film, *An Inconvenient Truth* and within the context of national political inaction. Unlike Transition Towns, CAGs are not based on a particular centralized and standardized model of development (Bailey *et al.* 2010), and their potential for wider adoption and spread may be limited by this fact (Hielscher 2013). There appears to be a hiatus in the growth of CAGs. Seeding groups in new areas has proven difficult and some have suffered decreased membership or have disbanded. Unless more widespread replication of CAGs can be stimulated across and within communities, their potential to influence political actors at the local, state and national levels will be limited.

As CAGs arise from within their own communities, subject to their particular identities, values, contexts and capacities this could lead to more widespread replication of evolving grassroots collectives. The Lock the Gate Alliance provides a relevant example here. Coal seam gas development is focused around particular, mostly rural, communities and has generated significant community concern resulting in the rapid development of grassroots groups. Although there are coalitions with CAGs based on issue-linkages, Lock the Gate members were initially drawn from their distinct communities facing threats to their property through the expansion of CSG exploitation. The emergence of different grassroots groups forming around newer and more immediate threats, such as CSG extraction, creates the potential for diversity and fragmentation at the grassroots (Ostrom 2010), thus revealing the potential for the incorporation of other climate discourses that can create more widespread political action and influence on climate change-related issues. The fragmentation, replication and issue linkage of differing climate change-related issues offer greater prospects for shifting the established regime towards a lower carbon emission trajectory.

Scale of influence and how change occurs

For the most part, it is engaging with their local community in order to build support for political action that is most important to CAGs. However, groups varied to the extent to which their sphere of action extended from the local community level. For some groups, action has come to focus more on national politics as they argue that it is at this level that major legislative and economic reform must be created. For others, the focus is on winning over more members from their local community to the climate change 'cause':

> *I'm trying to influence the political masters by showing that there is a consensus for action and they needn't be scared. They'd be voted in if they act on the environment and they'd be voted out if they don't. So it's a whole chain of people, you've got to influence the local community but the end goal is to get serious commitment, political action which means building big infrastructure and changing laws and regulations and transport systems and everything else to make sustainability possible.*
>
> (Wayne, 68, NSW4)

CAGs that are more established and that undertake strategic planning[9] appeared to have a clearer notion of their targets for action, membership and advocacy. Groups without such plans may be tempted to try to achieve too much with their limited resources and often this became a point of frustration:

> *I feel that we have a very amateurish approach. We spend enormous amounts of energy, say leafleting a neighbourhood, putting out hundreds of leaflets and getting two or three people to come. That is a huge waste of our energy.*
>
> (Jeffrey, 64, VIC3)

Trying to influence sceptics or people not attracted to the issue was perceived to be unlikely to succeed and as Daphne (65, VIC3) points out, bringing about social change by influencing public opinion is necessarily a long-term endeavour:

> *about the public education and changing public opinion, I think that takes a long time. I've been a community activist in various areas for a number of years and I know that it takes at least ten years to turn public . . . opinion around*

For Louis (2009) collective action needs to influence the general public in order to influence public policy and create broader scale social change. CAGs may need to devise their strategies more in line with this view, that is, they may need to seek to develop a community consensus to drive political action on climate change as a precursor to their other political aims.

A few groups expressed ambitions to influence climate change at a global level but this was a minority view. The forms of influence stated included participating in international days of action (such as those organized by 350.org or Earth Hour):

> *I think one of the things that we also hope is that we have a world presence 'cause we did things like the 350 day of action which we did with millions of people, the largest concerted action in the world ever and we were part of that. I think we were acting on the world stage, I thought I was . . .*
>
> (Jacob, 53, NSW3)

However, as these are largely symbolic gestures, the effectiveness of CAG participation in achieving broader scale influence is likely to be minimal. As previously discussed, organizing on a national level has now become more established among CAGs. National annual summits and other organizing and skills building opportunities have contributed to a higher degree of national information-sharing and strategizing. The development of the Solar Citizens campaign is one example of community organizing with a national emphasis that has arisen from the grassroots with the potential to generate national political outcomes. However, global networking and the connection of issues around climate change between grassroots organizations transnationally were not significantly evident.

Grow outside their 'elite'

Grassroots innovations can influence the dominant regime by growing the spread and influence of their networks and increasing the diversity of actors involved (Seyfang & Haxeltine 2012). In all cases the CAGs demonstrated an involvement with a broader range of local community actors. Some CAGs with memberships bedded deeply within their local community institutions (government, business and third sector organizations) spoke of strong ties with local councils, churches, educational institutions, other non-government community sector organizations and local businesses. This enabled the spread of ideas and collaboration on projects of mutual interest and benefit. In this sense, reformist rather than radical approaches might work better to influence regimes. However, the lack of diversity of participants within and across groups was a compelling characteristic of the CAGs. Active and engaged members of CAGs represent a particular subset or 'elite' dominated as they are by middle class, well educated and financially secure citizens who hold post-materialist values. This limits the reach and penetration of CAG influence within their own communities and also raises the broader question of whether other communities (based on locality, interest and capacity) will seek to actively engage with climate change as an issue.

I sense this could be highly problematic for generating the broad scale community involvement required to address an issue such as climate change whose causes are ingrained in current systems that support unsustainability. I believe there is a role here for extending the notion of niche projects (described above) that harbours the potential for the development of 'global' niches. Aggregation of diverse groups (acting as niche projects) into networks that support a pluralism of actors and opinions (reminiscent of Torgerson's green public sphere) may break down or otherwise dilute the elite nature of current grassroots collectives active on climate change such as CAGs.

Translate their ideas into mainstream settings

The development of a national network of groups and annual summits since 2009 is an important development within the grassroots climate action movement for organizing, strategizing and mobilizing among CAG members. However, CAGs face significant challenges in penetrating the extant politico-economic regime. Recent debates over the introduction of a carbon tax in Australia demonstrate the polarization of community views around climate change both in the climate action movement and in the wider Australian society (Tranter 2011; Jones 2010). Given the power of entrenched 'business-as-usual' positions and organized scepticism (Geels 2014; Klein 2014), this currently presents as a difficult obstacle to surmount.

However, CAGs have proven to be flexible in taking up new national initiatives, especially those which portray a positive community vision and have political traction (such as the Solar Citizens Campaign). As community organizing and outreach skills develop within the climate action network there is greater potential for the grassroots climate action movement to broaden and diversify its membership and support base in order to shift public opinion and create more mainstream buy-in.[10]

Social learning

One further element, social learning, determines the successful niche growth and emergence from the grassroots. Social learning refers here not to the acquisition of knowledge and skills but to the deeper, transformative and reflexive learning whereby people challenge the values and norms of present business-as-usual trajectories. Empirical evidence shows that CAGs enhance social learning (Moloney *et al.* 2010). CAGs support members' abilities to learn about climate change within its collective (local and community) and social (national and international) contexts. CAG members also develop and extend their skills in a number of important arenas: for some groups the emphasis may be to understand how innovative technology can be effectively applied to their local community setting; for others, skills relate to community organizing, awareness raising, networking, promotion and communication; others still are engaged in developing the confidence and skills of activism and coordination of high impact non-violent acts of civil disobedience that directly challenge state hegemony. CAG members displayed their reflexive learning ability tangibly within the research focus groups, demonstrating their capacity to evaluate the effectiveness of their voluntary acts and commitment to climate change actions both strategically and affectively.

Conclusion

> *So we've got to get some runs on the board and to get runs on the board we've gotta do it as a community, it's gotta ... have an impact across the community and you want to say you don't have to wait for government to work out what the hell they're doing ... for nations to work out between them what's happening. You do it at a local level and it's easy to actually just encourage other[s] through the network of councils or whoever, and I think that's empowering because the people at a grassroots level can say yep, we can do something.*
>
> (Marcia, 36, NSW4)

CAGs act as grassroots innovators for regime transition; that is, they are locations of radical social innovation and alternative practices that emerge from civil society at the grassroots (local/community scale). CAGs consist of a particular elite and their potential to disseminate wider into the mainstream of their local communities may be limited by this fact. They come together under specific formative conditions and, therefore, only certain communities will have the capacity to support CAG creation. Their impact and longevity follow a phased development pattern stimulated at a particular historic/social 'moment' into action. It may be that CAGs in their current form are short-lived. However, this does not mean that their influence in creating regime change is negligible or insignificant.

When CAGs are conceptualized as niche projects, within a broader-scoped sustainability/energy transition niche, the potential for regime change may be realized. Five possible means by which CAGs can influence the extant regime were discussed. First, through replication, niches can bring about aggregate changes. Second, through growth in scale and influence niches can attract more participants. Third, diffusion occurs through translation of niche ideas to broader mainstream audiences. Fourth, niches (as aggregates of niche projects) can build networks of wider support throughout their local communities and facilitate broader stakeholder engagement. And finally, through the processes of social learning knowledge is built and shared, and deliberative skills and practices are nurtured in groups. This accelerates both individual and collective political agency on climate action and creates the conditions for these niche practices to translate into regime change.

CAGs are currently failing to grow and spawn new groups, and the number of members within existing groups is not increasing. Nor are they replicating by emerging from different communities, though there has been an expansion of other types of grassroots innovations in response to more immediate threats to local communities, such as Lock the Gate. CAGs are characteristic of niche projects in this regard; they are one type of grassroots innovation within a broader sustainability niche. Should another significant 'moment' arise (as it did in 2006) to generate a social scare and/or moral shock around climate change, there is no doubt potential for future CAG growth and replication.

CAGs are developing linkages with other groups and organizations, extending their influence beyond their local communities. The Solar Citizens campaign is one example where CAGs are now working together across Australia with an ambitious policy agenda and influencing national political outcomes. The Lock the Gate Alliance provides another example, demonstrating the aggregation of niche projects. The Alliance has grown rapidly through the involvement of CAGs that see the links between their climate change campaign objectives and the rapid development of CSG within Australia. This evident coalition of interests between groups has also enhanced opportunities for social learning so that deliberation, campaigning and advocacy skills are being developed and shared.

Notes

1 This participant did not provide his actual age.
2 http://grassrootsinnovations.org/2012/04/13/gi-briefing-7-seeing-community-climate-action-through-the-eyes-of-mainstream-actors/, accessed 8 June 2015.
3 www.campaigncc.org/node/1185#global, accessed 8 June 2015.
4 http://lockthegate.org.au/, accessed 8 June 2015.
5 www.solarcitizens.org.au/, accessed 8 June 2015.
6 http://lockthegate.org.au/groups/, accessed 8 June 2015.
7 http://peoplesclimate.org/lineup/, accessed 1 June 2015.

8　I have excluded niche performance in my analysis as my research has not specifically addressed measures of CAG performance and effectiveness.

9　Both NSW2 and VIC1 mentioned that their groups had engaged in strategic planning, for example. This is consistent with Hielscher's (2013) findings that groups which articulated a broader vision were more successful.

10　This may well be the case as the fossil fuel divestment movement, led by 350.org (http://350.org/, accessed 8 June 2015) gains significant traction.

References

Avelino, F. 2009, 'Empowerment and the challenge of applying transition management to ongoing projects', *Policy Sciences*, vol. 42, no. 4, pp. 369–90.

Bailey, I., Hopkins, R. & Wilson, G. 2010, 'Some things old, some things new: the spatial representations and politics of change of the peak oil relocalisation movement', *Geoforum*, vol. 41, no. 4, pp. 595–605.

Beck, U. 1992, *Risk society: towards a new modernity*, trans. M. Ritter, Sage, London.

Dryzek, J.S. 2009, 'Democratization as deliberative capacity building', *Comparative Political Studies*, vol. 42, no. 11, pp. 1379–1402.

Dryzek, J.S., Downes, D., Hunold, C., Schlosberg, D. & Hernes, H.-K. 2003, *Green states and social movements: environmentalism in the United States, United Kingdom, Germany and Norway*, Oxford University Press, Oxford.

Dryzek, J.S., Norgaard, R.B. & Schlosberg, D. 2013, *Climate-challenged society*, Oxford University Press, Oxford.

Feola, G. & Nunes, R. 2014, 'Success and failure of grassroots innovations for addressing climate change: the case of the transition movement', *Global Environmental Change*, vol. 24, no. 0, pp. 232–50.

Foderaro, L.W. 2014, 'Taking a call for climate change to the streets', *New York Times*, 22 September 2014, p. A1.

Geels, F.W. 2005, 'Processes and patterns in transitions and system innovations: refining the co-evolutionary multi-level perspective', *Technological Forecasting and Social Change*, vol. 72, no. 6, pp. 681–96.

Geels, F.W. 2011, 'The multi-level perspective on sustainability transitions: responses to seven criticisms', *Environmental Innovation and Societal Transitions*, vol. 1, no. 1, pp. 24–40.

Geels, F.W. 2014, 'Regime resistance against low-carbon transitions: introducing politics and power into the multi-level perspective', *Theory, Culture & Society*, doi. 0263276414531627.

Grin, J., Rotmans, J. & Schot, J. 2011, 'On patterns and agency in transition dynamics: some key insights from the KSI programme', *Environmental Innovation and Societal Transitions*, vol. 1, no. 1, pp. 76–81.

Grin, J., Rotmans, J. & Schot, J. 2010, *Transitions in sustainable development: new directions in the study of long term transformative change*, Routledge, New York.

Gross, M. & Mautz, R. 2015, *Renewable energies*, Routledge, UK.

Hanson, F. 2011, The Lowy Institute Poll. Australia and the world: public opinion and foreign policy, Sydney, Australia.

Hielscher, S. 2013, *Carbon rationing action groups: an innovation history*, Project report. University of Sussex; University of East Anglia, accessed 4 June 2015, http://sro.sussex.ac.uk/53354/.

Hielscher, S., Seyfang, G. & Smith, A. 2011, *Community Innovation for Sustainable Energy*, Centre for Social and Economic Research on the Global Environment (CSERGE), CSERGE Working Paper 2011–03, Norwich, UK.

Hoffman, S.M. & High-Pippert, A. 2010, 'From private lives to collective action: recruitment and participation incentives for a community energy program', *Energy Policy*, vol. 38, no. 12, pp. 7567–74.

Howaldt, J., Schwarz, M., Henning, K. & Hees, F. 2010, *Social innovation: concepts, research fields and international trends*, IMA/ZLW.

Hulme, M. 2010, 'Cosmopolitan climates: hybridity, foresight and meaning', *Theory, Culture and Society*, vol. 27, no. 2–3, pp. 267–76.

Jones, B. 2010, *Democratic challenges in tackling climate change*, Whitlam Institute, University of Western Sydney, Australia.

Kirwan, J., Ilbery, B., Maye, D. & Carey, J. 2013, 'Grassroots social innovations and food localisation: an investigation of the local food programme in England', *Global Environmental Change*, vol. 23, no. 5, pp. 830–7.

Klein, N. 2014, *This changes everything: capitalism vs. the climate*, Simon and Schuster, New York.

Louis, W.R. 2009, 'Collective action – and then what?', *Journal of Social Issues*, vol. 65, no. 4, pp. 727–48.

Meadowcroft, J. 2011, 'Engaging with the *politics* of sustainability transitions', *Environmental Innovation and Societal Transitions*, vol. 1, no. 1, pp. 70–5.

Middlemiss, L. & Parrish, B.D. 2010, 'Building capacity for low-carbon communities: the role of grassroots initiatives', *Energy Policy*, vol. 38, no. 12, pp. 7559–66.

Moloney, S., Horne, R.E. & Fien, J. 2010, 'Transitioning to low carbon communities – from behaviour change to systemic change: lessons from Australia', *Energy Policy*, vol. 38, no. 12, pp. 7614–23.

Neilsen and Environmental Change Institute 2007, Climate change and influential spokespeople: a global Nielsen online survey, accessed 7 April 2011, www.eci.ox.ac.uk/publications/downloads/070709nielsen-celeb-report.pdf.

Ornetzeder, M. & Rohracher, H. 2013, 'Of solar collectors, wind power, and car sharing: comparing and understanding successful cases of grassroots innovations', *Global Environmental Change*, vol. 23, no. 5, pp. 856–67.

Ostrom, E. 2009, *A polycentric approach for coping with climate change*, 5095, The World Bank Development Economics Office of the Senior Vice President and Chief Economist, Washington.

Ostrom, E. 2010, 'Polycentric systems for coping with collective action and global environmental change', *Global Environmental Change*, vol. 20, no. 4, pp. 550–7.

Pattberg, P. & Stripple, J. 2008, 'Beyond the public and private divide: remapping transnational climate governance in the 21st century', *International Environmental Agreements: Politics, Law and Economics*, vol. 8, no. 4, pp. 367–88.

Rauschmayer, F., Bauler, T. & Schäpke, N. 2015, 'Towards a thick understanding of sustainability transitions – linking transition management, capabilities and social practices', *Ecological Economics*, vol. 109, no. 0, pp. 211–21.

Raven, R., Bosch, S.v.d. & Weterings, R. 2010, 'Transitions and strategic niche management: towards a competence kit for practitioners', *International Journal of Technology Management*, vol. 51, no. 1, pp. 57–74.

Reeves, A., Lemon, M. & Cook, D. 2014, 'Jump-starting transition? Catalysing grassroots action on climate change', *Energy Efficiency*, vol. 7, no. 1, pp. 115–32.

Scoones, I., Leach, M. & Newell, P. (eds) 2015, *The politics of green transformations*, Routledge, London.

Scott-Cato, M. & Hillier, J. 2010, 'How could we study climate-related social innovation? Applying Deleuzean philosophy to transition towns', *Environmental Politics*, vol. 19, no. 6, pp. 869–87.

Seyfang, G. & Haxeltine, A. 2012, 'Growing grassroots innovations: exploring the role of community-based initiatives in governing sustainable energy transitions', *Environment and Planning C: Government and Policy*, vol. 30, pp. 381–400.

Seyfang, G., Haxeltine, A., Hargreaves, T. & Longhurst, N. 2010, *Energy and communities in transition – towards a new research agenda on agency and civil society in sustainability transitions*, CSERGE Working Paper EDM 10–13, CSERGE, Norwich, UK.

Seyfang, G. & Smith, A. 2007, 'Grassroots innovations for sustainable development: towards a new research and policy agenda', *Environmental Politics*, vol. 16, pp. 584–603.

Shove, E. 2010, 'Social theory and climate change', *Theory, Culture & Society*, vol. 27, no. 2–3, pp. 277–88.

Smith, A. 2007, 'Translating sustainabilities between green niches and socio-technical regimes', *Technology Analysis & Strategic Management*, vol. 19, no. 4, pp. 427–50.

Tranter, B. 2010, 'Environmental activists and non-active environmentalists in Australia', *Environmental Politics*, vol. 19, no. 3, pp. 413–29.

Tranter, B. 2011, 'Political divisions over climate change and environmental issues in Australia', *Environmental Politics*, vol. 20, no. 1, pp. 78–96.

Ungar, S. 1995, 'Social scares and global warming: beyond the Rio Convention', *Society and Natural Resources*, vol. 8, pp. 443–56.

7 Future pathways for community action on climate change

Negotiating the risk society in the anthropocene

As an interlocking issue that respects neither national borders nor political timescales, climate change creates 'a world of fluid heterogeneity, where scale becomes transient and Cartesian space easily subverted' (Hulme 2010, p. 563). It becomes another of the expanded global risks that individuals increasingly encounter (Beck 2006, 2010). Climate change is not just a problem for nations, institutions and civil society in the public sphere to resolve; it has become a focus for individualized responsibility and private-sphere action (Carvalho 2010; Paterson & Stripple 2010). Climate change has become the symbol of our times, blending the local and the global, the past with the future, the 'us' and the 'them': a heuristic for examining not only the modern condition, but ourselves.

Beck's *Risk Society* (1992) acknowledges the centrality of risk and the individualization of responsibility in attending to global 'bads' such as climate change. Contemporary society, according to Beck, is full of contradictions that he delights in exposing, ridiculing and critiquing. However, at the core of Beck's thesis is a serious intent: for social evolution to occur, society must proceed to a second reflexive modernity. Modern scientific and technologically mediated risks and man-made catastrophes underpin this modernity, epitomized by climate change. According to Beck (1992, p. 24): 'Risk society is a *catastrophic* society.' Yet it is under these conditions that hegemonic power and authority can be disrupted and the vision of a reflexive modernity and cosmopolitan society can be realized, as 'political modernization disempowers and unbinds politics and politicizes society'. Risk and individualization break down the extant institutions and structures, opening fractures in the regime and exposing the contradictions of individualised responsibility where 'one can do something and continue doing it without having to take personal responsibility for it' (Beck 1992, p. 33).

Evident in Beck's thesis is the central role of citizens in addressing state irresponsibility in the face of contemporary global risks. Nowhere is this more evident than in the issue of climate change where growing citizen distrust in politicians and political institutions has been matched in recent years with the emergence of community collectives active around climate change. Within Australia where the politics of climate change has attained a special significance (Jones 2010), even notoriety, a community-based movement for action on climate change has emerged. CAGs fill a particular position within Australian climate politics. They have risen from local communities across Australia to undertake various forms of voluntary action with the intention to generate widespread community awareness and support. They target their political action towards governments in order for them to take responsibility for climate change through strong action and to diminish the threat of dangerous climatic change.

The individualization of responsibility for social change on climate change

In Beck's thesis, the individualization of responsibility under the conditions of global risk create the conditions where sub-political entities operate as counter-agents to state authority and institutions. According to Beck (2010), climate change 'releases a cosmopolitan momentum' as risk conditions break down and subvert the prevailing institutions of modernity creating an 'interconnectedness' between people. As life situations become increasingly cosmopolitan, the progression to social change becomes realized. The 'social scare' (Ungar 1995) of 2006 created a set of conditions that complement the social forces identified by Beck. A series of coalescing events led to widespread and heightened public concern on climate change, which permeated societies internationally. This 'cosmopolitan moment' shifted the political, economic and social landscape, opening the potential for change in the prevailing regime. Community collectives such as CAGs grew rapidly at this time.

Notwithstanding Beck's contribution, there are important caveats to be considered in promoting an individualization of responsibility for climate change action. The individualization of responsibility has become pervasive in Western discourse and government policy aligned with neoliberal thinking. The individualization of responsibility for voluntary climate change action emphasizes an *individualist* approach rather than a *situated* approach (Middlemiss 2010). An individualist approach relies on people taking action on climate change irrespective of the significant structural constraints embedded in the current regime that perpetuate unsustainability. Further, an individualist approach emphasizes personal- and private-sphere action reflected in individual lifestyle choices and household carbon reduction actions. A structuration approach engages 'authoritative actors' in voluntary action on climate change within the public sphere. It follows then, that for social change on climate change to be successful, individuals need to come together in collectives to overcome structural constraints, such as a lack of empowerment, distrust in governments and politicians, and lack of reflexivity.

My investigation into CAGs tested these normative hypotheses. Little prior research has been conducted with CAGs and this research contributes to understanding: the motivation of members of these groups (as individual agents) for undertaking voluntary action on climate change; why they join grassroots collectives; the nature of their individual and collective actions; how working together assists them in overcoming constraints to action; and how their actions contribute to broader social change. The model developed (Figure 5.2) explains the virtuous circle of this progression whereby CAG members shift from their personal agency through to collective agency and as political agents undertake voluntary action within the public sphere.

STT assisted in further explicating how community-based collective action can lead to social change. A further extension of this literature examines sustainability transitions in relation to grassroots social innovations engaged in sustainability projects, such as climate change action. This literature makes an important contribution to understanding how innovations that arise at the grassroots level of civil society can influence and potentially overcome the dominant, unsustainable regime (Geels 2014; Grin *et al.* 2010). In applying STT I have endeavoured to uncover how individuals, as 'active agents' (Rosewarne *et al.* 2014) within their communities, come together on climate change in order to influence other community members, politicians and governments. Australian CAGs are not a unique case here. They arose under the same landscape conditions that led to an 'upsurge' (Rosewarne *et al.* 2014) in climate action globally. While there is no doubt fewer people are now involved in CAGs within Australia today since their height in 2009, and many groups have folded (and this relates equally to other groups such as CRAGs and Climate Camps), as the frontiers for climate activism have shifted new collectives have risen. CAGs have swung their support behind other initiatives, so whereas their form may differ they still provide an outlet for local concerned citizens to engage in climate change praxis. Some continue to create a strong focus for climate change action within their local community;[1] while others have aligned with broader citizen movements (e.g. Lock the Gate alliance; Solar Citizens); still others are situated at the frontlines of fossil fuel production.[2] I briefly recap below the major findings from my research on CAGs as an illustration of how broader community action on climate change may be achieved.

People feel responsible for climate change

People understand that they have a personal responsibility for climate change and express high levels of concern about its impact. However, people are failing to engage with climate change and to take social action on the issue as they perceive the disparity between their individual empowerment and their capability in light of the enormity and complexity of the problem. They believe that responsibility needs to be shared with others and that governments need to take the lead.

CAG members assume that they have a personal responsibility for climate change but that this responsibility is shared with others, in particular, governments. In contrast with the majority within their communities, CAG members were motivated to take action based on their knowledge of climate change science but underpinned by a strong sense of moral obligation. In 'doing the right thing', CAG members came together in their collectives to influence governments and politicians to take concerted action and work to prevent dangerous climate change. CAG members perceived their forms of voluntary action as legitimate in the face of government inaction and that their role extended to making governments accountable for climate change mitigation.

As active agents on climate change, CAG members possess a spatial responsibility for climate change that creates a link between their local actions and global effects. They understand that they have an intergenerational responsibility as the effects of climate change extend from past (historic) emissions into future (unknown) impacts. This *cosmopolitan* responsibility for climate change exposes important ethical mores of fairness, equity and justice and condemns inaction. This chain of responsibility is a thread, which links local and personal action with the global. Singer (2011) expresses this as an expanding circle of responsibility that emanates from the central layers of human concern to encompass all human beings (and life) as an essential societal goal. Responsibility rises in relation to social risks and creates allied rights. Actors at all levels have an obligation to respond to climate change.

People act responsibly to mitigate climate change

Citizens are tangibly demonstrating their acceptance of their responsibility for climate change through their actions in their personal and private spheres, in their households and lifestyle choices. They also act in the public sphere as economic actors or citizen consumers, and through their political actions as democratic agents. Individual actors, moreover, place preference on their local action over global action as they perceive that this is the level at which they can effect change (Feola & Nunes 2014; Norgaard 2011).

CAG members demonstrate their responsibility both through their personal- and private-sphere actions but also within the public sphere. They are undertaking significant actions around their households and lifestyle practices that often extend well beyond current social norms of behaviour, enacting an 'environmental politics of sacrifice' (Maniates & Meyer 2010). These actions include: no longer flying, reducing personal showering routines and turning off their hot water systems. CAG members are leading by example as one tangible expression of their individual responsibility, linking their lifestyle choices to a critique of social unsustainability, such as overconsumption and social injustice through inequitable access to a share of the global atmospheric commons. They come together in groups in order to express their collective and political agency by: lobbying their local politicians; taking direct action at the sites of carbon pollution such as coal mines and power stations; buying solar panels in bulk; and raising awareness within their local communities.

Individual actors acquire agency through voluntary action

People perceive their responsibility for climate change as a shared obligation with governments. However, they also express strong feelings of distrust of governments' ability and willingness to undertake the actions required for global warming to be addressed and dangerous climate change averted. People see a lack of political conviction around climate change action and the incapacity of nations to come to a global agreement. This has led to disempowerment, denial and apathy in the general community (Norgaard 2011). Only certain people acquire individual agency through their voluntary actions in order to engage with climate change. Moreover actors acquire agency by overcoming the societal constraints proffered by the structural conditions of disempowerment, political distrust and lack of reflexivity.

CAG members have overcome these constraints to individual agency expressed in broader community apathy and inaction. They believe that the barriers to taking action on climate change lie in the more practical limitations of their lack of time and money. CAG members are both individually and collectively empowered to take action on climate change. Their involvement within their group creates a virtuous circle of increasing capability, enhancing their individual and collective agency so that they enact political agency (Figure 5.5). They see their role as being in political action, which is outside but not against the state. They have legitimacy and their actions are targeted to ensure government accountability, authenticity and transparency.

Pathways from community action to social change

Three potential pathways for the individualization of responsibility to create social change under conditions of risk have been exposed. First, faced with impending catastrophic climactic change, actors become fearful and disempowered, leading to inaction. Second, 'agency-oriented' (Middlemiss 2010) actors act within their personal and private spheres, making lifestyle choices and implementing changes within their households, though these may only consist of small and inconsequential steps. In this 'thin cosmopolitanism' (Linklater 1998a) actors fail to connect to, or otherwise challenge, the structural constraints that embed the continuing unsustainable regime. Third, actors that come together in groups such as CAGs demonstrate a collective agency and are able to take action within the public sphere.

Such collectives are thus a sign of 'thick conceptions of cosmopolitan citizenship [that] attempt to influence the structural conditions' (Linklater 1998b, p. 206).

If these different pathways are acknowledged, it can be seen that the individualization of responsibility is creating the conditions for social change but only where individuals, as 'active agents', are able to overcome the significant structural constraints to their individual agency. CAGs demonstrate this. They are individually empowered to take voluntary action on climate change. They are 'actors with authority' who base their action on a personal and moral obligation. They come together with like-minded people to form collectives that express collective agency. The group supports and enhances their individual and collective agency, creating a virtuous circle of increasing agency. CAGs act collectively on voluntary climate action as grassroots niches with the potential to influence the hegemonic regime.

Much is being made of community-led initiatives as not only the forerunners of transformational change but also as sites for cut-through social, technological, economic and political innovations (Barry 2012; Scoones *et al.* 2015). While these are exciting times, the following caveats need to be considered: grassroots innovations will need to extend beyond their social elites in order to engage broader mainstream uptake; structural constraints should not be underplayed – our carbon-based economy is firmly embedded and will require significant 'destructive' (Geels 2014) forces before an alternative, clean and safe economy can come into place; neoliberalist states continue to promulgate an individualization of responsibility on climate change action and are failing to enact strong climate policies that would cap their GHG emissions at a level that avoids dangerous climate change; and finally, the risk remains that the efforts of individuals, households and their communities will continue to be subverted to capitalist imperatives that sustain 'growth-at-all-costs' economies fuelled by endless cycles of unsustainable consumption.

How can individuals' actions on climate change at the local level link up to create global-level change?

I have created a detailed argument on how individual agency is commuted to collective agency in climate change engagement, facilitated through group involvement. I argue that CAG members as individual agents have overcome the structural barriers that face individual actors in climate change mitigation. The ability of CAGs to move from their grassroots niche into regime change has been explored as grassroots social innovations with social change potential (see Chapter 6).

The CAG 'niche' however consists of a certain 'elite'; that is, only certain 'privileged' communities (Middlemiss & Parrish 2010) have formed CAGs and only certain (mainly post-materialist) members of those communities become active CAG members. Based on Seyfang and Haxeltine

(2012), I proposed five ways that CAGs as a niche of voluntary grassroots climate action can influence the existing regime: by replication resulting from fragmentation; through their scale of influence and development of networks; by growing outside their 'elite'; by translating their ideas into mainstream settings; and through social learning.

What remains uncertain is the linking mechanism, the 'in-between substance' (Hoyer & Aall 1995 cited in Lindseth 2004, p. 327) that would realize the connections from local-level action to the global. Smith (2007, p. 429) argues there is a bewildering number of potential points of connection and synchronization for the change required in the extant regime to achieve the normative goal of sustainability. Current understandings moreover consider such linkages 'to be "haphazard and coincidental"' and there remains no 'theory of "linking"' to draw on (Smith 2007, p. 431). Change needs to be conceptualized as a 'messy' process (Bulkeley & Newell 2010; Ostrom 2009).

Recent accounts of climate change governance have stressed the significance of these 'messy' change developments as increasing numbers of players enter into the governance of climate change at all scales – global, regional, national, state and local (Bulkeley *et al.* 2015; Hoffmann 2011; Stevenson & Dryzek 2014). While STT has played a key role in my analysis of how change can occur from the grassroots, in Chapter 4 I introduced two further theoretical frames that seek to explain the role of community-based collectives in transformational change: Ostrom's polycentrism and Torgerson's green public sphere. Both approach environmental change from different and, I would argue, complementary perspectives. Polycentrism provides understanding of how individual to collective linkages can occur built on critical aspects of social capacity and community resilience such as trust, cooperation and social learning. The green public sphere, on the other hand, is concerned with more vertical linkages from the individual/collective to the global based on citizen discourse and deliberation within the public sphere. Conceptualizations that incorporate these additional theoretical frames and that employ a transdisciplinary ontology may be needed in order to gain further understanding of the 'in-between' substance that links local-level community action to global-scale response on climate change.

Horizontal versus vertical transition

Related to the above is the question of how change that comes from the 'bottom up', that is, from the grassroots, links to 'top-down' processes evident in the global governance of climate change. According to Giddens, horizontal *social systems* are distinguished by deliberative processes and vertical *social structures* by more formal institutional practices that, for example, NGOs might engage in and are focused on challenging extant power and social norms. Accordingly, to take advantage of both horizontal and vertical transition potentialities, 'social movements should operate both inside and outside the state' (Dryzek *et al.* 2003, p. 155). In a similar way, Lidskog and Elander (2010) call for a cosmopolitan democracy as an alternative global governance as it distributes power horizontally through greater civil society involvement and possesses far greater potential for the type of horizontal linkages required in transnational decision-making (p. 36). Acknowledging the need for both horizontal and vertical governance pathways, Lidskog and Elander suggest dual climate change governance arrangements: vertically aligned formal institutions such as now exist in the current global climate governance system; and informal horizontal and transnational networks drawn from civil society (p. 38).

This provides another potential avenue for conceptualizing sustainability transitions from the grassroots to the global. In the horizontal plane informal grassroots organizations can replicate through growing their networks and coalitions across their local communities while the engagement of more politicized actors occurs through more formal and bureaucratized organizations (Doyle 2009; Dryzek *et al.* 2003; Lidskog & Elander 2010), which can operate on the vertical plane of shifting established social norms and political constituencies. Dryzek *et al.* (2003) note that environmental movements derived from the grassroots are often 'self-limiting' (p. 15) because they tend to operate outside of the state and thus outside of regime power, but their influence may nonetheless have an indirect impact through their ability to influence public opinion, enhance social learning and change power distributions:

> As Torgerson (1999: 140) puts it, 'the public sphere does not directly govern, but influences government in an indirect fashion through the communicative power of opinion' . . . The collective outcomes that social movements can influence are not confined to public policies. Changes in the terms of political discourse can take effect not just in the state, but directly in society's political culture. Movements can be educational, and change the distribution of power in society.
>
> (Dryzek *et al.* 2003, p. 133)

For Dryzek (Dryzek 2008, 2009) it is not so much the *form* of such institutional arrangements as the *processes* involved that link the local and global in the governance of climate change. Discourses are for Dryzek (2009) the horizontal social structures that enable or otherwise constrain political agents (p. 480). It is in discursive democracy, 'a species of deliberative democracy' (p. 483), that people come together to discuss and debate 'problem sets'. These deliberations do not need to be structured but can form freely across horizontal and vertical scales and where matters of common identity or ideology bear no importance (p. 483). I see such small group deliberations as an important focus for future and more detailed research.

Arborescence and rhizome

The application of the horizontal and vertical allegory for transition processes that incorporate grassroots and institutional actors is further provoked by the work of Deleuze (as cited in Scott-Cato & Hillier 2010). Deleuze also plays with the tension between the vertical and horizontal scales through the imagery of arborescence and rhizome (Scott-Cato & Hillier 2010, p. 872). Arborescence according to Deleuze is 'a tree-like structured hierarchy, epitomized by institutions of the State' while the rhizome is the 'antithesis of arborescence', consisting of 'a horizontal underground plant stem with lateral shoots and roots, such as ginger', a 'decentred set of linkages between, multiple branching roots and shoots, i.e. "a proliferating, somewhat chaotic, and diversified system of growths" (Grosz 1994, p. 199)' (Scott-Cato & Hillier 2010, p. 872). This creates a rich picture of an underground root system connecting and binding together to form a mat-like impenetrable mass, as explained below by Bogue (1989, p. 107):

> Arborescences are hierarchical, stratified totalities that impose limited and regulated connections between their components. Rhizomes, in contrast, are non-hierarchical, horizontal multiplicities that cannot be subsumed within a unified structure, whose components form random, unregulated networks in which any element may be connected with any other elements.
>
> (cited in Scott-Cato & Hillier 2010, p. 872)

Deleuze and Guattari (1987) further explicate the role of rhizomes as providing the 'in-between substance' (Hoyer & Aall 1995, p. 327 as cited in Lindseth, 2004) in processes of change that may link the local to the global. They connect social struggles and when broken can start up again so that ideas incorporated within a protest movement, for example, will remain after the protest is disrupted and so the cause can be taken up by others:

> 'The fabric of the rhizome is the conjunction – "and"– connecting elements, issues and ideas. "AND" is neither one thing nor the other, it's always in-between, between two things' (Deleuze 1995, p. 45). To think rhizomically is to reveal the multiple ways possible to assemble thoughts and actions in immanent, always-incomplete processes of change and innovation, or becoming.
>
> (Scott-Cato & Hillier 2010, p. 872)

This provides additional explanatory weight to what Hoyer and Aall (1995, cited in Lindseth, 2004) describe as the 'in-between substance that links the local and the global' (p. 327). As Scott-Cato and Hillier (2010) propose, these courses of innovation and change are not necessarily realized through a steady process of movement building over time but rather there are disjunctions where movements may wax and wane but the ideas continue. This extends community-based collectives engaged in climate change action from their role as niche projects to be considered within a broader sustainability context. Grassroots innovations involved in their particular sustainability projects within their local communities could over time seed bigger change as post-materialist values are taken up by wider publics, expressed through their local community concerns. It also allows for future landscape-level changes or 'social scares' to stimulate the re-assembly of disparate movement elements around the increasingly complex global 'problem sets' (Dryzek 2005) that are a feature of the second modernity (Beck 1992).

Is there empirical evidence to suggest that grassroots climate action collectives such as CAGs are taking on some of these niche project and transition characteristics? I have already identified that climate change is conceived by CAG members as an idiom for the prevailing conditions of societal unsustainability. Yet in recent times there have been calls to expand the 'problem set' (Dryzek 2005) of climate change to incorporate broader sustainability concerns.[3] The rise of the Occupy movement, for example, prompted some to call for linkages between the Occupy and the grassroots climate action movements.[4] Rosewarne *et al.* (2014) identify how the Camp for Climate Action has been a model for Camp Frack,[5] responding to the widespread threat of CSG fracking to local communities. The fossil fuel divestment movement is gaining increasing momentum, largely under the auspices of 350.org and modelled on successful divestment movements against apartheid in South Africa in the 1980s. These examples of global 'issue-linkages' between grassroots climate action and more widespread sustainability concerns possibly presage the acceleration of niche project activity into a 'complex contagion' (Centola & Macy 2007). Central to this 'contagion' is the ability to 'rhizomically' proliferate through social learning (Reed *et al.* 2010) and discursive deliberation (Dryzek 2008, 2009; Hendriks 2006). Discursive deliberation is exemplified by inclusive and non-hierarchical decision-making of the type popularized in the World Social Forum, Climate Camps and the Occupy movement (Doyle 2009). I have shown that CAGs, apart from creating collective agency, enhance social learning among their members in the democratic skills that allow political engagement. Through their deliberations, CAGs develop shared meanings and values around climate change and sustainability more broadly. Grassroots community innovations thereby have a critical role in building a *complex contagion* that can lead to widespread social change.

Further questions for future research

This leads to several lines of enquiry that deserve further attention. First, as indicated above, there is a need for further examination of the role of small group deliberations in social change utilizing group-based research methods, such as focus group discussions. The potential of the inclusive collective democratic decision-making processes utilized by the World Social Forum, Climate Camps and Occupy movement is worthy of investigation to determine how these could inform a type of broader scale citizen engagement on climate change and its root causes.

I have considered one type of grassroots innovation, Australian Climate Action Groups, as my research focus and have identified an expanding and evolving literature that considers different types of grassroots collectives involved in various sustainability projects (exemplified in the work of Seyfang, Smith and others). There are several questions that follow, such as: what are the differing routes of niche formation? How are different niche actors characterized? And what motivates their collective action within their own local communities? This opens up the potential for comparative investigations into the different routes of grassroots niche formation and whether, for example, niche formation characteristics differ across different societal and cultural contexts.

In the same way that niches may possess different formation pathways, what characterizes individual niche actors? In my research it was evident that a particular type of person is attracted to becoming a CAG member and Tranter's (2010, 2011) research extends this notion to characterizing people who get involved in environmental action more generally. Further evidence from the work of Seyfang (with others), Howell (2010) and Krakoff (2011) for example, indicate significant similarities in their research cohorts. However, this does not preclude other types of grassroots innovations attracting different niche actors. Moreover, determining different groups of actors with the capability to form sustainability niches will be an important precursor for generating broader scale social change targeted towards a future sustainable society. The question arises whether different types of grassroots innovators are similarly drawn to their issue of concern as a heuristic for a more expansive concern. In my research CAG members often pursue their interest around climate change as it represents an idiom for the wider existing societal conditions of unsustainability. This opens up the question of what motivates grassroots collective action around different sustainability issue niches. The recent, rapid growth in community-supported agriculture through farmers markets and local food production through community gardens and allotments in Western nations, along with the trajectory of community renewable initiatives (Gross & Mautz 2015), are pertinent examples, ripe for investigation.

As I noted in Chapter 6, my research was not specifically formulated to determine the characteristics of the communities that CAGs are situated in and this represents a potential area for further research on community-based climate change. As grassroots niches are unique to their local communities, the questions raised by Middlemiss (2010) around the varying capabilities of communities to support niche formation and what capabilities grassroots

niches may offer to their local communities are relevant. There are complementary framings and research endeavours within the field of third sector
research (Onyx & Edwards 2010; Rauschmayer *et al.* 2015) that raise
questions around the role of such collectives in building and/or extending
social capital and contributing to community resilience. This line of questioning will be of particular importance to researchers interested in the
capacities of communities to adapt to climatic change.

Conclusion

> There are examples of individuals becoming responsible citizens through
> collective action. Whether these movements are also able to transcend
> the local context within which they are embedded, take issues of
> environmental justice and the North-South divide into consideration
> and proceed to a responsibility for global development remains to
> be seen.
>
> (Räthzel & Uzzell 2009, p. 334)

In Chapter 1, I positioned climate change as a complex 'wicked'/'super-
wicked' problem, which presents as not only the greatest challenge to
humankind but the greatest moral challenge. At the core of the climate
change issue are deeply moral considerations such as fairness, equality,
justice and democracy. How we respond to climate change as individuals,
collectively and globally, therefore, goes to the very root of the human
condition itself. Or, in Beck's words, 'how do we wish to live?' becomes the
critical question for contemporary society facing the impacts of anthropo-
centric global 'bads'. The challenge of unsustainability that faces the planet
sits well beyond the purview of science, technology and the market. As
Marshall states, climate change 'is already part of our inner lives and dreams
... our inner awareness and unconsciousness' and 'we cannot feel dis-
passionately about it' (Marshall 2011, p. 3).

I have argued that CAG members, prompted by a 'moral shock', choose
to come together with like-minded people in order to take collective action
for climate change mitigation. CAG members distinguish themselves from
others within their local communities as empowered, trusting and reflexive
agents able to overcome structural constraints to collective and political
action. I have argued that in this way CAG members act as political, legitimate and cosmopolitan agents who enact the skills of democratic citizenship
enhanced through their group trust and cooperation and through their
group deliberations act out a discursive democracy. Moreover CAGs, as
singular niche projects of community-based collective climate action, can
develop into broader coalitions of climate action, clustering with other niche
projects in order to develop rhizomically. This coalition of niche projects
has the capacity to become a *complex contagion* of grassroots concern that
promulgates an alternative and sustainable societal vision.

CAGs for the most part show an essential faith in the political system, despite the fact that they are highly concerned about its effectiveness and doubt whether it has the political willpower to enact strong climate change mitigation reforms. CAGs do not seek overtly to overthrow the state, nor are they proposing a radical reorientation of society. In this sense they do not act as an ideologically driven grassroots social movement. They differ from similar grassroots movements such as Transition Towns that direct their collective agency towards building skills in local provisioning, turning their efforts more inward towards a relocalization. Instead, CAGs direct their action outward towards the political orientations of the state. CAGs are not concerned with relocalizing, but neither do they demonstrate any significant globalizing affinities through a concern for global climate justice. CAGs do not appear to have a radical reform agenda. Although CAG members are taking up sustainability initiatives, which sit outside current social norms, for the most part they do not challenge capitalism and the role of market mechanisms in carbon emissions reduction. Nor are they seeking political alternatives that sit outside of the state.

Under the individualization of responsibility model of climate change agency, the extant regime makes adjustments solely to take continued advantage of the economic and political imperatives of 'unsustainability'. It merely translates individual practices in ways that continue to support regime power and dominance (Paterson & Stripple 2010). An essential dilemma then for grassroots community-based CAGs is that they need to change the existing regime conditions without being co-opted within them. I find this a particularly difficult problem to decipher, because for CAGs to remain outside the state but not against (unsustainable) state objectives would seem to defeat their regime change prospects. CAGs do have a role, nevertheless, in addressing the continuing erosion of public trust in governments and politicians, opening the way, as cosmopolitan agents, to bolster state surety in a future cosmopolitan regime (Archibugi & Held 2011; List & Koenig-Archibugi 2010).

Despite the normative potential for regime shift, grassroots-initiated social change faces concerted barriers. Meadowcroft (2011) observes that changes towards sustainability face significant locked-in and path-dependent resistance from embedded political institutions and power structures that support current societal unsustainability and underpin the existing global climate governance regime:

> These struggles involve not only established political actors (such as political parties and major economic groups) but also emergent forces associated with new technologies, experimental practices and social movements. And since sustainability transitions may take decades, there will be repeated cycles of interaction, with all sides drawing lessons from previous rounds.
>
> (Meadowcroft 2011, p. 73)

While no doubt this lag in achieving sustainability transitions will not suit the need and desire of community-based climate action organizations to see rapid change in order to prevent the worst effects of a warming world, the 'political lives' (Torgerson 1999) cultivated through the collective action of CAGs can be celebrated.

Notes

1 Climate Change Balmain Rozelle for example continues to coordinate a range of voluntary community-based action. See www.climatechangebr.org/, accessed 8 June 2015.
2 Front line action on coal (http://frontlineaction.org/, accessed 8 June 2015) maintains a blockade at the Maules Creek coal mine development in Leard Forest, NSW. The blockade commenced on 5th August 2012 and is the first coal mine blockade camp in Australia.
3 'Need to broaden the conversation', CANAchat thread, canachat@cana.net.au, accessed 28 October 2011.
4 Buckland, K., 'History in motion', 350.org, organizers@350.org, accessed 27 October 2011.
5 www.campaigncc.org/campfrack, accessed 8 June 2015.

References

Archibugi, D. & Held, D. 2011, 'Cosmopolitan democracy: paths and agents', paper presented to the *Global Governance: Political Authority in Transition. ISA Annual Convention 2011*, Montreal PQ, 16–19 March 2011.
Barry, J. 2012, *The politics of actually existing unsustainability: human flourishing in a climate-changed, carbon constrained world*, Oxford University Press, Oxford.
Beck, U. 1992, *Risk society: towards a new modernity*, trans. M. Ritter, Sage, London.
Beck, U. 2006, *Cosmopolitan vision*, Polity, Cambridge.
Beck, U. 2010, 'Climate for change, or how to create a green modernity?', *Theory, Culture and Society*, vol. 27, no. 2–3, pp. 254–66.
Bulkeley, H., Castan Broto, V. & Edwards, G.A.S. 2015, *An urban politics of climate change. Experimentation and the governing of socio-technical transitions*, Routledge, London.
Bulkeley, H. & Newell, P. 2010, *Governing climate change*, Routledge, London.
Carvalho, A. 2010, 'Media(ted) discourses and climate change: a focus on political subjectivity and (dis)engagement', *Wiley's Interdisciplinary Reviews: Climate Change*, vol. 1, no. 2, pp. 172–9.
Centola, D. & Macy, M. 2007, 'Complex contagion and the weakness of long ties', *American Journal of Sociology*, vol. 113, no. 3, pp. 702–34.
Deleuze, G. & Guattari, F. 1987 [1980], *A thousand plateaus*, trans. B. Massumi, University of Minnesota Press, Minneapolis, MN.
Doyle, J. 2009, 'Climate action and environmental activism: the role of environmental NGOs and grassroots movements in the global politics of climate change', in T. Boyce & J. Lewis (eds), *Climate change and the media*, Peter Lang, New York, pp. 103–16.

Dryzek, J.S. 2005, *The politics of the earth: environmental discourses*, 2nd edn, Oxford University Press, Oxford.

Dryzek, J.S. 2008, 'Two paths to global democracy', *Ethical perspectives*, vol. 15, no. 4, pp. 469–86.

Dryzek, J.S. 2009, 'Democratization as deliberative capacity building', *Comparative Political Studies*, vol. 42, no. 11, pp. 1379–402.

Dryzek, J.S., Downes, D., Hunold, C., Schlosberg, D. & Hernes, H.-K. 2003, *Green states and social movements: environmentalism in the United States, United Kingdom, Germany and Norway*, Oxford University Press, Oxford.

Feola, G. & Nunes, R. 2014, 'Success and failure of grassroots innovations for addressing climate change: the case of the transition movement', *Global Environmental Change*, vol. 24, no. 0, pp. 232–50.

Geels, F.W. 2014, 'Regime resistance against low-carbon transitions: introducing politics and power into the multi-level perspective', *Theory, Culture & Society*, doi. 0263276414531627.

Grin, J., Rotmans, J. & Schot, J. 2010, *Transitions in sustainable development: new directions in the study of long term transformative change*, Routledge, New York.

Gross, M. & Mautz, R. 2015, *Renewable energies*, Routledge, UK.

Hendriks, C.M. 2006, 'Integrated deliberation: reconciling civil society's dual role in deliberative democracy', *Political Studies*, vol. 54, pp. 486–508.

Hoffmann, M. 2011, *Climate governance at the crossroads*, Oxford University Press, Oxford.

Howell, R.A. 2010, 'Lights, camera . . . action? Altered attitudes and behaviour in response to the climate change film The Age of Stupid', *Global Environmental Change*, vol. 21, no. 1, pp. 177–87.

Hulme, M. 2010, 'Problems with making and governing global kinds of knowledge', *Global Environmental Change*, vol. 20, pp. 558–64.

Jones, B. 2010, *Democratic challenges in tackling climate change*, Whitlam Institute, University of Western Sydney, Parramatta, Australia.

Krakoff, S. 2011, *Planetary identity formation and the relocalization of environmental law*, Working Paper 03-11, University of Colorado, Boulder, CO.

Lidskog, R. & Elander, I. 2010, 'Addressing climate change democratically: multi-level governance, transnational networks and governmental structures', *Sustainable Development*, vol. 18, pp. 32–41.

Lindseth, G. 2004, 'The cities for climate protection campaign (CCPC) and the framing of local climate policy', *Local Environment*, vol. 9, no. 4, pp. 325–36.

Linklater, A. 1998a, 'Cosmopolitan citizenship', *Citizenship Studies*, vol. 2, no. 1, pp. 23–41.

Linklater, A. 1998b, *The transformation of political community: ethical foundations of the post-Westphalian era*, University of South Carolina Press, Columbia, SC.

List, C. & Koenig-Archibugi, M. 2010, 'Can there be a global demos? An agency-based approach', *Philosophy & Public Affairs*, vol. 38, no. 1, pp. 76–110.

Maniates, M. & Meyer, J.M. 2010, *The environmental politics of sacrifice*, The MIT Press, Cambridge, MA.

Marshall, J.P. 2011, 'Climate change, Copenhagen and psycho-social disorder', *PORTAL Journal of Multidisciplinary International Studies*, vol. 8, no. 3, pp. 1–23.

Meadowcroft, J. 2011, 'Engaging with the *politics* of sustainability transitions', *Environmental Innovation and Societal Transitions*, vol. 1, no. 1, pp. 70–5.

Middlemiss, L. 2010, 'Reframing Individual Responsibility for Sustainable Consumption: Lessons from Environmental Justice and Ecological Citizenship', *Environmental Values*, vol. 19, no. 2, pp. 147–67.

Middlemiss, L. & Parrish, B.D. 2010, 'Building capacity for low-carbon communities: the role of grassroots initiatives', *Energy Policy*, vol. 38, no. 12, pp. 7559–66.

Norgaard, K.M. 2011, *Living in denial: climate change, emotions, and everyday life*, The MIT Press, Cambridge, MA.

Onyx, J. & Edwards, M. 2010, 'Community Networks and the Nature of Emergence in Civil Society', *Cosmopolitan Civil Societies Journal*, vol. 2, no. 1.

Ostrom, E. 2009, *A polycentric approach for coping with climate change*, Report no. 4, 5095, The World Bank Development Economics Office of the Senior Vice President and Chief Economist, Washington.

Paterson, M. & Stripple, J. 2010, 'My Space: governing individuals' carbon emissions', *Environment and Planning D: Society and Space*, vol. 28, pp. 341–62.

Räthzel, N. & Uzzell, D. 2009, 'Changing relations in global environmental change', *Global Environmental Change*, vol. 19, no. 3, pp. 326–35.

Rauschmayer, F., Bauler, T. & Schäpke, N. 2015, 'Towards a thick understanding of sustainability transitions – Linking transition management, capabilities and social practices', *Ecological Economics*, vol. 109, pp. 211–21.

Reed, M.S., Evely, A.C., Cundill, G., Fazey, I., Glass, J., Laing, A., Newig, J., Parrish, B., Prell, C., Raymond, C. & Stringer, L.C. 2010, 'What is social learning?', *Ecology and Society*, vol. 15, no. 4, pp. 1–10.

Rosewarne, S., Goodman, J. & Pearse, R. 2014, *Climate action upsurge. The ethnography of climate movement politics*, Routledge, London.

Scoones, I., Leach, M. & Newell, P. (eds) 2015, *The politics of green transformations*, Routledge, London.

Scott-Cato, M. & Hillier, J. 2010, 'How could we study climate-related social innovation? Applying Deleuzean philosophy to transition towns', *Environmental Politics*, vol. 19, no. 6, pp. 869–87.

Seyfang, G. & Haxeltine, A. 2012, 'Growing grassroots innovations: exploring the role of community-based initiatives in governing sustainable energy transitions', *Environment and Planning C: Government and Policy*, vol. 30, pp. 381–400.

Singer, P. 2011, *The expanding circle: ethics, evolution and moral progress*, Princeton University Press, Princeton, NJ.

Smith, A. 2007, 'Translating sustainabilities between green niches and socio-technical regimes', *Technology Analysis & Strategic Management*, vol. 19, no. 4, pp. 427–50.

Stevenson, H. & Dryzek, J.S. 2014, *Democratizing global climate governance*, Cambridge University Press, Cambridge.

Torgerson, D. 1999, *The promise of green politics: environmentalism and the public sphere*, Duke University Press, Durham, SC.

Ungar, S. 1995, 'Social scares and global warming: beyond the Rio Convention', *Society and Natural Resources*, vol. 8, pp. 443–56.

Index

For Product Safety Concerns and Information please contact our EU
representative GPSR@taylorandfrancis.com
Taylor & Francis Verlag GmbH, Kaufingerstraße 24, 80331 München, Germany

www.ingramcontent.com/pod-product-compliance
Ingram Content Group UK Ltd.
Pitfield, Milton Keynes, MK11 3LW, UK
UKHW021611240425
457818UK00018B/492